# IN SEARCH OF
# NOMADS

By the same author

*Cucumber Sandwiches in the Andes*
*Prince Henry the Navigator*
*The Trail of Tamerlane*
*The Quest for Captain Morgan*
*Trespassers on the Amazon*
*A Bird on the Wing*
*Diplomatic Bag* (editor)
*The Cossacks*

# IN SEARCH OF
# NOMADS

## AN ANGLO-AMERICAN OBSESSION FROM
## HESTER STANHOPE TO BRUCE CHATWIN

### John Ure

'To live in one land, is captivitie,
To runne all countries, a wild roguery.'
John Donne, *Elegie III*, c. 1595

CARROLL & GRAF PUBLISHERS
New York

Carroll & Graf Publishers
An imprint of Avalon Publishing Group, Inc.
245 W. 17th Street
11th Floor
New York, NY 10011
www.carrollandgraf.com

First Carroll & Graf edition 2003

First published in the UK by Constable,
an imprint of Constable & Robinson Ltd, 2003

ISBN 0-7867-1320-8

Printed and bound in the EU

For Caroline
who shared in the prologue and so much else

# Contents

---◆---

# CONTENTS

# List of Illustrations and Maps

Tuareg preparing for a Saharan camel race (*Paul Harris*)

Freya Stark (*John Murray archive*)

On the Karakoram Pass

Alexander Gordon Laing

Hugh Clapperton

A Tuareg guide in the Sahara

Sir Harry 'the Caid' Maclean

The Hoggar Mountains (*Tom Owen Edmunds*)

## Maps

# Acknowledgements

———⸻◆⸻———

Parts of this book are a personal chronicle of encounters with nomads and journeys made in their company or among them. For these experiences my thanks are due to those who helped me on my way and befriended me along the route. If they read what I have written, they will recognize themselves; but most of them are not into reading books – particularly not in English. My thanks are therefore no less sincere for being expressed in a void and after a long time lapse.

The greater part of the book is, however, based on research into the travels of others. For this I have more explicit thanks to express. Dr John Hemming (formerly director of the Royal Geographical Society) pointed me in some useful directions, as did Professor Carole Hillenbrand (Head of the Department of Islamic and Middle Eastern studies at Edinburgh University), Dr Shirley Kay, Colin Thubron and Nicholas Crane, who also cast a helpful eye over some of the text. Eugene Roe (the librarian of the RGS) gave me great help in identifying sources, particularly when the library was temporarily closed for reorganization; and Sarah Strong (archivist in the RGS) took much trouble to track down an account of a journey with the Bakhtiari. Pamela, Lady Egremont (who has herself travelled with the Bakhtiari), was generous in sharing her recollections with me. Robin Hanbury-Tenison (the explorer) was similarly helpful about the Tuareg. And as always the staff of the London Library took immense trouble to locate works on their own shelves and elsewhere.

I am grateful to Locker Madden of Aberdeen University for the photograph of his ancestor Sir Harry Maclean in full Moroccan attire, and to Nigel Nicolson of Sissinghurst Castle for the photograph of his mother Vita Sackville-West taken in the year she made her journey with the Bakhtiari.

I am also grateful to Mrs Drue Heinz DBE and the Hawthornden Institute for inviting me to work on the book in the delightful surroundings of Casa Ecco on Lake Como.

In a more general sense, I am grateful to the late Bruce Chatwin for his evocative writing around the subject of nomads, and to his biographer, Nicholas Shakespeare, for putting what Chatwin did, thought and wrote into an intelligible context. The deeper I have delved into the subject of nomads, the more I have sympathized with Chatwin's dilemma in writing about them, and the more grateful I have been that my own subject was as much their English-speaking fans as the elusive nomads themselves.

# Introduction and Definitions

—⫸◆⫷—

NOMADS are notoriously difficult to define. Are they pastoralists who move with the seasons from one pasture to another? Or are they Romanies who have no fixed abode and are for ever on the move? Is returning to a homeland after travels a disqualification for true nomadism? Is being a nomad a frame of mind, or is it a physical activity?

Bruce Chatwin wrestled with these questions intensively for three years when under contract to write *The Nomadic Alternative* (which eventually proved to be unpublishable) and never quite stopped wrestling with them to the end of his life. He took the romantic view: nomads moved because it was natural to do so and they liked being in motion. 'Nomads of today,' he wrote, 'are truck drivers, *gauchos*, *vagueros*, *mafiosi*, commercial salesmen, shifting migrants, and those possessed of the samurai spirit, mercenaries and guerilla heroes.' All this was totally at variance with the views of professional anthropologists. One such – Jeremy Swift, who was a friend of Chatwin – took issue with him. For Swift, nomads travelled under the compulsion of seeking fresh pastures; they would willingly have travelled less if the climate and the supply of grass had allowed it. 'It's hell on wheels taking all your possessions and children' was Swift's verdict, having spent six months migrating with the Bakhtiari and the Qashqai (who did not in fact have wheels) in southern Iran.

Certainly I shall not attempt to adopt Chatwin's broad, all-embracing vision: this is not a book about truck drivers and guerilla fighters. But at the same time I shall not forgo the romantic side of nomadic existence, both because this is a real element in the lives of those who make migrations, and because it is what first attracted me to the subject. So neither will this be a treatise for anthropologists: too many have been written already, and I am not qualified to add to the number. But problems of definition do not end here: even if some general categorization is agreed, difficult problems of selection remain.

It is impossible to codify all the remaining nomadic peoples of the world. Should any account of nomads include the reindeer herders of the Arctic Circle who move with their herds for a few months every year and then settle into a life of bourgeois comfort and conformity in northern Scandinavia (or of less comfort in Siberia)? Should it include the Australian Aborigines who drift to their own rhythm across the outback? If the Bakhtiari and Qashqai tribes who migrate with their flocks to the highlands of central and southern Iran every year are eligible for inclusion, are not the Turkana warriors of the semi-arid deserts of the Rift Valley in northern Kenya also eligible? And there are smaller tribes, whose migrations are sporadic or unpredictable, and who might sometimes be considered as nomads and sometimes not. Even if one reached an adequate definition of a nomad, to be inclusive in one's treatment of the surviving species would be an almost impossible task, and would result in a book that would be diffuse to the point of lacking any focus. Chatwin's problems were real ones and not wholly the product of his chameleon-like character and fertile imagination.

So any terms of reference have to be somewhat arbitrary. In my own case I have decided to make the criterion for inclusion a subjective one: I have included only those nomads who have traditionally fired the imagination and attracted adventurous spirits over the centuries from the

English-speaking world. Highest on this list are four groups: the bedouin of Arabia, the Tuareg of the Sahara, the Mongol-descended horsemen of the Central Asian steppes, and the Qashqai and Bakhtiari of the Persian plains. If anyone doubts the fascination that these people have had for my fellow countrymen, I hope the tales related in the book will quell such doubts. And the tales are worth telling for their own sake: I shall write as much about my compatriots' travels as I shall about the journeys of the nomads themselves.

But analysing what constitutes that fascination is more difficult. It can be argued that the attraction has in part been one of region rather than of role – that is, the desert itself rather than the migrant nature of its peoples has been the draw. I recognize that this sometimes has been the case, but I think it will emerge from the pages of this book that the concept of movement has played the decisive part in drawing English-speaking travellers into the nomads' orbit. The reason for this is perhaps to be found in the romantic literature on which nineteenth- and twentieth-century Britons were reared: Byron's heroes – Childe Harold and Don Juan – were always on the move; Tennyson wrote of 'that untravelled world, whose margin fades for ever and for ever as I move'; Flecker declared it was 'sweet to ride forth at evening from the wells'; the adventurers of Kipling and Buchan were for ever pressing on 'beyond the last blue mountain'. The sands of the desert and the dust of the plains may have had an appeal in themselves, but it was the movement across them that captivated the imagination of readers and dreamers. And nomads are the essential movers.

It must also be confessed at the outset that there is another and more personal reason for my arbitrary choice of these four particular nomadic peoples. It happens that the groups that I have nominated above for inclusion coincide with the groups of nomads with whom I have myself travelled at different times and for different reasons. So I have some personal experience of all of them and some affection for all of them. This is hardly a coincidence. As a Scotsman, living in England and partly educated in English-speaking North America, I have myself experienced in a marked degree that fascination with the nomads of Arabia, the

Sahara, the steppes and the Persian plains that I have found exercised such a hold over my compatriots: their obsession is mine too.

It all began with a sandstorm in southern Morocco thirty years ago.

# IN SEARCH OF
# NOMADS

# Preface: Legacy of a Sandstorm

———————◆———————

THEY said there would be a camel market the next day in M'Hamid el Ghouzlane, the gateway to the Sahara. We had already crossed the High Atlas south of Marrakesh and had passed the gaunt, deserted Glaoui fortress of Telouet before passing through Ouarzazate and along the Draa Valley to the end of the metalled road at Zagora. Beyond here a sandy track lurched through overhanging rocks: it was biblical-looking country; Moses would have felt at home here, or Bunyan's pilgrim on his way through the Slough of Despond. But we were neither in Sinai nor in some desolate allegorical land. We were in southern Morocco in January 1972, and we were on our honeymoon.

The idea of attempting to find the Tuareg – the blue men of the desert – had come to us slowly as we meandered through Morocco in a small hired car. We had talked to Berbers in the silver markets of Taroudant and to carpet merchants in the souks of Fez. Everyone knew of the blue men – so called on account of the blue robes they wear as they ride their fine Hoggar camels through the desert – but few had encountered them.

When they emerged from the desert, it was usually to attend a camel market, we were told. Their life in the Sahara was still shrouded in some mystery. Their black goatskin tents were secret and private places into which few outsiders were invited. The possibility of finding them and of penetrating the fringes of the Sahara had appealed to us as a contrast to the Arabian luxuries of the Mamounia Hotel and the international splendours of the Gazelle d'Or. So when the camel market at M'Hamid had been suggested to us as a possible location for an encounter with Tuareg (unusually far north-west for them in Reguibi country) we had cheerfully set out through the Slough of Despond.

We had nearly reached M'Hamid when disaster struck. Being inexperienced in the ways of the desert, we had no warning. What was one moment a clear and sunny winter day suddenly became as dark as evening; what had been a still and warm afternoon suddenly became a howling and bitter gale; what had been a quiet and tranquil track suddenly became a noisy and whirling cascade of sand and rock particles. The gallant but inadequate hired car lurched off the track and showed no sign of being inclined to further motion. Even with all the windows wound tightly shut, it leaked like a colander: sand penetrated our eyes and ears, our nostrils and hair, our pockets and money-belts, our cameras and binoculars, our suitcases and hand-luggage. Weeks afterwards, when safely back in England, we were to open wallets and come across packets of sand, to open books and receive a shower of rock particles in our laps. We were temporarily blinded, immobilized and discomforted.

We had even more nearly reached M'Hamid than we realized. During a temporary slackening in the velocity of the sandstorm, between whirling cascades of sand, we saw the outline of a square block of rock or masonry ahead. We made our way towards it on foot. As we approached, the outline became clearer: it was a kasbah or fortress, in fact quite possibly originally a Foreign Legion garrison fort. In normal circumstances it might have seemed a forbidding and uninviting edifice; in a sandstorm it looked like welcome shelter.

I remembered some advice I had been given at our embassy in Rabat on a previous visit to Morocco: 'When in difficulty, seek the assistance of the local Caid.' The Caid - as I understood it - was the representative of central government. In former times he would have been an independent chieftain, but now I imagined he was more likely a provincial official, dark-suited, pedantic, surrounded by files and forms to be filled in triplicate. But any port in a storm, I thought. It seemed likely that the most solid building in M'Hamid would house the Caid, and if the price of shelter was filling out a few forms, so be it.

We walked around three sides of the fort before we found an entrance - a wide arch leading into a bleak courtyard. Desolate as it might be, the sand whirled less savagely here and we could see on the far side of the courtyard another gateway, this time closed and guarded by two sentries muffled up to the eyes with cloaks over their *djellabas* and carrying antiquated weapons which looked more like muskets than rifles. We approached them diffidently, privately wishing we were still safely ensconced in the comforts of the Mamounia Hotel.

'Can you take me to your Caid?' I shouted as politely as I could in French above the roar of the storm. Shouting seldom sounds polite, and in a language foreign to both speaker and listener this seemed more than usually to be the case. For good measure, I gave the taller of the guards a letter, with which I had been supplied by the British embassy, requesting all and sundry to give us any help we needed. Presumably, I thought, this was exactly the sort of occasion that the writer had had in mind when he offered us this highly embossed missive. It would now be put to the test.

The guard to whom I had given the letter turned on his heels and, opening the heavy wooden door just wide enough to allow himself but not too much sand to pass through, disappeared from view; the other watched us with evident suspicion. Neither had spoken. I gestured towards the whirling sand and made some inane remark about inclement weather. There was no flicker of response.

After what seemed like an eternity of standing in cold, discomfort

3

and embarrassment the first guard returned and motioned us through the gates into a smaller and covered court. Benches with saddlebags serving as cushions lined the tiled walls. A fountain base, long since dried up, stood in the centre of the court. We settled ourselves on saddlebags expecting another long wait.

My mind turned to what little I knew of the activities within Berber or Glaoui fortresses in this part of the world. I recalled Gavin Maxwell recounting how less than ten years earlier he had been exploring the kasbah at Telouet (which we had passed the previous day) and 'found my torch shining upon white but manacled bones in a dungeon . . . they could have been either a hundred or less than five years old'. What was in store for us uninvited intruders I wondered. Probably, I concluded, nothing worse than an eventual summons to an office and a bureaucratic interrogation as to why we were here, so far from the normal tourist routes.

Quite suddenly the double doors at the far side of the courtyard were flung open and a tall, robed figure with a silver dagger in his waistband stepped forward to greet us. This was no *petit fonctionnaire*: he looked more like Omar Sharif playing his role in *Lawrence of Arabia*. With his entry, what had been a tiresome misfortune was transformed at a stroke into an intriguing adventure.

The Caid – for this indeed was he – extended a warm welcome in impeccable French and led us into a richly carpeted room where coffee and sweetmeats were laid out on a low central table surrounded by deeply cushioned benches. He invited us to sit while barefoot servants poured out coffee from a vast silver-spouted vessel into diminutive cups. We explained how we had had to abandon our car, and the Caid suggested that we stayed at his fortress until the storm abated: it could be a matter or hours or it could be several days, he said. Meanwhile, he would send someone to bring our luggage from the car. M'Hamid was a lonely post, he said, and he would be glad of our company at dinner.

Among the cases that were duly fetched from our nearly silted-up vehicle was a slim leather box with expensive gilt fastenings. We saw

4

the Caid eyeing it curiously: did he think it was a pistol-case, we wondered. To reassure him, we opened up this newly acquired wedding present, and the moment his eyes rested on the backgammon board he looked visibly relieved: this was the answer both to entertaining us and to diverting him.

For the next two days the storm raged intermittently around us and we stayed in the fort, grateful for the shelter and hospitality. The Caid insisted that we were his guests, and we felt instinctively that any suggestion of payment would have been viewed as the grossest bad manners. But the Caid had his own way of exacting a modest toll for our board and lodging. The fun of backgammon is doubling the stakes when you think you are ahead of your opponent, so (as in poker) an element of gambling for monetary stakes is required. We would take it in turns to play against the Caid for modest sums of local currency, and we always lost. It did not take us long to find out why: our host's pieces were moved fast and with more attention to the desired destination that to the numbers thrown up by the dice; dice were declared 'cocked up' when they showed disappointing numbers, and in a score of other little ways the Caid quietly manipulated the game. He was, after all, playing on his own home ground and no doubt by 'local rules'. To have protested would have seemed ungrateful or even dangerous: one thought of the manacled skeleton up the mountain pass at Telouet. So we smiled and smiled and lost more and more.

On the third day the winds began to drop and the sky lightened. Our car had been dug out of its sand drift and was little the worse for its immersion. It was time to move on, and the Caid asked us about our plans. We explained that we had come in hopes of seeing the Tuareg at the camel market, as we had always been intrigued by the nomadic tribes of the Sahara. Now it seemed the camel market had been overtaken by the sandstorm, and we would have to retrace our steps. We were mildly disappointed but – thanks to his kindness – none the worse for our adventure.

The Caid became thoughtful. Did we seriously want to meet the

Tuareg? Had we ever ridden camels for any long distance ourselves? Would we be prepared to try? We could see that an idea was forming in his mind which had nothing to do with backgammon, and our answers seemed to encourage his line of thought. Slowly he came out with a proposal.

It seemed that before the sandstorm broke he had been on the point of sending a small camel caravan, under command of a Moroccan army sergeant, a few days' ride into the desert, to take provisions to a Tuareg encampment about which he had recently become aware. We had the impression that he was nervous about what the Tuareg were up to and felt that the best way of finding out their plans was to send out a military patrol, under the guise of a charitable mission, to bring supplies and to enquire whether the Tuareg had crossed into Morocco over the unmarked frontier from Algeria or Mauritania, and if so where they were now heading. Settled authority is ever mistrustful of nomadic peoples.

If we really wanted to see the Tuareg in their true habitat – the desert – rather than as awkward strangers attending a market, then we could go with his patrol. We would be safe. The sergeant was a reliable man and he even spoke some French. His camels were tried and in good shape. The only problem was that we would have to take all our own food (he could lend us a sleeping bag) and there was very little time since the moment the sandstorm was over the patrol must set out as it had already been unduly delayed and the Tuareg had a practice of slipping away into the sand-dunes never to be seen again. We could go down to the square in the centre of M'Hamid and buy what we required.

We needed no second invitation but shuffled the backgammon pieces back into their case and headed on foot to the so-called *grande place* – an indeterminate open space ankle deep in shifting sand after the storm. After days of doing nothing, suddenly everything was a rush. Our objective was not made easier by the fact that there were no shops. Instead there was a circle of some dozen men sitting on the ground in

6

their *djellabas* with rugs laid out in front of them covering their wares from the still-drifting sand. The two or three other potential customers would approach one of the squatting figures and tap him on the shoulder, after which the merchant would raise the corner of his woven rug and reveal beneath it whatever it was he was selling. The system worked up to a point if you knew what the merchant was likely to be selling, but naturally we had no idea.

We did the rounds, tapping shoulder after shoulder and getting a glimpse from one of a few oranges, from another of some tins of sardines, or some grubby-looking packets of cigarettes, or bottles of Fanta lemonade, or a mountain of dried dates. Time was against us: the Caid had told us to be back in half an hour. We bought fast and indiscriminately, bundling our wares into an old canvas bag we had rescued from the car.

When we got back to the fort we found the sergeant, plus four other motley soldiers in robes with rifles slung over their shoulders, and eight rather mangy-looking camels, gathered by the gate. The Caid was there to see us off, flashing his Omar Sharif smile and doubtless thinking what suckers the English were when it came to backgammon. Our inadequate provisions were dropped into a copious saddlebag. We clambered on to the sitting camels and survived their jerky, seesaw lurch on rising. The sky looked blue and innocent, as if the storms of the past few days must have been figments of our imagination. In a matter of another half-hour M'Hamid was an indistinct line of mud walls and a tower on the horizon while ahead of us stretched an undulating sea of sand.

Just as we began to think that we were Lawrence of Arabia, we had our first nasty shock. My camel, which had been plodding in line with that rhythmic swing that has given rise to the expression 'ship of the desert', suddenly gave a snort and took off at a gallop towards the horizon. I clung on to every bit of superstructure I could lay my hands on, and avoided – just – falling off. When the initial crisis was over, I managed to crane my neck around and see our little caravan already an

7

alarming distance away, but – to my relief – the 'reliable' sergeant was in hot pursuit of me on his own ever faster galloping camel. Soon he caught up and headed mine back to the caravan, explaining to me on the way what had happened. Apparently I had, inadvertently, crossed or uncrossed my legs on the camel's hump and thus given the order to charge. For the rest of the journey I was to sit, frozen hard with cramp, unmoving to avoid any repetition. Meanwhile, the sergeant's gaze was for ever roaming the horizon in search of the Tuareg.

Before nightfall we saw the expected black goatskin tents on the sheltered side of a low sand-dune. A cluster of camels, paler and less mangy-looking than ours, was hobbled nearby. Figures came tumbling out of the tents: a few blue men in the expected indigo robes, but mostly a horde of scantily clad small children. Although we could not follow anything of what was said, it was clear that the meeting was a friendly one. Soon everyone was squatting around a fire chattering and drinking sweet tea from tiny cups, in a circle that had been generously extended to include us. Our camels were unloaded. Some military-style bell-tents were erected at a short distance from the more ramshackle Tuareg ones. A cauldron bubbling with dubious parts of sheep's anatomy was placed over the fire. The sun went down in a red ball over the dunes. One's limbs were slowly thawing out from the constrained rigours of the ride. All seemed well with the world on this our tenth night of married life.

While we had been seated, careful not to expose the soles of our feet to our hosts, around the fire, the soldiers had pitched a tent for us and had laid out our scant belongings. Our military escort ate separately from the Tuareg, and we felt we should do the same: this was, after all, why we had bought our own curious selection of rations. The dates felt rather more appropriate to the surroundings than the sardines. As the sun had gone down, the temperature had dropped dramatically; already the sand, which had been hot underfoot, felt cold and, having been in shirtsleeves all day, we were glad of sweaters and anoraks.

Around us in the fading light camels farted, goats nibbled at nonexistant grazing and children whispered. It was a timeless scene – biblical in its beauty and simplicity, but packed with the minutiae of living. The burble of conversation was hypnotic. There seemed no reason ever to leave the fireside.

But there was: sheer weariness, and eventually we retired to our bell-tent and crawled into the double sleeping bag that the Caid had thoughtfully provided. We were glad that among the wedding presents we had brought – along with the backgammon set – was a silver hip flask, filled with brandy for emergencies. We declared a state of emergency and passed it avidly between us, hoping that we would not be discovered consuming alcohol in the midst of a highly Islamic community.

It was now quite dark outside. There was a gap between the bottom of the canvas sides of our tent and the sand below, and in this gap was a line of tiny pinpoints of light – glistening reflections of the flickering fire outside. At first we thought this sparkle was fireflies. But they seemed oddly in pairs. A flash from our torch revealed that we were mistaken: lying on their tummies on the cold sand, a complete circle of small Tuareg children were watching our every move under the edge of the canvas. It was a rather more public post-nuptial night than we had anticipated.

From first light the next morning all around us was activity. We had scrupulously buried our sardine tins, orange peel and other rubbish, so it was with some chagrin that we observed the Tuareg children digging up our debris and distributing it among themselves as treasure-trove: sardine tins were already being beaten out to make crude knife blades. I recalled Owen Lattimore's remark that 'the pure nomad is a poor nomad' and thought how properly this applied to the Tuareg.

The plan that appeared to have been agreed the previous evening around the fire was that our small military party and a slightly larger Tuareg group – mostly consisting of men – should travel together via a nearby oasis back to M'Hamid, where they would await the next opportunity to sell some camels and to buy provisions. We would take two days to complete the return journey by this more circuitous route. The purpose of going out of our way to include the oasis was not altogether clear to me: it seemed there might be a chance of meeting some other Tuareg tribesmen there or of buying melons from the custodians of the wells. Some of the extended Tuareg families would remain behind in our camp, with most of the children and all the goats.

The packing up was done remarkably quickly, with the women doing most of the work. As we moved off I found myself riding beside the sergeant. We were far enough ahead of the others to be able to talk freely, and it was doubtful whether anyone else understood a word of French anyway. He declared himself well pleased with the information he had gleaned the previous evening. It seemed that the Tuareg we had met had become local to this part of the Sahara; the fact that they had so many goats with them was sure indication of the limited range of their migrations; they might have been wandering for months across the dimly demarcated region where Morocco shaded off into the western Sahara, Algeria and Mauritania, but they had not been making the trans-Saharan journey from Mali in the south. (We had seen signs at M'Hamid saying that Timbuktu was a mere forty-seven days' camel ride away.) Down there, he said ominously, even the rulers of the country came from nomadic stock; their camels could travel for five days in summer with no water and for weeks in winter. How could you control a country like that? It was said, he went on, that there were over half a million nomads scattered over the whole western and central Sahara if you included some of the Moors like the Hammunat tribe from Mauritania. They might surge out of the desert at any time and shake the whole fabric of the kingdom of Morocco. They were living in the past. They had no roots anywhere. What could you do with people like that?

His words were falling on deaf ears. I could not see these people as an anachronism or a regrettable occurrence – still less as a threat to established order. My two or three days with the Tuareg had awakened in me an awareness of a different sort of life from any I had known

10

before. Home to the Tuareg was wherever they were, not where they came from or were going back to. Possessions – be it a camel or a knife blade – were for using and enjoying and not for hoarding: as Anatole France once said, 'it is good to collect things, but it is better to go on walks'. Food, like the warmth of a fire, was for sharing. Life to them was a bridge: one should cross over it, not build a house on it. All these thoughts – few of them original – churned in my head, but I knew they were not for me: I was embarking on married life, on setting up home, on building houses real or metaphorical.

But when I got home I found that my fascination with the way of life I had so briefly glimpsed was not unique to me. Many of my compatriots shared it. If one could not live as a nomad, perhaps one could at least explore that world through reading and travel. And there was so much to read and so many places and peoples to visit.

# BOOK I

# THE MIGRATORY TRIBES
# OF SOUTHERN PERSIA

'A fruitfull countrey, inhabited with pasturing people, which dwell in summer season upon mountaines, and in winter they remoove into the valleyes without resorting to townes or any other habitation: and when they remoove, they doe journey in carravans or troops of people and cattell, carrying all their wives, children and baggage upon bullocks.'

Anthony Jenkinson, trader and envoy of Queen Elizabeth I, quoted in Hakluyt's *Principal Navigations, Voyages and Discoveries of the English Nation* (1698)

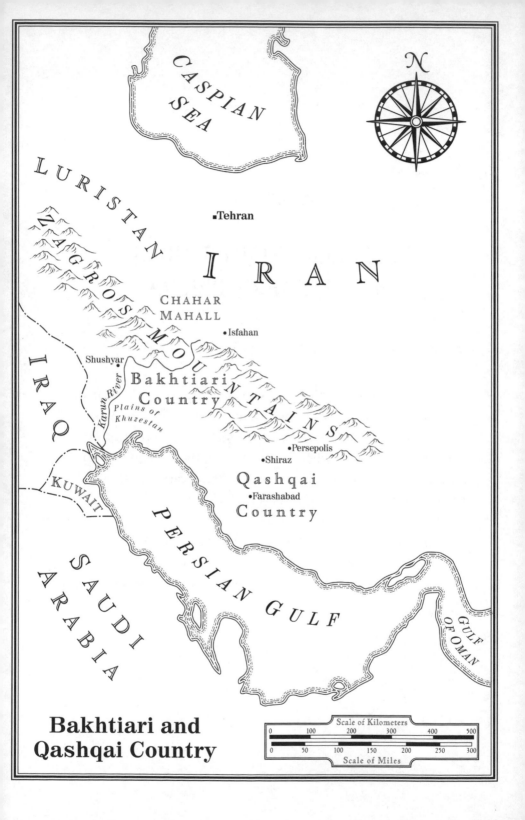

CASPIAN SEA

N

LURISTAN

ZAGROS

.Tehran

IRAN

CHAHAR MAHALL

•Isfahan

IRAQ

Shushyar•

Karun River

Bakhtiari Country

MOUNTAINS

Plains of Khuzestan

KUWAIT

•Persepolis

•Shiraz

Qashqai

•Farashabad

Country

PERSIAN GULF

SAUDI ARABIA

GULF OF OMAN

# Bakhtiari and Qashqai Country

Scale of Kilometers
0    100    200    300    400    500

0    50    100    150    200    250    300
Scale of Miles

# 1

## The Bakhtiari

—◆—

I look back as through a telescope, and see, in the little bright circle of glass, moving flocks and ruined cities.

Vita Sackville-West

THE Bakhtiari pastoral tribes of southern Persia have always been a magnet to English – and sometimes American – travellers. To understand why, it is necessary first to learn something of their origins and history; but this is not as straightforward as it sounds. Lord Curzon wrote of the Lurs, of whom the Bakhtiari are a part, that 'a people without a history, a literature, or even a tradition, presents a phenomenon in the face of which science stands abashed'. Be that as it may, some things are known.

To start with, the Bakhtiari are probably the largest of Iran's pastoral tribes. It has never been easy to estimate their numbers because no official figures are available, and the periodic censuses carefully avoid any assessment of the tribes as such. But in the 1960s it was calculated (by people who travelled with them) that those who made the twice-yearly migration – to and from the winter grazing by the Persian Gulf and the summer grazing beyond the Zagros Mountains in the hills above Isfahan – numbered some 150,000 strong.

Their origins are, as Curzon implied, obscure. The Lurs may have moved into Persia with the Medes at the end of the second millennium BC – probably from the Caucasus. Certainly they were firmly established in their present location in southern Iran (see map, page 14) by the time of Alexander the Great's invasion. They subsequently resisted the Arab invasions, but it is only in the early eighteenth century that they emerge from their mountain fastnesses into the flickering light of history. From then onwards their story has been one of periodical rebellions against the Shahs of Iran, usually followed by harassment and suppression by the Shah's troops.

Some of the tribal revolts have threatened or even toppled the imperial crown. Twice they rose up against their rulers in the 1730s, but already they were showing signs of the internal divisions that were to frustrate their success; not only were the Bakhtiari divided between the Haft Lang ('those of the seven feet') and the Chahar Lang ('those of the four feet') branches, but many lesser schisms and sects bedevilled their solidarity. An occasional Il Khan, or supreme chief, united the whole tribe. One such was Mehemet Taki Khan in the 1840s: at the height of his power he could put over 12,000 mounted riflemen into the field, but eventually he was tricked into putting himself in the Shah's power and ended his life being dragged in fetters from one castle dungeon to another – a particularly tragic end for one who had led a free-ranging life in the mountains. The next great Bakhtiari chief – Hussein Quli Khan – emerged in the 1850s and, after thirty years of guiding his people and leading them on their migrations, he, too, attracted the jealousy of the Shah – Nasr-el-Din – and in 1882 was lured to Isfahan and strangled at a dinner given in his honour by the Shah's son.

The most dramatic flash of insurrection against the Qajar dynasty in the twentieth century came in 1908 when the Shah, having revoked the constitution, bombarded the Majlis (parliament building) with mercenary Cossack artillery and provoked a full-scale revolution. The following year the Bakhtiari khans swept down from the hills and occupied Isfahan, going on to march on Tehran itself. The Shah fled for

16

protection to the Russian legation and was deposed by popular demand. For several years the Bakhtiari dominated the political scene, filling the capital with their horsemen and establishing one of their number as Prime Minister and another as Minister of War; but by 1912 most of the Bakhtiari had slipped away back to their tribal pastures on either side of the Zagros Mountains.

Reza Shah, the founder of the last – Pahlavi – dynasty, was always highly suspicious of the tribes. They did not fit his model of a new Iran: they were misfits in his schemes of health, education, taxation and conscription. Even the fact that a plot against the Shah was frustrated by one of the Bakhtiari khans – Sadr-e-Azam – did not reconcile the Shah to this traditional and maverick force within his own modernistic and disciplined state. Far from being grateful to Sadr-e-Azam, he contrived his murder a few years later in the bath-house of a Tehran gaol.

In 1923 Reza Shah divided the Bakhtiari's land into different administrative regions and, more crucially, withdrew the right of the tribesmen to be armed. The right might have been withdrawn, but the weapons themselves remained in the hands of the tribesmen, and in 1929 six thousand armed Bakhtiari laid siege once again to Isfahan. The Shah persuaded them to withdraw to the hills, but in 1933 he decided he was strong enough to strike decisively against them: on a cold December night, government troops moved simultaneously in Isfahan, Tehran and Chahar Mahall (the Bakhtiari heartland) to arrest seventeen of the leading khans. Some were summarily executed and others imprisoned for life, seven of them dying shortly afterwards in captivity. The office of Il Khan was abolished, arms were confiscated, troops were garrisoned in the region, and the fortresses that the Bakhtiari had built in their highland summer grazing grounds were dismantled. Most drastically of all, the Shah attempted to settle the tribesmen and prohibit their migration, without making any attempt to provide year-round grazing or other provision for their herds and flocks. In consequence, the later 1930s saw a sad diminution in the

number of sheep, cattle and even horses – in fact, in all that constituted the wealth of the tribe. Old men and babies had often been
victims of the rigours of the migration through the steep and snow-
covered Zagros Mountains; now they died not of exposure but of
malnutrition and disorientation.

But the Bakhtiari had not even then altogether given up
their capacity to cause trouble. In the Second World War the
tribesmen, encouraged by the abdication and exile of Reza Shah in
1941 and by the release of some of their khans, again took to the
hills and started collecting arms. Government garrisons were attacked,
and the blandishments of German agents fell on receptive ears. But,
as so often in the past, internal quarrels frustrated the Bakhtiari's
capacity for action. With the help of the Allied powers, the Iranian
army rounded up the German agents and once again disarmed the
tribesmen.

Not surprisingly, the new Shah – Mohammed Reza, who was to be
the last of the Pahlavi line – inherited his father's mistrust of Bakhtiari
independence and tried to subsume tribal life into the pattern of an oil-
rich modern state. This was the condition that persisted in the 1950s
and 1960s when there was a renewal of interest in the tribes among
intrepid English travellers.

But one such traveller – Sir John Russell, the counsellor at the
British embassy in Tehran in the 1950s – wrote: 'The Bakhtiari
country today still has something of the Highlands after Culloden or
the Deep South after Sherman had marched to the Sea.' A proud but
divided people had been humbled, if not destroyed, by forces that can
be described as 'enlightened' or 'politically correct' depending on one's
viewpoint. With the fall of the Shah and the installation of the Islamic
Fundamentalist regime at the end of the 1970s, the pressure on the
Bakhtiari and other tribes eased somewhat, but still a pastoral existence
and a nomadic tribe seemed an anachronism in the warring world of
the Middle East.

Today the goat bells are fainter among the lush pastures of the plains and the barren hills of the Zagros Mountains. But they are still to be heard.

THE first really detailed account we have of an Englishman among the Bakhtiari is that of Sir Henry Layard, who was later in life to become celebrated as the discoverer of Nineveh and as a distinguished diplomat. His prolonged travels among the Bakhtiari in 1841 and 1842 came about largely by chance.

Having studied law in a solicitor's office in London for six years from the age of sixteen, he had decided that a more adventurous life called and that he would pursue a career – at the Bar or in the Civil Service – in Ceylon, where he had a relative in high office in the British administration. He had a friend – Edward Mitford – who had similar intentions but 'had a dread of a voyage by sea', so the two young men set off overland through Central Europe, Dalmatia, Montenegro, Albania and Bulgaria to Constantinople. From there they intended to cross Asia Minor (Turkey), Syria, Palestine and the Mesopotamian desert to Baghdad; the last lap of this ambitious journey was to be through Persia and Afghanistan to India and ultimately Ceylon.

Such a journey would have been challenging at any time. In the early nineteenth century – with much of the Middle East in turmoil, with Central Asia in the grip of the Great Game between imperial Russia and the British Raj in India, and on the eve of the First Afghan War – it was rash to say the least. They sought advice from Sir John MacNeill, who had until recently been the British envoy to the court of the Shah of Persia; his counsel was sound: 'You must either travel as important personages, with a retinue of servants and an adequate escort, or alone, as poor men, with nothing to excite the cupidity of the people among whom you will have to mix.' Layard and Mitford could not afford to adopt the 'important personages' route, so they set off as – relatively – 'poor men'.

The Royal Geographical Society, which they also consulted, suggested that instead of taking the route to Herat and Afghanistan through northern Persia, they should try to reach Kandahar (in southern Afghanistan) through Isfahan and Yezd (in southern Persia) since 'that part of Central Asia had not then been visited', and even the intrepid Sir Henry Rawlinson had been unable to visit the highlands inhabited by the Bakhtiari tribes 'who were always more or less in open rebellion to the Shah'. Layard promised therefore to try to visit the Bakhtiari mountains.

By the time he came to publish his narrative of the journey more than forty years later (in 1887, in two volumes from the already well-established house of John Murray), his time spent with the Bakhtiari had assumed the central and most exciting part of his *Early Adventures*, which were indeed subtitled as 'a residence among the Bakhtiari and other wild tribes'.

After a whole year of travelling together, Layard parted from Mitford, since the latter had decided to cross Persia by the northern route after all in the interests of getting to India more quickly. (Perhaps he also had 'a dread' of a journey through totally unknown country.) Layard therefore set off for the Bakhtiari country without a companion but furnished with a 'firman' – an open letter from the Shah stating that 'at every place where I stopped for the night provisions for eight persons' were to be provided at the Shah's expense. The Shah also attached an officer to accompany him and his servants. The Shah's attitude towards Englishmen was ambivalent: he declared he liked the English but loathed their Foreign Secretary – Lord Palmerston – who had rudely withdrawn his envoy to Persia. Finally he was given a letter from the Shah's chief minister to the Il Khan of the Bakhtiari – Mehemet Taki Khan – recommending him for 'special protection'. He appeared to have changed from travelling as a poor man to travelling as an important personage. But letters and firmans from the authorities were of dubious value among a tribe in 'more or less open rebellion' – as Layard was soon to discover.

The first intimation of just how inadequate his protection was occurred when Layard found himself within sight of the black tents of the Bakhtiari and the man in charge of his horses refused to risk himself or his mounts among 'these savage people'. Indeed, Layard was frequently warned that the Bakhtiari had the worst reputation in Persia as robbers – 'treacherous, cruel and blood-thirsty'; while he might succeed in getting into their country, the 'chances of getting out again were but few'.

On leaving Isfahan, Layard adopted Bakhtiari dress and took to carrying a long matchlock musket, a sabre and a pistol in his belt, which may have helped to commend him to his new hosts; but his travelling companions told him he should regard such accoutrements as 'not for show but for use'. Despite their attitude to the Shah, the Bakhtiari chiefs, 'like all nomadic tribes', considered themselves bound by the desert code of hospitality to strangers. Layard was plied with Shiraz wine and sweetmeats, with pilaus and savoury stews. They were disconcerted to find he was a Christian – most of them never having met such an infidel before — and they conspicuously refused to eat out of the same dish; Layard was at great pains to say nothing that could have been construed as blaspheming against the Prophet lest he 'might have been torn to pieces'.

Being not only a Christian but a 'Frank' (a Western European), Layard was thought to be 'a cunning physician'. Despite their distaste for infidels, the tribesmen came to him for help with all sorts of medical complaints, and he was even invited into the ladies' quarters, where he was received unveiled by the chiefs' wives. Their main preoccupation, however, was one about which he could do little: they wanted charms for securing the affections of their husbands and to make them conceive male children. Sometimes the mullahs had to be consulted to pronounce on whether it was safe to allow Layard to prescribe, and on one occasion he had to mix his medicine (usually quinine) with water that had been passed over a text from the Koran.

During the many months that Layard was to travel in Bakhtiari country – with his archaeological and political antennae always alert for classical inscriptions or tribal news – he was to experience a bewildering and alarming series of contrasting responses. In the villages he was provided with sustenance in response to the Shah's firman, but with reluctance and resentment because his accompanying officer never paid the villagers, so – in fact – he was their involuntary guest rather than the Shah's. In the more thickly populated tribal areas, among the black tents, the Bakhtiari chiefs themselves were usually hospitable towards him – more despite than because of his credentials. But in the less frequented mountains, individual tribesmen or wild marauding gangs frequently robbed, cheated or even stripped him of his clothes and few valuables – his watch and compass, for instance, without which he found it impossible to orientate himself.

The worst occurrence was when he stayed with a dissident Bakhtiari who tried to persuade him to resume his journey before dawn the following morning. Layard was convinced that the plan was to ambush and rob him in the dark, so he refused to leave before daylight. It availed him little, because he was ambushed nonetheless in a steep defile and his sole servant, who had gone on ahead with his horse, showed that he was a party to the plot by promptly helping himself to the contents of Layard's saddlebags. His assailants brandished their swords in his face and demanded his valuables, showing that they knew where he kept these hidden and thus revealing that they were in league with his so-called hosts of the night before. His servant deserted him and he was left bare and defenceless on a mountain pass above the Karun River, which he eventually swam, narrowly avoiding being washed away. It was typical of the Bakhtiari that after his wretched experience, when eventually he regained the friendly tents of the Bakhtiari chief and reported his misfortunes and loss, the chief was furious at this breach of tribal hospitality and sent out a punitive party to retrieve Layard's possessions – an operation quickly and successfully accomplished.

An added hazard of travelling alone in these regions at that period was the abundance of fierce animal – as opposed to human – predators. In addition to wolves, which were much dreaded by the shepherds, there were lions, snow-leopards, bears, wild boar, hyenas and jackals – all hunting for food, and all being in turn hunted by the Bakhtiari. Bustards were hunted with falcons from horseback, and a skilled falcon was – then as now – a highly prized possession. Not surprisingly, the Bakhtiari's horses were terrified by lions, so the young warriors accustomed their horses to the frightening sight and scent of lions by riding them up to stuffed lions' skins. Layard took part in several lion hunts and witnessed great courage by Mehemet Taki Khan when confronted with a wounded beast that was about to kill two fellow tribesmen.

In fact, Layard became an admirer and good friend of Mehemet Taki Khan – the Il Khan of the Bakhtiari at that period. He discussed with him the possibility of the Bakhtiari adopting a more sedentary lifestyle and developing trading links with neighbouring countries, where there was a market for Bakhtiari rugs, indigo, goats' hair and other tribal products. But it was to no avail. The internal feuding within the tribe, and their antagonism towards the Shah's government (and of the Shah's government towards them), ensured continual strife. While Layard was in Persia, the Shah finally declared Mehemet Taki Khan to be in a state of rebellion and – despite the latter's attempts to raise revenue from his tribe for the Shah – he was eventually enticed to a meeting with the Shah's chief eunuch, seized and fettered by the neck, wrists and ankles. Layard later visited him in prison and took messages to his family. But by now open war had broken out between the Bakhtiari and the Shah's army. Layard himself joined in a desperate but unsuccessful night raid to rescue Mehemet Taki Khan, and was shortly afterwards himself captured and imprisoned by hostile tribesmen; he escaped during the night from a robber baron's castle and fled for his life. It was little wonder that after so many scrapes he abandoned his original plan to reach India and Ceylon, returned to Constantinople and secured an honorary post at the British embassy there. His discovery of the lost city of Nineveh was to lie in the future.

Layard had not come to Persia to study nomads or to share their life:

he had found himself in the Bakhtiari country at the request of the Royal Geographical Society because it happened to be – like Central Africa – an unusually unknown region in the 1840s. But having once encountered the Bakhtiari, like so many of his later compatriots, he became totally fascinated by a people to whom migration was a necessary way of life. The twice-yearly challenge of crossing the mountains between the coastal plains and the high summer pastures around Isfahan appealed to his sense of challenge and adventure – even when his maps and notebooks were soaked in crossing the Karun river. It was fortunate for his successors that those notebooks survived their drenching, as they served as an inspiration for later travellers. Less fortunate was his overt support of the Bakhtiari and their Il Khan, and his active involvement in their cause; this was to be an enduring factor in the suspicion of successive Shahs of any contact between the Bakhtiari and the British – a suspicion that was to make further contacts always difficult and sometimes impossible.

SO difficult and fraught with hazard was contact with the Bakhtiari that very few British travellers (or indeed travellers from elsewhere) attempted it for most of the rest of the nineteenth century. But one English lady did succeed in travelling extensively for several months among – though not with – the Bakhtiari in 1890. She was a most unlikely adventurer.

Isabella Bird, although she had made some strenuous journeys, was considered to be a lady of uncertain health, much given to charity work. She married a husband – Mr Bishop – ten years her junior in age, but despite her apparently frail health she outlived him. Then, released of other responsibilities, she took off on foreign travels 'to improve her health'. Travelling on horseback across Persia with a minimum of guides and a servant, she was more than once robbed. On one occasion a thief came to her tent in the night and took, among other things, her cork sun helmet, her gloves, her sun umbrella, her thimble, her 'mask' and her revolver-case. The list conjures up an engaging vision of the lady's accoutrements. But it was not the loss of any of these which really upset her: the tragedy was that her embroidery had gone, and now she had no way of relieving 'the tedium of the long wait during the pitching of my tent'. After this experience she grew more circumspect and decided 'to rope the table and chair, on which I put my few remaining things, to the bed, taking care to put a tin can with a knife in it on the very edge of the table, so that if the things are tampered with the clatter may awake me'.

The highlight of her Persian travels was her time among the Bakhtiari. She spent three and a half months riding along, and frequently crossing, the Karun river and reckoned that some of 'the crude forts here and there which the tribesmen attribute to mythical heroes of their own race' were probably built by earlier Greek or Roman invaders. Her journey coincided with Bakhtiari movements from the warm plains of Khuzestan, where they had spent the winter, to the mountainous terrain consisting of lofty ranges, gorges and alpine pastures which 'they invariably spoke of as "their country"'.

Part of the attraction for Mrs Bishop was the wildlife; she could never see enough of it, and complained that 'the only animals seen' were a bear and its cubs, wild boar, ibex, blue hares and some jackals. The 'noxious forms of animated life' were more abundant: snakes and venomous spiders in particular could have been dispensed with. But having read Layard's account of his travels, she was clearly disappointed at not encountering lions and snow-leopards: for Isabella Bishop the *frisson* of excitement far outweighed the possible dangers of such encounters.

She was fascinated by the Bakhtiari, but not uncritical of their ways. She found that 'in religion, they are fanatical Moslems of the Shiah sect, but combine relics of nature worship with the tenets of Islam'. She admired them as horsemen and marksmen, but pointed out that, while in inter-tribal wars from 10,000 to 12,000 men might tackle the field, they would probably field only about half that number if called on to face an external threat. She found them predatory by inclination and tradition, and continually indulging in blood feuds. And she had particular sympathy for the problems of Persian tax collectors sent among such belligerent people. No wonder successive Shahs found them awkward subjects.

Even more than Layard, she found herself besieged with requests for medical assistance. In vain she tried to explain to them that she was not a doctor, 'scarcely even a nurse'. When confronted with a child dangerously ill with pneumonia, she 'put on a mustard poultice, and administered some Dover's powder'. Indeed, the mysterious Dover's powder seemed to be a general panacea. The fame of her 'Burroughes and Wellcome's medicine chest' spread far and wide. The greatest number of patients were – as always – suffering either from eye complaints or from a requirement for love potions to make them more attractive to their husbands. Apart from the obvious difficulty of prescribing for the latter category, Mrs Bishop found that one major obstacle to all her cures was the reluctance of the Bakhtiari women to apply soap and water to themselves or to their children.

But however limited its success, her medical ministrations greatly increased her popularity and acceptability among the tribes. When she was robbed in Bakhtiari country by two men who came into her tent while she was sleeping and removed her trunk, which contained 'some English gold and 1,000 *krans* for four months' travelling', the local khan – whose guest she had been – promised that 'the money would be repaid, and that the village would be levelled with the ground'. She reckoned that in fact the village would be left standing but that the khan would levy a fine on the village for many years to come. Meanwhile, although her 'washing apparatus and medicine bottles were neatly arranged on the ground outside', the moneybags were nowhere to be found. The khan had the villagers searched and ordered that as long as Mrs Bishop remained in his territory she was not to be allowed to pay for anything.

Nothing daunted, Mrs Bishop continued on her way. Soon once more she was among 'nomadic tribes moving with vast flocks and

herds'. She was always happier when among these tented peoples than
in the settled villages, where she found much to criticize. In one such
village, the khan's house looked like 'a second-rate caravanserai' and
the rest was 'a miserable hamlet of low windowless hovels' surrounded
by 'narrow dirt-heaped alleys, with bones and offal lying about; gaunt
yelping dogs; bottle-green slimy pools, and ruins'. And she found the
people in the villages as dirty as their houses.

Mrs Bishop always had a special interest in the Bakhtiari women.
She felt they missed out on much of the excitement of life: while the
men were splendidly spirited horsemen, the women 'merely sat on
horses' and usually only then if they were pregnant or nursing babies,
otherwise they walked. They spent much time 'in quiet contemplation
of cooking pots'. But she admired the looks of some of them: three
young Bakhtiari wives in particular appealed to her as having 'a style of
beauty novel to me – straight noses, wide mouths, thin lips, and long
chins . . . their hair hangs round their wild, handsome faces . . . in
loose, heavy, but not unclean masses'.

Her curiosity about the women was matched by theirs about her.
They asked her if she could read, and if she made carpets – their own
occupation in winter being 'a little carpet-weaving, which takes the
place of our "fancy-work"'. On being told that Englishwomen liked
dancing, they thought this strange as 'here, our servants dance for us',
and men and women dancing together was considered 'contrary to the
elementary principles of morality'. They invariably asked if she had a
husband and children, and on hearing that she was a widow and child-
less 'they simulate weeping for one or two minutes, a hypocrisy which,
though it proceeds from a kindly feeling, has a very painful effect'.
They also wanted to hear her advice about how to take away wrinkles,
how to whiten teeth and how to hang on to their husbands when they
themselves reached the age of forty. One unfortunate young wife, who
was 'poorly dressed, very dejected-looking, and destitute of ornaments',
pleaded for something to bring back her husband's love.

It was not only the women who were curious about Mrs Bishop and the reason for her travelling. She was sometimes asked if she was searching for herbs that would convert base metal into gold. Others thought that she was mapping the country with sinister intent. She was reminded by the khan on one occasion that the English 'under the dress of a merchant often conceal the uniform of a soldier'. But whatever their suspicions, she was generally treated with respect. Presents of apricots and curds, of pickled celery and sour cream all arrived at her tent flap. When she asked for milk, she was given a cow. The khan complained that she made too few requests and that she should not 'feel as if you were in a foreign land . . . we love the English'. Apart from folk memories of Sir Henry Rawlinson and Sir Henry Layard, they had had little enough exposure to the English, so the remark was a considerable compliment to the intrepid Mrs Bishop and her medicine chest.

One of the reasons she was so popular with the Bakhtiari was undoubtedly her courage and disinclination to grumble. The fact that she was stout-hearted on the march comes across in passages in her letters: 'On reaching the snow I found Rustem Khan's horse half-buried in a drift, so I made the rest of the ascent on foot . . . the snow was three feet deep, but for the most part presented no difficulties.' She refers cheerfully to crossing a fast river 'on a twig bridge' and then 'fording a turbulent effluent'. And she was equally impervious to difficulties in camp: although her own tent was described by some of the tribe as 'fit for Allah', it was in fact open-fronted and devoid of any privacy, added to which 'sometimes their horses stumble over the tent ropes and nearly bring the tent down'. When robbed, she explains to her host that robberies occur everywhere, and that the unusual thing about her experience with the Bakhtiari was their prompt willingness to make restitution. Whingeing was not in this Victorian lady's nature.

Another of her endearing qualities was a quiet respect for all things Islamic, and a disinclination to flaunt her Christianity in any way that might appear provocative. She respected the frugalities of Ramadan and tried to lighten the load on her followers when they were hungry or exhausted as a result of fasting. She did not press reluctant ladies to be photographed. And she treated the mullahs with respect even when – as sometimes – they looked like thriving merchants and carried weapons.

Mrs Bishop may not have been a nurse, but she was certainly not squeamish. When not coping with human ailments – including gangrene – she was prepared to turn her self-taught skills to veterinary matters. On one occasion she was called before dawn to sew up a mule that had been gored by a wild boar – 'and awfully gored it was . . . a broad wound the depth of my hand and fully a foot long extended right into its chest, with a great piece taken out', she recorded. Among a people whose wealth was their livestock, a woman who could turn her hand to sewing up the entrails of animals was at a premium.

To the Bakhtiari Mrs Bishop must have seemed in every way a strange contrast to their own women. Many of the latter worked extremely hard in pitching and dismantling tents, cooking and performing other camp functions. But the more exalted khans' wives – Mrs Bishop's social equals – spent their time competing with each other for their husbands' affections, and at one and the same time currying favour with the favourite wife and trying to undermine her influence behind her back. When not so occupied, they were busily hiring professional storytellers to entertain them with love stories, or re-dyeing their hair and their eyebrows. Meanwhile, the English traveller in their midst had altogether different preoccupations: 'a pair of stout gardening gloves' was proving quite inadequate to stop her hands from blistering on the high mountain passes of the Zagros, and her spectacles 'with wire gauze sides' had to be abandoned as they threatened to roast her eyes. (Perhaps the stolen mask was being missed?)

But the Bakhtiari seemed to appreciate her qualities. When she arrived unescorted at one settlement, to treat some ailing women, the men of the tribe led her horse into the camp, and one of them made a step of his back while another made a lower step of his knee, to help her dismount elegantly. When on the same occasion a fierce guard dog attacked her horse, 'fixing its teeth into my stirrup guard and hanging on', the local khan shot the dog and threatened to beat its owner. All Bakhtiari women were safe from assault when travelling between villages, but the courtesies extended to Mrs Bishop went far beyond the usual and, being a widow, she did not risk being stoned to death if she was suspected of infidelity. Not that such suspicions would ever have been likely in her case. 'Your presence purifies the house," said her host, leading her into his tent after the incident with the dog – an unusual tribute to an 'infidel'.

Mrs Bishop's account of her travels with the Bakhtiari fill a substantial part of the two volumes she wrote – in the form of letters to a friend – about her Persian travels. Right throughout the summer of 1890 she was having a series of adventures, all of them exciting, but with a certain repetitive nature: precipitous paths over mountain passes, tricky river crossings, uncertain reception from new branches of the tribe, the theft of her possessions in camp and threats of highway robberies or worse, being mobbed by the sick and the dying in need of medicines . . . the pattern goes on and on.

But through it all shines her commitment to the nomadic life that she was experiencing at first hand. She raves in her book about 'the true Bakhtiari country, a land of mountains which rumour crests with eternal snows, of unexplored valleys and streams, of feudal chiefs, of blood feuds, and of nomads'. Always she comes back to the virtues of nomadic life: 'it was a real refreshment to be away from the mud of villages . . . their [nomadic] tents are barely a shelter from the wind and rain, but in them generations are born and die, despising those of their race who settle in villages.' She was aware that she was breaking new ground, at times journeying where no European had been before. Others were to come after her, but never very many in any one decade, and none more imbued with the recurring English obsession with migration.

The Bakhtiari could never quite work out why she was there: only her compatriots – who had elected her as the first lady Fellow of the Royal Geographical Society – could understand her strange calling.

MRS BISHOP may have been the first English lady to penetrate the Bakhtiari country, but she was by no means the last, as the subsequent pages of this book will show. But the most enraptured and uncritical of all lady travellers in the region must surely have been Mrs E. R. Durand who made *An Autumn Tour in Western Persia* in 1899. She went with her husband and a Mr Rennie, who was a member of the British legation at Tehran, with her lady's maid, a butler and a small group of other servants; and wherever they pitched camp they set up 'a small flagstaff flying the Union Jack in the daytime and a hanging lantern at night'. Mrs Durand was used to being a hostess in imperial Simla, and things tended to be compared with the standards of the British Raj.

The purpose of including the Bakhtiari country in their more wide-reaching tour was to make contact with the nomadic tribes or, more particularly, since this was a very social party, with 'the chiefs'. She wanted to see what sort of people they were. A further but subsidiary purpose seems to have been exploring the possibility of a new trade route 'through their rugged highlands'. Everything they encountered was seen by Mrs Durand through agreeably rose-tinted spectacles.

When Mr Rennie was 'splashed with mud from a wandering bullet' she commented that it 'was all very picturesque and charming'. The local khans 'could not have been more kind and hospitable . . . they behaved with the greatest courtesy and were so polite and agreeable that they made me feel at once I was among gentlemen'. She described a fight in which 'I believe some people had been killed' but went on immediately to add that the clansmen were all quite friendly again. When it transpired that some of the khans' sons had been educated abroad but not in England, Mrs Durand thought that 'this seems a pity . . . an English public school training is just what an Oriental boy wants'. But despite their failure to attend the right schools, the boys transpired to be 'dear little dignified, well-mannered creatures'.

31

Mrs Durand's cheerful outlook extended to the physical dangers of the trip. She describes crossing a 'narrow bridge of wicker work, forty feet above the water, with no rail . . . it was tipped over sideways, and looked very shaky altogether'; nothing deterred, Mrs Durand reported that she crossed without difficulty and 'had a very pleasant afternoon'.

In true Victorian style, Mrs Durand expected equal sang-froid from animals. When her husband's horse reached the worst place on a rocky mountain path and 'looked despairingly round, and down at the water, and up at the overhanging precipice', he gave her a moment's anxiety. But sure enough 'the well-bred sensible horse stepped forward and walked quietly across the rickety wicker bridge'. Good breeding was rewarded: the horse was brought home to England with them. On another occasion, however, the ending was less fortunate: 'we lost a horse drowned . . . its head came up three times, poor beast, with the eyes staring wildly, and then it sank into the dragging under-current.' One feels it was a less well-bred horse.

On another river crossing a rope broke and one of the Durands' servants was left dangling over a fast-flowing river; he was eventually pulled to safety but 'much upset'. However, a teacupful of 'old Scotch whisky from Dalgairns' of Dundee' restored him; Mrs Durand added that no other medicine was regarded as nearly so efficacious. Like all travellers in these parts, she and her husband were subjected to a regular flow of sick and injured people wanting medicine, and when she commented that many of the nomadic tribesmen looked very poor and unhealthy, she was readily reassured by her guides that 'there is no water and air anywhere like the water and air in the Bakhtiari country . . . there are no unhealthy people in our mountains'. All was well, really.

Characters who to other travellers would doubtless have appeared as sinister and menacing were to her all part of life's rich tapestry. On one occasion a wild man leapt out and forcefully stopped her husband's horse, gesticulating frantically and showing scars around his neck from the chains in which he had been restrained after a recent killing of a fellow tribesman, and protesting to the visitors 'after all, one must kill people sometimes'. Mrs Durand took it in her stride and reported that 'the party broke up with laughter all round, and everyone seemed satisfied'. She comments wryly that 'men are fond of carrying knives in Persia, and sometimes the results are serious' – just a little local colour, in fact.

Mrs Durand's interest in the migratory Bakhtiari nomads was conditioned at every step by her social awareness. The khans were gentlemen and the rest were colourful natives as far as she was concerned. She was no anthropologist. She had heard reports of earlier compatriots – particularly Sir Henry Layard – who had ventured into these parts, and she felt she had not let them down by any show of feebleness. Indeed, 'our kind Bakhtiari chiefs' had shown their appreciation of her by presenting her with a box of bulbs – and it was only unfortunate that one of her servants had inadvertently left them behind somewhere in the mountains. The only real anxieties that were allowed to appear in her book did not concern the plight of the local people or the hardships of the route, but concerned the news from South Africa where her son was fighting for the British army with the 9th Lancers in the Boer War; the only 'bad news' in this positive tale was that she discovered on emerging from the fastness of the Zagros that 'our troops are shut up in Ladysmith'. When she finally left the Bakhtiari hills behind her on 5 November 1899, she confessed to the greatest hardship she had experienced: 'Tea without milk is a thing I could never get reconciled to. Some people like it, and the Persians drink it in great quantities . . . but it always seemed to me to be quite horrid.'

The Bakhtiari had been mystified by Mrs Bishop: one wonders what on earth they could have thought of Mrs Durand.

SIR HENRY LAYARD was by temperament and practice a scholar, but he had had no formal higher education. One of the next of his compatriots (after Mrs Bishop) to explore the Bakhtiari country had – on the contrary – not only achieved first-class honours at Oxford in modern history in 1888, but was the first woman ever to do so (although despite her success in the examinations, the regulations of the university did not at that period allow her formally to take up her degree).

Gertrude Bell devoted most of her life after Oxford to exploring the Middle East, and acted as a political agent for the British government in the region during the First World War. In the early 1890s her travels took her to Persia, and on her return she published 'a book of travel' entitled *Persian Pictures*. In it she devoted a chapter to the nomadic tribes whom she describes as 'dwellers in tents'. Unlike Layard, she gives no detailed account in this of her adventures among the tribes, nor of their pattern of life, physical hardships and political problems. But what she does do is to put into words something of the romantic appeal to herself and to her fellow countrymen of Persia's (or now Iran's) nomads. She says that while philosophers may claim that every man is a wanderer at heart, it is more accurate to say that every man loves to fancy himself as a wanderer.

She lyricises about the landscape through which the tribes pass on their migrations:

> Here are steep valleys . . . strewn with rocks, crowned with fantastic crags, scarred by deep watercourses; here the hawks hover, the eagle passes with mournful cry, and the prisoned wind dashes madly through the gorge. Through the middle of the plain flows a river, its strong bed cut deep into the earth . . . flocks of goats feed along its banks, and from some convenient hollow rises the smoke of a nomad camp.

She notes the contrast between the landscape when the tribes are passing through it – when it is strewn with black tents, when horses and camels crop the grass by the edge of the stream, and the air is full of the barking of dogs and the cries of women and children – and the solitude that remains when 'the nomads have moved onward' and silence has spread itself like a mantle from mountain to mountain.

She gets near to analysing the appeal of such nomadic life when she describes 'the delightful sense of irresponsibility' that comes with passing through a landscape on which man has made no mark. Equally, she finds a profound loneliness in surroundings that give no hint that humanity has ever passed that way. Unlike Layard again, she feels no kinship for the Bakhtiari: 'the nomads can no more give you a sense of companionship than the wild goats: they are equally unconscious of the desolation that surrounds them.' Even the romantic appeal of a Bakhtiari camp at night, when the red light of the fires flickers between the tents, has a sinister aspect for her: 'the tribesmen flit like demons backwards and forwards . . . you find yourself transplanted into a circle of the Inferno . . . shaggy dogs leap out barking to meet you . . . dark eyes glisten through the dusk.'

Gertrude Bell tries in vain to imagine herself akin to 'the tented races', but finds that the whole life is too strange for her, too far away. 'It is half vision and half nightmare'; she has no place among dwellers in tents, she declares.

DESPITE Gertrude Bell's reaction – or possibly because of it – the Bakhtiari appear to have exercised a particular fascination for English lady travellers. A quarter of a century after her contact with them, another remarkably strong-minded and eccentric Englishwoman set out with four men friends to cross the Bakhtiari country in 1927: she was Vita Sackville-West, poet, intimate friend of Virginia Woolf, creator of Sissinghurst gardens and wife of Harold Nicolson.

The idea of travelling across southern Persia (as Iran was still known) did not come to her out of the blue. Harold Nicolson was posted to the British legation in Tehran and – although she firmly declined to share his diplomatic life abroad with him – she was attracted by the idea of traversing a wild tract of country virtually unknown to her compatriots, and seeing something of pastoral nomadic life. Her interest in the mutation of the seasons and the relationship of countrymen and crops, which had found expression in her long poem *The Land*, published the previous year, was well established. The Bakhtiari were a people permanently in search of fresh grass, whose movements were dictated by the seasons of the year, and who regularly braved the rigours of snow-covered mountains and raging torrents to achieve their 200-mile twice-yearly migration. Although addicted to the comforts of life and no horsewoman, Vita Sackville-West braced herself for an adventure.

Apart from her husband, her companions included Gladwyn Jebb (later Lord Gladwyn and ambassador to the United Nations and to France), to whom seems to have fallen much of the practical administration of the trip: Vita refers to 'his calm and haughty efficiency'. The expedition was made possible only by some assiduous courting of the Bakhtiari leadership and of the relevant Persian officials by the diplomats involved. The reluctant authorities swung wildly in their attempts to dissuade the travellers: one moment the Bakhtiari route was described as passable for a motorcar (a blatant lie) and therefore not worth traversing; and the next moment it was said to be so dangerous that an escort of armed guards would be needed, and therefore better not attempted. Research into the realities of the route was hampered by the fact that they could find no detailed books on the subject more recent than Sir Henry Layard's account of almost a century before, which was not altogether surprising as there had been so few intervening travellers.

Vita and her companions made their journey in spring, but in the reverse direction to the migrating tribesmen: the visitors were descending to the plains having crossed the Zagros Mountains, while the tribesmen were driving their flocks into higher pastures for the summer grazing. This had the effect that Vita's party were forever going against the tide of all that moving life, being always confronted with faces and never with tails. She memorably describes '. . . the long, silly faces of sheep, the satyric faces of goats with their little black horns; the patient faces of tiny donkeys, picking their way under heavy loads; and then, six or eight little heads of newly born kids, bobbing about, sewn up in a sack on a donkey's back'.

Interested as she was in the people and animals through whom she was moving, Vita was possibly even more interested in the effects of nomadic life on the terrain through which the Bakhtiari passed. She wrote that it seemed right that the mountains should witness the great pilgrimage in the two temperate seasons 'and right also that the mountains should be left to their own loneliness during the violence of summer and the desolation of winter'. Here was the author of *The Land* as fascinated by the interplay of itinerant tribesmen and their barren hillsides as she was to be by the interplay of English yeoman farmers and the rich soil of their Weald of Kent.

Indeed, Vita's account (recorded in her book *Twelve Days*, published by Leonard and Virginia Woolf in 1928) is highly orientated towards her own sensitivities. She had at first wondered if there was sufficient material in her trip of less than a fortnight to warrant a whole book. There would not have been, had she not turned her focus so frequently inwards. The nomadic life – however briefly sampled – had a sharp appeal to her:

Dawn, the hour at which one started; dusk, the hour at which one stopped; springs, at which one drank; beasts of burden, to which one bound one's moving home; a beast from the flock, which one slaughtered and ate fresh; fire; a story; sleep. There was nothing else.

The sensitivities were sometimes less introspective and more squeamish. When a Bakhtiari chief brought in a young lamb to kill for their supper, complete with a copper bowl to catch the blood from its slit throat, Vita pleaded that it should be spared: 'though what we really meant was that we ourselves should be spared the horrid sight.' And sometimes the sentiments aroused, as when a Bakhtiari in a white cloak galloped past on a white horse while they were dining, were a surrender to the purest romanticism.

But while sensitive to their own reactions, Vita and her companions were not always equally sensitive to the Bakhtiari's reactions to them.

There were several incidents when Vita's attempts to photograph Bakhtiari girls caused terror (could the camera be an evil eye?) in the objects of her attention. One Bakhtiari chief who accompanied his gift of a lamb with an invitation to dine in his tent and stay in his camp as his overnight guests, had the lamb accepted and the invitation rejected – it would have been too much trouble re-pitching the tents. And a chief who asked for medical help was quickly abandoned with some quinine tablets when his temperature was discovered to be 108 degrees – 'lest the man should die before our eyes, and we be blamed'. There was a stronger element of curiosity than of participation in this elite little group of travellers.

CURIOSITY about the Bakhtiari was not confined to English-speaking people in the Old World: across the Atlantic, too, there was a fascination with their way of life. In the early 1920s a film crew (or a 'motion picture' team, as it was then known) determined to film an annual migratory ride. Three Americans – Marguerite Harrison, Ernest B. Schoedsack and Merian C. Cooper – attempted first to film the Kurds, but the Turkish authorities blocked this plan, so they moved south across the desert to Baghdad, where Sir Arnold Wilson and Miss Gertrude Bell advised them to try the Bakhtiari country.

Their purpose was to screen a drama that, they considered, would have almost universal appeal: 'When man fights for his life, all the world looks on. And where does man have to fight harder than when he finds his opponent the unrelenting and stern forces of Nature? We decided to throw on the screen the actual struggle for life of a migratory people.' Schoedsack was the cameraman; Mrs Harrison helped with organization, interpreting and providing medical assistance; Cooper wrote a book (published in New York in 1925) about the expedition, which was very much the 'book of the film' rather than the other way round. Both film and book were entitled *Grass*.

Cooper and his companions joined the Bakhtiari in their winter grazing grounds near Shushtar at the northern end of the Persian Gulf.

As the winter grass withered, they joined the tribe in crossing the Karun river and traversing the snow-covered Zagros Mountains before their descent on to the summer uplands west of Isfahan. At their own request, they travelled with a group of the tribe who had been allocated one of the toughest routes through the mountains. Cooper got to know the khan of his particular group, and his two wives and close relations, fairly intimately. He decided that the khan was a rascal, but a brave and engaging one.

His description of the Karun river crossing is detailed and dramatic: a bend in the river was chosen where the current tended to wash men and animals safely on to the other shore, rather than carrying them indefinitely downstream. Flotation rafts were made of inflated skins, to which were attached children, newly born animals and goats (the only full-grown livestock not expected to swim). Even with all the precautions, and with the khan himself repeatedly swimming to and fro to supervise the crossing, there were losses: 'every day dozens of animals – principally sheep – have been drowned, and tonight the women of our camp are wailing in the tent of the mother of a young tribesman, who was carried on down past the landing-place into the rapids below.'

But Cooper's most purple prose is reserved for the mountain ascent: 'Like flies against the almost vertical mountainside clung the struggling horde.' He describes how the advance party waded barefoot through the snows, probing the ground with long poles to detect any crevice since 'it was all up with man or beast who fell . . . down its black depths'. On some stretches the tribes were stumbling up the passes 'encased by snow walls' cut by the advance party, and any who ventured off the narrow track risked sliding to their deaths below. Most of the tribe slept in the open air even at these altitudes, rather than struggle to unload and pitch tents; indeed, most of the tents had been left behind at the winter grazing, because they had different tents awaiting them on the summer uplands and could not face the extra weight of portage required to provide shelter on the migratory journey.

One theme recurs repeatedly in Cooper's account: the value the

Bakhtiari attach to preserving and using their weapons. He reports one khan as saying that every man of his tribe would die rather than give up his arms. There were rumours current among the tribes in the 1920s that a Cossack army – in the Shah's pay – was marching towards the Bakhtiari lands to disarm the tribesmen. The rumours were not without foundation, and the bravado of the tribes was not without justification, as subsequent events were to show.

Cooper's book is written with a mixture of hyperbole and repetition which makes it a less convincing read than it might otherwise be. But the film is still extant and provides one of the best records that exists of the hardships of the migration. It contributed in no small measure to the spread across the Atlantic of the traditional preoccupation with nomads that already existed in England. If a pastoral tribe who kept tents at both ends of their migratory ride were not – in the strictest sense – nomadic, that did not dim the attraction these people were to exercise over sedentary Anglo-Saxons.

IN 1959 a very small and elite group of spirited English travellers, who had seen the film *Grass* and who had read Vita Sackville-West's account of her journey with the Bakhtiari, were determined to undertake a similar adventure. The problem, as always, was getting the consent of the Shah to allow them to travel and mix with the Bakhtiari, whose migratory habits were anathema to the monarch and his government. But the group in question had two great advantages. One of them was Pamela Wyndham, a notable society beauty who was the chatelaine of Petworth House in Sussex and whose husband – John Wyndham (shortly to become Lord Egremont) – was political private secretary to his close friend, the then Prime Minister, Harold Macmillan. Mrs Wyndham had private connections with the Bakhtiari and the Shah's court, and she shrewdly chose the moment in the run-up to the Queen of England's state visit to Iran to put their request.

The other advantage was that another member of the party was counsellor at the British embassy in Tehran. John Russell was no ordinary diplomat. The son of Russell Pasha (a former head of the Egyptian police) and himself a kinsman of the Duke of Bedford, he was married to a former Greek beauty queen, and the couple were endowed with a sizeable personal fortune. Russell was a keen horseman: a Master of Foxhounds (MFH) in England, when subsequently posted as ambassador to Ethiopia he used to exchange thoroughbred stallions as birthday presents with the Emperor Haile Selassie. Russell was also – almost uniquely among members of the Tehran diplomatic corps – a personal friend of the Shah. Additionally, he had the great advantage of residence in Tehran and thus the opportunity to establish the necessary contacts and make the complex arrangements required for the expedition.

And it was no casual or small undertaking, consisting as it did of two khans from the Bakhtiari, two of their Persian ladies, Pamela Wyndham, Harry (Viscount) Hambledon, John Russell and his wife Aliki, three *kalantars* (organizers of the caravan), six sons and brothers of the *kalantars*, a radio operator, three cooks, eight domestic servants, five *farrashes* (literally 'carpet spreaders') and three grooms. To these were added six stallions belonging to the khans, six tribal mares belonging individually to the *kalantars*, two horses for the radio and batteries, twelve riding mules, thirty baggage mules, a number of (soon-to-be-eaten) sheep and a small pet dog. In all, the party consisted of forty-five people and fifty-six animals. It was no wonder that even John Russell referred to the 'by no means trivial question of expense'.

The objective was not just to achieve the migratory ride from the coastal plains of Khuzestan, at the head of the Persian Gulf, over the Zagros Mountains to the upland summer grazing; it was also to experience at first hand the nomadic way of life and to gain some understanding of the Bakhtiari peoples. For this reason they chose to make the journey in company with the tribe, moving in the same direction and at the same time (unlike Vita Sackville-West, who was always heading in the opposite direction). Because John Russell and his party were better mounted and supported than the tribesmen and did not

41

have to graze flocks as they went, they naturally moved faster; but they camped at greater leisure and in greater comfort, so they were for ever overtaking and being overtaken by the stream of tribesmen with their families, flocks, herds, accoutrements and baggage. Many of these – who were no part of their own special group – became familiar and friendly figures.

John Russell told me in graphic detail about this trip when (as a young diplomat on leave from Moscow) I visited him in Tehran later the same year. He also kept a diary on his journey, writing it up at rest stops en route and around the camp-fire after dinner. It is probably the fullest record ever made of the minutiae of this great migration.

The party took only fourteen days over the journey, riding some twenty-six kilometres a day but totalling only some three hundred and twelve kilometres in all, as they spent two days resting and hunting in the middle. They averaged about six hours in the saddle each day, but on the more perilous mountain tracks they preferred to dismount and walk the horses. Roads are unknown to this region of the Zagros Mountains, which have never been crossed by wheeled vehicles. Like the makers of the film *Grass*, they watched the tribes crossing rivers on inflated goatskin rafts. And when they reached the mountains they found that even the rough tracks of the trail had fallen into disrepair as the tribes now travelled in smaller units than previously; the steps cut in the tracks up the passes had worn 'as smooth as temple steps . . . and as dangerous'. Animal droppings made the steps more slippery still, and the path tended to slope outwards towards the abyss. At some points there were sheer rock faces of 2,000 feet below and above the track. The Monar Pass was some 5,000 feet above sea-level, and the highest point on the route was over 8,750 feet. For Westerners accustomed to the comforts of embassies and stately homes, this was no easy picnic.

But John Russell and his khanly hosts had determined that what comforts could be provided along the route should be. They took with them five double sleeping tents and two big mess tents, in addition to the kitchen tents and the tents for the servants. Most of these tents were military (Indian army) in origin and had come to them through the good offices of oil companies. The tents were sent ahead, so that not only was the camp pitched and ready for the khans and their guests at the end of the day's travels, but a luncheon tent and another for the post-luncheon siesta – the latter sited to provide a cooling wind-tunnel – were also sent ahead each morning. When it rained, as it did on the first night, the tents had to be dried out in the morning sun before they were light enough for the mules to be able to carry them. The food, drink and cooking paraphernalia were packed up by the chefs in huge padlocked wooden boxes – in the manner of a nineteenth-century explorer's retinue.

The horses that the khans had provided were sure-footed and courageous and caused no problems to the party, although one of the baggage mules kicked Pamela Wyndham on the knee and she was lucky not to be seriously injured. The good nature of the horses was all the more remarkable when the design of their bits was taken into account; these were of a savage local pattern that ensured that, when reined in, the metal tongue of the bit jabbed painfully into the horse's palate, thus ensuring an instantaneous application of the brakes. The members of the party all had different ideas about saddles, Russell preferring an Indian army troop saddle (complete with Queen Victoria's head on the breastplate) with a high front and back which kept the rider sitting 'as straight up as a clothes peg'; it was festooned with big brass rings for hanging things on. But Russell (as an MFH) and his companions were deeply shocked by some aspects of the Bakhtiari's treatment of their horses; in particular, when one riderless horse (not in their own party) stumbled and fell over a cliff, it was not shot to put it out of its agony but left to the tender mercies of the vultures.

The little cavalcade of distinguished travellers and their escort at times resembled a sporting expedition setting off to the North-West Frontier of the British Raj in India. And sport was to be a major part of their activities. Spare moments in the evenings and the two mid-journey 'rest' days were largely devoted to shooting and fishing. Game included partridge, wild duck, boar and even ibex. Shots were fired into the mouths of caves in the hope of flushing out bears that might be sleeping or sheltering therein. Around the evening camp-fires, there were endless stories of encounters with bears in these mountains: a bear was said to have carried off a woman and kept her prisoner in its cave, rolling a heavy stone across the entrance whenever it went out hunting. One of the khans claimed that his father had a stuffed bear – shot in these hills – which stood 2.3 metres high. Once a large black bear emerged and was pursued until it sought sanctuary in protective ravines. Leopards were reputed still to prowl around the migration trail, in the hope of finding stragglers. A yellow wolf was spotted and shot at from the saddle. On one occasion when wild boar were sighted, Russell and his Bakhtiari companions set off at a wild gallop after them, 'bullets whistling in all directions . . . like one of the rougher Irish point-to-points, with firearms added'.

But some game were already extinct in these hills even by the 1950s. The red deer, which had been heavier and as handsome as any in the Scottish Highlands, were no longer to be seen here (although they were still found in the forests of Khorassan); and of course the maneless Persian lions, which had been a feature of the plains as recently as Lord Curzon's visit at the turn of the nineteenth-twentieth centuries, were now only a memory, but a vivid memory: the Bakhtiari maintained there were two sorts of lion – 'Shiah' lions that could be exorcised by calling on the name of Allah, and 'kafir' lions that were man-eaters and beyond redemption.

To further encourage (if encouragement were needed?) these sporting and hunting instincts in the tribesmen, Russell organized a shooting competition, offering his own Winchester rifle to all comers and a selection of beer cans as targets at a distance of two hundred metres. All the Bakhtiari preferred to shoot without the use of a tele-scopic sight, and the older men proved better shots than their younger relatives, as they had learnt to shoot in the days before the Shah had disarmed the tribes and denied this sport to the younger generation. The khans told Russell that their men would talk about his event with nostalgia for years to come: profligacy with bullets was a sure way to their hearts.

All this shooting was very confusing to one small contingent that was attached to the Bakhtiari for the duration of their migration. This was the gendarmerie 'escort', provided by the Iranian government to protect the foreign visitors from any hazards they might encounter from the tribesmen. In reality, as Russell was quick to observe, it was the foreign visitors who were providing protection for the gendarmerie, because the Bakhtiari tribesmen had no love of the military or of the state authorities, and there were old scores to be settled resulting from past excesses by the military. Had the khans and their well-connected band of foreign visitors not been present, the gendarmes might have found their reception at the hands of the tribesmen was none too peaceful; as it was, they kept themselves to themselves and rode as bewildered observers among the marching hordes. Russell wryly recalled of them that the Persian word for soldier was *sarbaz* – 'one who gambles with his own head as the stake'. Without the protection of the foreign observers, these *sarbaz* would undoubtedly have been gambling with their lives.

But the greatest fascination for the visitors – even more than the scenery or the wildlife – was the nomadic way of life revealing itself to them as they journeyed onwards. At the early camps, before they reached the mountains, the tribesmen would not go to the trouble of pitching their black tents, but would erect a screen of woven reeds, rush matting and quilts, behind which the family would squat for the night. There were no looms for rug weaving among their frugal possessions, as these were too cumbersome to carry over the passes. At the first camp, Russell found one old woman perched on a high rock, with a scooped-out hollow top, grinding corn. He speculated that the rock had probably been used in this manner during the passing migration from time immemorial.

Because of the continual leapfrogging of the families and their flocks, as the foreign party moved through them and then they moved past the party again, Russell and his companions became almost as familiar with them as they would have done if they had not been travelling in their own exclusive group. The Bakhtiari girls would joke and even flirt with them: one young mother, with a baby at her breast, another child on her back and a third holding her hand, asked Russell cheerfully if she could give him a lift! Sadly, a young woman did not keep her charms for long: Russell commented that 'after a brief flowering as a young bride, in a few years she is an ageless, sexless, shapeless beast of burden'. But during that brief flowering, the women – who wore no veils – were strikingly good looking, with their high cheekbones, broad faces and long narrow eyes, and they were full of virile activity, rounding up stray sheep and goats while balancing infants on their hips. The teeth of both men and women glistened white, despite the fact that toothbrushes were unknown. Families tended to be large: one young girl with whom Russell spoke transpired to be her parents' sixth daughter and was called Amman Bas – 'Dear Heaven, enough'.

It was possible to tell the status of the men by their head-dress. The rank and file wore brimless caps in black or brown, while the caps of the chiefs were white. Men with aspirations to elegance sported crossed cartridge belts over their costumes. The status of the women was revealed by the profusion of gold or silver coins sewn on to their black attire, indicating wealth and position. If any doubt remained about the status of the chiefs, it was resolved for the visitors by witnessing the Mori tribesmen (a branch of the Bakhtiari) kissing the khan's knee as they held his stirrup for him to dismount. This was still a feudal society.

It was also potentially a violent society. Not only the Iranian military were traditionally at risk: little more than a decade before Russell's march, a British vice-consul and a doctor from the Church Missionary Society had been murdered as they travelled through this area by tribesmen coveting their sporting rifles. The case had been a brutal one: tracks were later to show that the doctor's young son had run off and hidden among rocks, only to be tracked down and murdered like his father. The culprits had never been caught.

As with earlier travellers, such as Mrs Bishop and Vita Sackville-West, there was a constant demand from the tribesmen for medical assistance. This fell particularly heavily on the ladies, especially Aliki Russell and Pamela Wyndham. Guessing what the demands would be, they had come provided with an extended first-aid kit and prepared for everything from sunstroke to frostbite: 'Dettol, Zambuk, iodine, aspirin and strong antibiotic cream are our best weapons in this country where medicine and doctors are unknown.' But some of the ailments they could not anticipate. A patient with gunshot wounds, inflicted during a quarrel over a woman (the husband had sent her back to her family after a few months), was one such. Another was a sixteen-year-old girl with a dead baby and internal pains which defied diagnosis. Other prospective patients were so unused to medicines that their likely reactions were unpredictable and not to be risked. Even an application of anti-scorpion serum gave rise to doubts. But on the other hand there were advantages in having built up no immunity to antibiotics: when the flesh around one man's open wound on his shin – after being kicked by a horse – was beginning to rot, it was felt that 'given these peoples' total virginity to medicine, a good squeeze of peni-cillin ointment will probably save the leg'. It did. Another happy story was that of the eighty-six-year-old cook who was so addicted to smoking opium ('after sixty years he was beginning to get into the habit') that he was believed to have reached a point where if a snake bit him it was the snake that died.

The sad fact was that it was not just first aid or emergency help that the visitors were providing: it was often the only medical help available to these tribesmen. There were no hospitals (just as there were no roads, bridges, schools, wells or telegraph poles) in the Bakhtiari country; and if the tribesmen ventured into a town or city, such as Shiraz or Isfahan, they could not afford to pay for treatment at the hospitals when they got there. The government's attitude to the problem was: 'Let them settle, then we will give them doctors.'

Apart from medical help, the visitors could not do a lot for the Bakhtiari tribesmen. Certainly, tips or any monetary presents were quite unacceptable among these proud peoples, although cartridges and cigarettes were popular with the men and sweets with the children. With the khans, the only acceptable presents were those that fell within the well-prescribed category of 'noble gifts' exchangeable between equals: hawks, rifles, hunting knives, greyhounds or – of course – horses. Doubtless in Lord Curzon's day a lion cub would have come into this category.

Second only to the fascination of getting to know the nomadic life, and indeed a facet of it, was the sense of stepping backwards in time and stepping outside the normal confines of space. Writing his journal alone in the fading evening light, Russell relished 'the enchanting and peculiar sounds of a camp going to sleep – the occasional neigh of a horse, the rattle of a mule's picket chain, the dry knock of a mallet securing a tent peg, the call of a little owl; and the river gently purring over the rapids'. It was moments such as this, or when a young shepherd boy was playing his pipe, or when the khans were telling tales of German spies and mysterious oil prospectors, or when one of them would read Persian poetry aloud around the fire at night, that the magic of nomadic life seemed its most intense to the English visitors. No radios blared out from the rough bivouacs (the only radio was the one lent to the visitors by General Bakhtiar – head of the Shah's dreaded secret police, the SAVAK – as an emergency link); no drunken songs emerged from the black tents of Islam. The shepherds slept with their flocks, as tied to their sheep as a ploughman to his plough. If the tribesmen dreaded the rigours of the long migration, they did not complain; for them, this was life as it had ever been.

For Russell, this was what had made the three years of planning, in every spare moment from his embassy work, worthwhile. This was indeed what had drawn Russell and his friends, like their compatriots over the centuries before, to come to throw in their lot – albeit briefly – with the migrating Bakhtiari.

# 2

# The Qashqai

―――≽◆≼―――

Any nomad migration must be organised with the precision and flexibility of a military campaign. Behind, the grass is shrivelling. Ahead, the passes may be blocked with snow.

Bruce Chatwin

A FEW years after Sir Henry Layard had undertaken his adventurous travels among the Bakhtiari in the 1840s, another Englishman – also on the fringe of the diplomatic world – made a memorable journey to the south of Shiraz in southern Persia: he turned his attention not to the Bakhtiari but to their rival migratory tribe, the Qashqai.

Consul Keith Abbott had the East in his blood – or at least in his family tradition. Both his brothers were educated at the East India Company college at Addiscombe in England, and both rose to become generals, one having come up through the Bengal Engineers, and the other through the Bengal Artillery, in the days before the Indian Mutiny. Both were knighted.

Keith Abbott's career was less glamorous but equally devoted. His most significant post was that of consul-general in Tabriz and he made himself the greatest expert of his time on the remoter parts of Persia. Perhaps because of the more spectacular careers of his brothers, or perhaps because of overexposure to the rigours of the Persian Gulf climate, Keith Abbott became a testy and cantankerous traveller, demanding in his expectations of hospitality and quick to see the inadequacies of lesser breeds.

In March 1850 he set out to explore, map and record an almost totally unknown part of the country south and east of Shiraz, having heard of the nomadic tendency of the tribes and being anxious to inform the Royal Geographical Society about them. Everywhere he went he took compass bearings and measured precise distances: his final report to the RGS is weighed down with columns of statistics that can have been of little interest to anyone (except possibly someone who was planning a military campaign through the country). He travelled with a retinue of servants whom he sent on ahead to secure suitable accommodation for himself.

Abbott had hardly left Shiraz when he ran into his first fracas. His team of scouts and servants reached a village – 'a group of miserable hovels', according to Abbott – and set about requisitioning the best of what was available for the consul. Their efforts were not appreciated by the locals: the inhabitants were 'indisposed to give us quarters', and later 'villagers collected with fire-arms and long heavy-headed bludgeons'. Abbott reported that on his arrival he managed to 'pacify the hags of the village' and then – having inspected the best billet available – declared that they were 'the abode of legions of vermin' and rejected them. Other villages received the same treatment and also reacted with the 'clubs armed with heavy knobs'; he was not the most popular self-invited guest.

When he moved out of the settled areas into the tribal regions, hovels gave way to black goatskin tents. Here he found, when not the subject of skirmishes himself, that he became involved in those of others. He was aware that the Qashqai claimed descent from a race transplanted by the Mongol invader Hulagu – a grandson of Genghis Khan – who swept through Kashgar and parts of Afghanistan in 1256. So he was not surprised by the evidence of marauding that confronted him. He reported without surprise how six mounted plunderers from the Baharlu tribe drove off fifty head of cattle from their neighbours and were pursued and a number of them killed. What few permanent habitations there were in this region tended to be turreted towers. Abbott got into the habit of firing off volleys of shots at the approach to any settlement to scare off potential ambushers and 'put himself in readiness to repel an attack'. He must – at the least – have seemed a nervous and slightly alarming visitor.

Sometimes he went further with his militant involvement. When the guest of one Qashqai (or 'Cashghau', as he spelt it) khan, he volunteered advice to his host about how he might capture a local fort that was holding out against him; he proposed tunnelling under the walls and blowing them up. Doubtless his military engineer brother had explained such operations to him, but his advice ignored the tribesmen's lack of high explosives. It did the trick nonetheless. When the beleaguered defenders heard that a European had arrived on the scene and proposed a plan that would bring about the fall of the fort within two hours, they immediately sued for surrender terms.

By early April the Qashqai had started their migration from the plains to their summer upland pastures. Abbott witnessed this and, despite his negative attitude to most local activities, was impressed despite himself:

This is a very difficult pass, the road leading generally over bare slippery rock, on which the cattle scarcely maintain a footing, and where ledges of rock crossing the path or steep rises or falls add to the difficulty . . . the sheep or goats moved together in large flocks; the asses, oxen, camels, dogs and the men, women and children, were all mixed up together . . . sometimes the children were intrusted [sic] with the care of young kids or lambs, which they carried in their arms; others were strapped on the backs of the beasts, and seemed perfectly at ease. The road was so encumbered with the tribes and their property that we were much delayed.

The last sentence gives – as always – some hint of Abbott's impatience with the local inhabitants.

The Qashqai women in particular aroused his disdain. He recorded that he had seen nothing approaching good looks in any of them and that they were further disfigured by the filth and rags in which they were clad. While 'there was nothing feminine in their appearance', he grudgingly concluded that 'any one of them is as good as a man in a fight'. Either his eye was prejudiced, or the Qashqai women have improved in looks dramatically over the past century and a half: recent travellers – myself included – have noted their shy charms.

Abbott was on his travels for nine months in all, and covered a vast tract of territory between Baghdad and Tehran, including most of Luristan. His curiosity had driven him to probe the Qashqai's nomadic way of life, but it was to be left to other Englishmen to strike any real rapport with this distinctive tribe.

IT was almost a hundred years later that another Englishman set out to live with the Qashqai. He also reported his findings in detail, not as in the case of Abbott to the Royal Geographical Society, but to an almost equally illustrious body – the Royal Central Asian Society. But he was a very different figure from Consul Abbott, and his impressions were more positive – possibly because he was not motivated exclusively or mainly by curiosity, but by an extremely practical desire and capacity to help the people among whom he travelled.

Captain Oliver Garrod, a doctor in the Royal Army Medical Corps, was sent to southern Iran in the middle of the Second World War with a brief to provide basic medical services in a part of the world where the British government was anxious to establish some influence. It was a curious mission. He was clearly to purvey medicine and goodwill; possibly also to keep a watchful eye on the sympathies and activities of the tribes with whom he was moving.

Iran (or Persia, as Winston Churchill insisted on still calling her at that date) had played an enigmatic role in the early years of the Nazi conflict. The Iranian rulers had shown a disturbing tendency to veer towards sympathy with Germany, and as a result the Russian Red Army had occupied large parts of northern Iran and the British army parts of southern Iran. Reza Shah (the first of the Pahlavi line) had been prevailed upon to abdicate in favour of his young son and go into exile in South Africa. As the German invasion of Russia advanced, it became increasingly important to be able to dispatch oil and other supplies from the Persian Gulf to the Red Army in the Caucasus. The tribal areas of the south had become strategically significant.

And the tribes themselves – particularly the Qashqai – were flexing their muscles. Reza Shah had been a scourge of the nomadic tribes; he had forcibly settled them in appalling conditions. Garrod describes how: 'Refuse rotted in the villages, polluting the springs and spreading typhoid and dysentery . . . the mud hovels were often no better than large dog kennels . . . indescribable fug was built up in which pneumonia and tuberculosis flourished.' After Reza Shah's fall and exile, the Qashqai took to the hills and their nomadic life again; their leaders returned to them from prison or exile, and they dug up or seized useful quantities of firearms. Suddenly they were a force in the land once more.

But they were not altogether a friendly force as far as Britain and her allies were concerned. The Qashqai khans continued to conspire with a German agent called Meyer who operated in and around Shiraz, just as in the First World War they had conspired with the German agent Wassmuss and had provoked the intervention of the South Persia Rifles commanded by Sir Percy Sykes.* In 1942 the British unearthed a plot that linked German agents with the disaffected Qashqai leadership, with a number of members of the Majlis (parliament) in Tehran, and with an even larger number of serving Iranian army officers. The co-ordinator and linchpin in all this anti-Allied activity was a certain

---

*Coincidentally, Brigadier-General Sir Percy Sykes, the celebrated historian of Persia, presided over the meeting of the Royal Central Asian Society on 25 May 1945 at which Captain Garrod presented his findings about the Qashqai.

General Zahidi, Governor of Isfahan. It seemed all too likely that at a word from him a widespread uprising would ensue, which the British garrison would have been quite unable to contain. If this happened, the supply line to southern Russia would be cut and the Red Army's ability to repel the German invasion put in jeopardy. There was everything to play for.

The British high command's solution, approved by General 'Jumbo' Wilson, was to dispatch Major Fitzroy Maclean of the Cameron Highlanders to kidnap General Zahidi from under the noses of his staff and guards and remove him from the scene. It was not an easy task, because if instead of a quiet abduction there were to be an exchange of fire, then the very revolt that the British wished to avoid might have flared up. How this remarkably dashing operation was accomplished is recorded in Sir Fitzroy's own book, *Eastern Approaches*, and forms no part of this story. But it does illustrate the unusual – indeed unique – circumstances in which Captain Garrod was dispatched to spend twenty months mostly in the Luristan and Fars provinces of Iran.

Unlike Abbott, Garrod was an enthusiast for what he found and saw. 'The Qashqai,' he declared, 'approach the highest level of nomadic civilization.' He found much to admire. In contrast to other tribes 'whose ambition was to possess their full legal quota of wives', the Qashqai with hardly an exception were monogamous. He encountered numerous instances of real family love and affection. Blood feuds were almost unknown and murder very rare, disputes being settled by recourse to tribal law. (All this was in marked contrast to the neighbouring Boir Ahmedi tribe whom Garrod found to be continually indulging in endless strife and bloodshed: their most common sickness was gunshot wounds, and they had a charming habit of disposing of unwanted rivals by 'using a preparation of finely ground leopards' whiskers which they conceal in their food', bringing on a lingering death from ulceration of the gut – the symptoms of which were slow to develop and thus made such murders hard to detect.)

Garrod found that the health of the Qashqai tribe was much

improved by their reversion to nomadic ways and could, in his view, be further improved by choosing migratory routes that avoided malarial areas. He found that venereal disease was almost unknown 'thanks to the very high level of morality', and only a few of the older generation smoked opium.

Garrod also admired the looks of the Qashqai. Although like Abbott he recognized that they were descended from a tribe who had been resettled by Hulagu from Kashgar (hence, he maintained, the name Qashqai) and, although some of them had some Mongol features, he detected a much stronger Turkish streak in them. He found the men tall and well built, and the women 'often very beautiful when young', though he admitted that they did not age well. He remarked that Qashqai women, 'like all nomads', went unveiled and showed little shyness in displaying their bosoms. He also remarked on their habit of hanging gold ornaments, sequins and sovereigns from their headcloths and their skirts, so that they jingled as they walked. Garrod also maintained that the women's skill of weaving was often a good gauge of the general civilization of a nomad people, and by this criterion he reckoned the Qashqai 'among the finest of all the nomads of Persia'.

While travelling with the Qashqai, Garrod had to acclimatize himself to long hours in the saddle. He did not find this easy, and one of the things he admired most about the Qashqai was their horseman-ship. He reported that their horses, mere ponies by European stan-dards, were of predominantly Arab blood but, notwithstanding this, were admirably suited to rough terrain. He had to try to keep up with them as they galloped flat out over the most atrocious country, and he witnessed their favourite stunt of shooting gazelle from the saddle at the gallop and executing – often simultaneously – an all-round traverse under the horse's belly. Although gazelle were plentiful on the plains and lower slopes of the mountains, Garrod expressed some concern as to how long this would remain the case 'at the present inordinate rate of destruction by nomadic hunters'. Everywhere there were wild boar, and on the higher ground Garrod found leopard, ibex, mouflon, brown bear and even an occasional snow-leopard – all prized as game but more elusive.

One feels that Garrod enjoyed the invigorating life of the Qashqai and celebrated with them their escape from the sterile hardships of settled existence under the Shah. He revelled in the joys of early summer, when the fresh grass grows to the height of a horse's girth, and when several thousand tents spread over a single plain. This was the season when the khans would organize great hunting parties, and doubtless the setting of broken bones after riding accidents comprised a fair proportion of Garrod's medical activities.

Although no doubt keeping an eye on any tribal propensity to flirt with German agents or stir up a general uprising of the sort that the Allies dreaded, Garrod seems to have adopted a more indulgent attitude towards their strafing of the Iranian army, under which the tribes had suffered so acutely in Reza Shah's reign. He reports how, even before he arrived, the tribes had driven out their former oppressors – army, gendarmes and officials – and had embarked on an orgy of stealing and looting firearms. But he saw this as a necessary prelude to resuming their own nomadic way of life after the years of enforced settlement: 'being great lovers of freedom, they prefer the hard life of the hills to loss of this and their self-respect.'

The modest doctor from the Royal Army Medical Corps – sent to succour the nomadic tribes and monitor their activities – had fallen under the spell of the Qashqai, and they for their part had taken him under their wing and made him their guest throughout the long six-week migrations, when they would cover a distance of over 350 miles – the longest migration of any Persian tribe. This mutual rapport was a pattern that was to recur.

CAPTAIN GARROD encountered the Qashqai at a period when they had been able to revert to their migratory habits, after the fall of Reza Shah and before the consolidation in power of his son, Mohammed Reza Shah.

Mohammed Reza was less ruthless than his father. Although he employed a savage secret police in the form of SAVAK, he did not authorize the murder of tribal chiefs as his father had done. But he shared Reza Shah's mistrust of those tribes who had taken advantage of his father's exile to rearm and return to their former ways. The Qashqai, just as much as the Bakhtiari, did not fit into his scheme of things for an oil-rich modern state.

So the Shah's army once again began to play cat and mouse with the tribes. They did not absolutely prohibit the migration, but they made it as difficult as possible. Where previously leopards and bears had waylaid tribesmen who strayed from their groups, now soldiers did so. Worse, they set up fortified positions on the Shiraz road where it passed between the mountains and where the Qashqai were at their most vulnerable as they crossed in open country from the cover of one range of hills to the next. The Qashqai took to crossing this dangerous strip of land at night; once safely into the mountains they felt themselves secure from ambush or pursuit.

This was the position in the late 1950s when an established English author – Vincent Cronin – decided he would like to join the Qashqai for their biannual migration. He had an introduction to one of the Il Khan's family, but found that nothing could be arranged at long range. He therefore visited Farashabad, where the Qashqai had their base and assembly point. Eventually he made contact and, instead of being able to undertake the migratory ride, he found himself the confidant of one of the khan's relations, who recounted to him in great detail the adventure described in Cronin's book *The Last Migration*.

It is a curious book – half fact and half fiction (and written before the term 'faction' was coined). In it Cronin tells a dramatic story of the Il Khan of the so-called 'Falqani' tribe – pseudonym for the Qashqai, whom he wished to protect from publicity that might have been damaging to them with the Iranian authorities. His hero had spent thirteen of his thirty years of life leading the migration – many thousands strong – from the lowland winter pastures to the upland summer meadows. The route involved crossing the exposed Shiraz road, with its military gun-towers, and the rugged Zagros Mountains beyond.

This model tribal leader is the prototype of the perfect khan: he is to the Qashqai what Cameron of Lochiel was to his Scottish clansmen during the 1745 rebellion – a father-figure, an inspiration and a warrior. He knows and loves his people, who reciprocate his trust; he endures their hardships himself and eschews privilege and comfort; he declines offers of subsidies and comfortable residences for himself as a price of 'settling' his tribe; he copes diplomatically with well-meaning do-gooders and officious army officers. But it is all to no avail. The 'last migration' ends with a pitched battle when the tribe is ambushed by the army: there can be no more nomadic life for the Falqani.

Cronin himself had become an advocate of the Qashqai, and his book is a staunch defence of their way of life. Although he wrote almost an obituary for his imagined Falqani, things were not quite so gloomy for the real-life Qashqai. Throughout the 1960s and 1970s the Qashqai continued their migrations, though in smaller groups and having in most cases been obliged to surrender their arms once more to the authorities. Then, with the fall of Mohammed Reza – the last Shah – the impediments to the migrations eased under the ayatollahs, though some Qashqai leaders still fell foul of Ayatollah Khomeini. And there were to be other Englishmen after Cronin who managed to travel on the migrations.

BRUCE CHATWIN did not limit his interest in nomads to the Qashqai: far from it, he was obsessed for most of his short life with the whole concept of nomadic life. It has been suggested that this was – at least in part – a consequence of his own itinerant childhood and early life. As the son of a wartime Royal Naval officer, he was brought up on the move from one house or lodging to another with his mother;

when later the family settled in Birmingham where his father was prac-
tising law, Bruce found little to keep him at home and was, in a sense,
a perpetual refugee. 'I never felt any real attachment to a home and fail
to produce the normal emotive response when the word is mentioned,'
he was later to write.

Having started his serious working life in Sotheby's the fine arts
auctioneers, and later having studied archaeology at Edinburgh
University, he finally turned to travelling and writing. His first major
commission was to write a book on a theme that had long absorbed
him: *The Nomadic Alternative*, he called it, and it was to become a
compendium of history, travel, philosophy and quotations – largely
developing the theme that nomadic life was not a poor relation of
settled agriculture but was a viable and often preferred alternative to
the sedentary life. Chatwin wrestled with his theme for three years, and
– although the manuscript he produced at the end of that period
proved to be unpublishable – he never really gave up his preoccupation
with nomads. The last book he published during his lifetime – *The
Songlines*, about the Australian Aborigines – was a variant on the
theme.

In the course of researching his nomad book – 'that wretched book'
as Nicholas Shakespeare calls it in his definitive biography – Chatwin
visited and travelled with various nomadic tribes. His adventures in
Afghanistan are recounted in another chapter dealing with those parts
of the world. But among his forays into the world of migratory tribes
was a visit in 1971 to the Qashqai in southern Iran.

Chatwin had stayed in Tehran with his friends the Oxmantowns
and had then borrowed an embassy vehicle and driven south to Shiraz.
He managed to make contact with the Qashqai while they were on
their spring migration and 'for five days filled a British Embassy Land
Rover full of sheep, tribesmen, women suckling their babies etc.'.

The encounter, though brief, made a deep impression on him and
he drew on it in his subsequent writings. Many years later in *The
Songlines*, for instance, he recounted how surprised he had been by

the single-minded preoccupation of the Qashqai with the journey in hand. His travels there had coincided with the period in which the last Shah had erected a tented city at Pasagadae (near Persepolis) in which to entertain a vast collection of royalty from all over the world, invited to celebrate the two-thousandth anniversary of the founding of the Persian monarchy. The migration had passed close by this latter-day Field of the Cloth of Gold, but the Qashqai had never diverted their gaze from the route ahead to wonder at the array of blue and gold marquees set out so improbably against the desert landscape.

Chatwin also wrote in his notebooks and subsequently published some lyrical passages about his time moving with the tribe:

> The Qashqai men were lean, hard-mouthed, weatherbeaten and wore cylindrical hats of white felt. The women were all in their finery; bright calico dresses bought specially for the springtime journey. Some rode horses and donkeys; some were on camels, along with the tents and tent poles. Their bodies ebbed and flowed to the pitching saddles. Their eyes were blinkered to the road ahead.
>
> A woman in saffron and green rode by on a black horse. Behind her, bundled up together on the saddle, a child was playing with a motherless lamb; copper pots were clanking and there was a rooster tied on with a string.
>
> She was suckling a baby. Her breasts were festooned with necklaces, of gold coins and amulets. Like most nomad women, she wore her wealth.
>
> What, then, are a nomad baby's first impressions of this world? A swaying nipple and a shower of gold.

The fascination of the nomadic way of life was greatly enhanced for Chatwin by this brief encounter with the Qashqai. His notebooks are stuffed with Qashqai sayings and proverbs: 'A good horse is a member of the family' is one such. Colourful material for the foreground of his forthcoming book was not in short supply.

It was the background philosophy that proved the difficult part. Chatwin pondered over the writings of Charles Darwin and was attracted by a passage in his *The Descent of Man* in which Darwin argues that the migratory urge is the strongest of all animal instincts, even outweighing the maternal instinct. He cites examples of migratory mother birds abandoning their fledglings in the nest to join the long flight south at the end of the summer. All this was grist to Chatwin's mill. Because he was a rolling stone himself, he wanted to believe that this was a superior way of life: home, settling down, making nests, parental responsibilities – all these were subsidiary activities in comparison with the life-enhancing necessity to keep moving, to respond to the call of the far horizon.

This philosophy might – just – have carried conviction if Chatwin had been able to define it more closely. But there was a deep-rooted confusion in his thinking which Desmond Morris, (author of *The Naked Ape*) to whom Tom Maschler (chairman of Jonathan Cape, the publishers who had commissioned *The Nomadic Alternative*) had sent Chatwin's synopsis, was quick to point out: this was the fundamental psychological difference between wandering away and then back to a fixed base, on the one hand, and wandering from place to place without a fixed base, on the other. Chatwin did not really acknowledge the distiction in his unpublished book, and nor did he acknowledge the distinction in his own life. He remained a wanderer, but a wanderer who returned at unpredictable intervals to a wife, a house and a circle of devoted friends – none of which (it emerges from Nicholas Shakespeare's thoughtful analysis) really amounted to a sense of home.

Chatwin not only demonstrated the appeal of nomads for Englishmen, but by his writings he added momentum to the appeal. His preoccupation with the subject runs like a *leitmotiv* through much of his widely read work, and a new generation of travellers set out on the sandy trail.

ONE subsequent traveller with the Qashqai who was not influenced by Bruce Chatwin was myself. When I set out in 1977 to retrace the epic military campaign of Tamerlane across Central Asia, Iran, the Caucasus and Turkey (a journey that resulted in *The Trail of Tamerlane* published three years later), I was unfamiliar with Chatwin's writing, which was not surprising as his first book – *In Patagonia* – was only published that year.

I stumbled on the idea of trying to join the Qashqai, and share a part of their migratory march, almost by chance. It had been our resolve (the other participant in the expedition, being my wife who – undeterred by recollections of our Saharan misadventures – had volunteered to act as photographer) to follow Tamerlane's route as closely as possible. Where he crossed the Elbruz Mountains in northern Iran, we did too; where he hovered on the plains of Qarabagh in the Caucasus, we did too; where he scaled Assassin castles, we did too; so when we came to a formidable stretch of desert to cross we had to think of a way of keeping to his tracks without losing our own way. With all this in mind, we had spurned the idea of undertaking the journey in our own vehicle, which could not negotiate the mountains and other hazards. So we progressed slowly by local buses, lifts on dusty trucks, the hiring of mules and guides, and whatever other means of locomotion came to hand and seemed appropriate for the terrain. The deserts of southern Iran, across which Tamerlane had had to make a rapid progress because he needed to regain his capital in Samarkand, where trouble was brewing in his absence, presented an unusually formidable obstacle. There were no buses, no trucks, no mules or camels to be hired (or even bought), and – while we might be able to get into the area by wheeled vehicle – parts of the route would be impassable even to a Land Rover and it was much too far to walk unsupported by companions or back-up. We were floored until we remembered the Qashqai.

The season of the year was late spring. The Qashqai could be expected to be well into their migration, and if we could only find them, and be permitted to travel with them for a few days or longer, we could not only cross this inhospitable tract of land in safety, but we could also – as a bonus – experience the sensation of travelling as Tamerlane and his army had done, with their women, their children, their horses, their camels, their flocks and all the impedimenta of a mighty army or tribe on the move.

But finding them was not to be easy. We knew already that the Shah did not look kindly upon contact between foreigners – particularly the British and more particularly diplomats (of which I was one) – and his southern tribes. There had been a long history of trouble arising from such contacts, from the time of Sir Henry Layard through until the time of Sir Fitzroy Maclean. The word had gone out that assistance and directions were not to be given by government officials.

Our frustration was increased by the ease with which we met in Shiraz the remnants of the Qashqai who had not, for one reason or another – usually ill health – joined the migration. We became familiar with the men of the tribe, in their strangely shaped felt hats, with earflaps sticking up like the wings on Mercury's helmet; and with the women in their brilliant multi-coloured and multi-layered dresses adorned with gold ornaments. It struck us that the reddish skin and high cheekbones of the Qashqai, features of their Central Asian origin, gave them the appearance of better-looking cousins of North American Indians as portrayed in Western films. But, even when we could find a common language, these stay-behind tribesmen were unable to tell us the whereabouts of their fellow tribesmen.

So we tried other sources of information about the route of the migration. We soon found that the governor's office and the office for 'administration of tribal culture and education' had predictably received negative instructions from Tehran. We spread our net wider. There was scarcely a bureau in Shiraz where we had not perched in the waiting room and sipped glasses of sweet tea while listening to repetitious speeches of courtesy and obfuscation. We were invited to visit tribal school projects outside the city; we were shown displays of tribal rugs; we were invited to talks on tribal customs; we were even told we could go to Firuzabad, where the Qashqai had spent the winter and been until recently. We began to empathize with Vincent Cronin in his similarly frustrating circumstances twenty years earlier.

Although a member of the British Diplomatic Service, I was on long leave and away from my own post. Unlike Bruce Chatwin, therefore, I had no access to an embassy Land Rover with which I could scour the surrounding hillsides for traces of the migrating tribe. But luck was on our side. In the course of our stay in Shiraz we encountered an Englishwoman called Rosie, the wife of an oil company executive working in the Gulf, who shared our wish to find the Qashqai. Her reasons were different from ours: she was teaching herself to weave carpets on a Qashqai loom and wanted to see first-hand how such looms were transported on the camels and donkeys of families on the move. She had a large-scale map on which she had worked out the likely routes of that year's march; already she reckoned the mountains were behind them, they would now be crossing the barren desert-like hills and soon they were likely to be fanning out on the broad sunlit uplands where they would spend the summer months. Rosie had her own Land Rover and was prepared to let us join forces with her in the hunt. The party was completed by the presence of her Great Dane – Jupiter – who took up considerably more of the Land Rover than any of the rest of us but turned out to be the greatest asset in our entourage.

Rosie had studied the ways of the Qashqai more closely than we had by that stage; she was in the tradition of Captain Garrod rather than Consul Abbott and was an enthusiast for everything to do with the Qashqai. She knew that they liked to keep well clear of roads and inhabited areas, where they might be accused of poaching grazing and where, as Cronin had so vividly described, they might risk brushes with the Iranian military. She also said that as the migration progressed and as the tribe reached the higher pastures, they would be likely to split into smaller, extended family-sized groups. The only hope of finding them in full cavalcade would be to patrol the crests of the hills in the Land Rover until we saw some signs of life in the valleys below.

Having put several hours of driving between ourselves and Shiraz, we left the tracks and started looking in earnest, climbing up on foot to crags we could not reach otherwise and scanning with binoculars the horizons for telltale plumes of dust from moving camels, horses, mules and sheep. After a long day of continual movement and unrewarding vistas of empty hillsides, we were beginning to wonder how tens of thousands of men, women, children and animals could disappear without trace into a seemingly endlessly rolling landscape. Eventually we saw a smudge of darker colour against the dun, dusty horizon. Could it be goatskin tents, we wondered. We headed straight for it, risking Lan Rover springs and the evident discomfort and restlessness of Jupiter.

We were not mistaken. As we got closer the ragged outline of tent-poles and tethered horses emerged from the blur. It was indeed a Qashqai camp, but an unusual one, consisting only of young men and horses – no families, camels, flocks or impedimenta. We had stumbled on an advance party, reconnoitring the route for the main body of a much larger tribal group who were following closely behind.

Our reception – unsurprisingly in the circumstances – was equivocal. Some of the men withdrew inside the largest of the tents, evidently for a rapid conference, while the others eyed us suspiciously from a wary distance. We dismounted from the Land Rover but kept Jupiter to heel. I recalled that the the laws of nomad hospitality are based on the assumption that a stranger is an enemy unless or until he has entered the sanctuary of somebody's tent. We waited anxiously for the upshot of the deliberations within.

When the men emerged, they had elected a spokesman who managed some English. With difficulty we gathered that his concern was as to whether we were government agents, or welfare officials, or social workers. We reassured him as best we could that we were none of these things. What convinced him that our protestations were true was undoubtedly Jupiter: interfering do-gooders just did not go around with Great Danes. We were accepted for what we were – curious

67

travellers in search of companionship and help. We were invited under the shade of the black awning: we had been admitted to the sanctuary of the tent. A kettle appeared from the shadowy interior recesses. The ritual of hospitality had begun.

It was not long before the rest of their part of the tribe appeared. First we saw on the horizon what appeared to be moving posts above the stony, scrub-covered dunes, like periscopes from submarines emerging from a tranquil sea. Then humps beneath the posts. Then camels beneath the humps. The Qashqai, their tent-poles projecting from their baggage like knitting needles from a ball of wool, were bearing down on us. They went on coming like an incoming tide: behind the camels were mules, goats, children on foot, young men on ponies, old men on donkeys, women jingling with ornaments; and tied on to the pack animals were black iron cooking pots clanking, live chickens fluttering, newborn lambs bleating and an occasional well-wrapped-up Qashqai baby gurgling contentedly. All the paraphernalia of nomadic life was here, unchanged in essentials since the days when Abbott had encountered them a hundred and twenty years before. It was what we had come for.

We had reckoned without the dogs. Sheepdogs in southern Iran do not fall neatly into the categories of Border shepherds or collies: they come in all shapes and sizes, from great white monsters that could see off a wolf, to diminutive wiry mongrels that work in scary packs. Many of them have their ears cropped as young puppies, in the belief that this will make them hear better. In this disparate crowd, Jupiter was the centre of much more attraction than we were. Tall, black and sleek, he looked like one of John Buchan's aristocratic Highland lairds who had inadvertently fallen in with a ragtaggle gang from the Gorbals of Glasgow. The tribal dogs circled him warily, and beyond the dogs a circle of tribesmen squatted admiringly. Short of bringing a peregrine falcon, we could hardly have found a more prestigious companion.

While the men admired Jupiter, the women got on with the serious work of setting up camp. Flocks were tended, ewes were milked, tents were pitched, curds were laid out to dry in what was left of the sunshine, camel and mule droppings were being collected as fuel for the evening's fire, and – when more pressing jobs were completed – looms were assembled and work continued on tribal rugs. We watched this last activity with special attention as we had long heard that Qashqai rugs were in many respects unique.

Weaving among the Qashqai is not limited to the making of fine rugs for the floors of houses or superior tents; simpler kilims are woven for humbler abode. And almost every object on the migration seemed to require some sort of cover: saddlebags, saddle rugs, baby bags, tool bags, knife bags and even Koran covers, all had to be woven with distinctive motifs. Some were intended as wedding gifts, some as a contribution to the dowry of a Qashqai maiden. Even in the 1970s, many rugs and artefacts were being woven with a wider market in mind: the bazaars of Shiraz would be kept provided with goods for visitors as well as for local and domestic use.

The origin of the motifs on the rugs is the subject of much learned controversy. Undoubtedly some are copied from traditional urban Persian carpets – formalized flowers and birds on ivory backgrounds are not uncommon. Other rugs have a more distinctively Caucasian flavour: geometric patterns in vivid colours that could have originated in the Shirvan, Kuban or Kazak regions, with their stars and elaborate borders. Yet others are characteristically tribal and nomadic: stylized lions, camels, dogs and even humans parade across the tightly woven fabrics.

The Qashqai have a reputation for having a quick eye for a new pattern. James Opie, in his handsomely illustrated book, *Tribal Rugs*, quotes a story told by Lois Beck (who made important anthropological studies of the Qashqai in the 1970s) of how she visited a Qashqai weaver one day with a notebook in her hand which had an unusual design on the cover. The weaver had only a few seconds in which to see the book cover, and appeared to pay no special attention to it. But on a subsequent visit to the region, Lois Beck found a rug woven in a pattern irrefutably based on her book cover. Such acute observation is responsible for many of the original and striking designs to be found in Qashqai weaving. High knot-counts and the best-quality wool – and even silk – add to the desirability of such rugs, as do vegetable (rather than chrome) dyes extracted from plants and sometimes beetles found along the migration route. The one feature that tribal rugs can seldom or never achieve is size; while looms need to be transported on animals' backs, there is no scope for weaving drawing-room-sized pieces.

So popular have Qashqai rugs become that the name is now extended to many products of a much wider region within Iran, and international dealers tend to label as 'Qashqai' most of their better southern Iranian examples. This being so, rugs have become the most valuable of the tribe's productions, as is witnessed by the fact that whereas spices, leather and even silver objects will be sold – after much bargaining – by Qashqai women in the bazaars of Shiraz and elsewhere, only men are empowered to handle the sale of rugs and similar woven artefacts. In fact, a rug is almost the only object other than a weapon which a male Qashqai would wish to be seen taking to market.

Some of these considerations passed through our minds as we watched a forest of tents growing up around us: where a moment before there had been a barren hillside, now there was a patchwork of black tents – awnings stretched at apparently haphazard angles attached to poles of unequal length, and very different from the uniform bell-tents and bivouacs we had seen at army encampments elsewhere on our route. Outside each tent, the family's horses and camels were tethered or hobbled, while young lambs were unpinned from their slings and reunited with their mothers or allowed to slip inside the tents to join the children. Even mares – we were told – were occasionally taken under the shelter of the tent to allow them to foal in the privacy and protection of the family tent. Perhaps the old Qashqai saying, 'Born in a tent, die in a battle', applied to horses as well as men. No wonder Bruce Chatwin had been told that a good horse was a member of the family.

The young Qashqai man who spoke some English and who had first welcomed us into his tent continued to keep a friendly eye on us. He asked if we would like to accompany them for part of the next day in the Land Rover; after that, he said, the terrain would become too difficult again. We consulted Rosie, who, her study of the looms completed, thought she should return to Shiraz, where her husband was expected back shortly from the Gulf. Even if she – and the much-admired Great Dane – had to go, our host said we were welcome to stay and travel with them over the next problematic piece of country – always provided we could ride a horse confidently. We could, and we accepted with almost indecent alacrity.

But first we had to see Rosie back to safety. We would have liked to have accompanied her all the way back to Shiraz, but she was adamant that she needed an escort only as far as the tarmac road, being accustomed to much longer drives alone with her Great Dane. She had a remarkable send-off: fourteen Qashqai horsemen rode flanking her Land Rover, for all the world as if she had been in a state landau trundling down the mall with its outriders of Household Cavalry, until she reached the tarmac.

When we returned to camp from this excursion, we found that a tent had been allocated to us. We had been accepted as part of the cavalcade. For the next days we were to travel not as spectators to a migration but as part of it. We were to learn the names and characteristics of men and of camels: of men like Amshar, who had lost all his sheep, chased over a precipice by a wolf, and had had his flock replaced by gifts from his extended family; and of camels like Arak, who could sniff out a well or a pool of brackish water from several miles away and lead a thirsty caravan to water.

We were treading, if not literally at least metaphorically, where our compatriots had trod before us. We felt that the ghosts of Henry Layard and of Gertrude Bell, of Vita Sackville-West and of Captain Garrod were riding beside us, chanting like Elroy Flecker's pilgrims: 'Lead on, oh captain of the caravan, lead on . . .'

We had either caught the English obsession with nomads in a big way . . . or more likely, we were suffering from mild heatstroke.

71

# BOOK II

# THE BEDOUIN OF ARABIA
# AND THE LEVANT

'I am to live among the Bedawin Arab chiefs. I shall smell the desert air; I shall have tents, horses, weapons and be free.'
Isabel Burton, in her journals (1869)

'Our camels sniff the evening and are glad.'
James Elroy Flecker, *The Golden Road to Samarkand* (1913)

'He is crazed with the spell of Arabia.
They have stolen his wits away.'
Walter de la Mare (1873–1956), *Arabia*

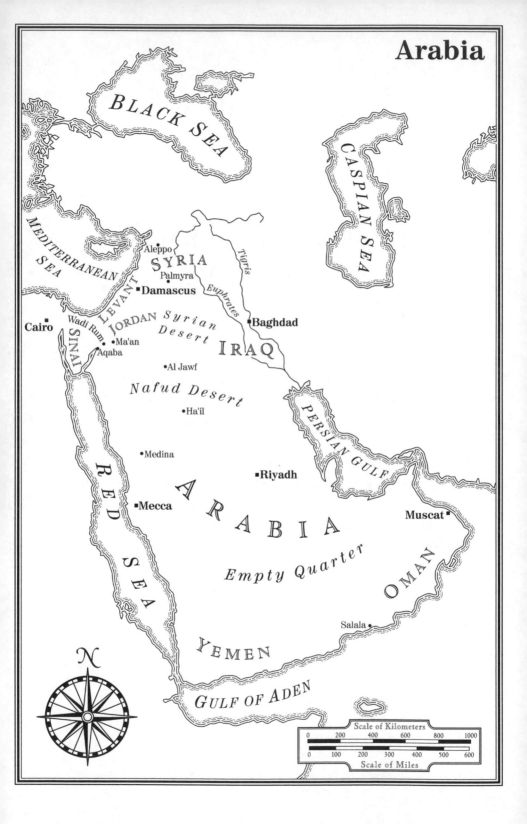

# Arabia

BLACK SEA

CASPIAN SEA

MEDITERRANEAN SEA

Aleppo
SYRIA
Palmyra
■ Damascus

*Tigris*

*Euphrates*

■ Baghdad

LEVANT

Wadi Rum
JORDAN
Syrian Desert

IRAQ

Cairo ■

SINAI

• Ma'an
Aqaba

• Al Jawf

Nafud Desert

• Ha'il

PERSIAN GULF

RED SEA

• Medina

■ Riyadh

A R A B I A

■ Mecca

Muscat ■

Empty Quarter

OMAN

Salala •

YEMEN

GULF OF ADEN

N

Scale of Kilometers

0    200    400    600    800    1000

0    100    200    300    400    500    600

Scale of Miles

# 3

# The Bedouin of Arabia: An Exotic Appeal

A RABIA was the home of the Prophet Mohammed and the birth-
place of Islam. As such it has – together with the Middle Eastern
desert lands to its north – always been the natural focus of Western
curiosity about the exotic East. But this curiosity has not always been
one of attraction; there have, at least since the time of the Crusades,
also been intermittently strong forces of rejection directed towards the
Islamic world. Islam was seen in the Europe of the Middle Ages and
indeed of the Renaissance as a negation of Christianity. The waves of
Arab and Moorish invaders that penetrated or threatened the very
heartland of Christendom were seen as potent anti-European forces.

The Western misconception – and frequently deliberate misrepre-
sentation – of the canons of Islam widened the gap. A society founded
on monogamy, despised (or sometimes envied) a society where wives
and concubines could proliferate and where the secrecy of the harem
was interpreted as a cloak for unbridled lasciviousness. The glimpses
seen, reported and painted by visiting artists of Eastern slave markets –

where nubile and frequently pale-skinned slave girls were much more often in evidence than the male manual workers who made up the bulk of the markets' wares – both repelled the righteous and titillated the prurient.

Literature reinforced these prejudices. In the early eighteenth century the body of oral tradition broadly known as the *Arabian Nights* (the thousand and one sexually orientated and often violent tales of Scheherazade) was first codified and translated into French by Antoine Galland. By the early nineteenth century the tales had been made available in English and were widely read in the English-speaking world too. Later in the same century, Richard Burton was to produce an unexpurgated edition that would shock elements of Victorian society. Although such works widened the perceived gap between western and eastern cultures, they also enhanced curiosity about the Orient.

Eighteenth-century British travellers in the Arab world tended to conform to the convention of writing descriptively about the landscapes rather than interpretively about their own impressions and feelings. Laurence Sterne in his *Sentimental Journey* (1768) had warned against 'vain travellers' who put too much of themselves into their books (though he was a prime example of this himself). But with the dawning of the Romantic Age, and the self-centred travellers' tales of Byron and others reaching a wider readership, the Arab world was opening up as a destination for the adventurous and the footloose. Those who chose to travel there were frequently restless themselves and particularly attracted by the lifestyles of pilgrims and migratory tribes, who shared their fascination with movement and far horizons: there was an urge 'to follow knowledge like a sinking star'.

Into this apparent void – an exotic region of the world only just beyond the frontiers of Europe – stepped a number of English characters as exotic in themselves as the regions they were to explore. Almost all of them were misfits in the society in which they were brought up. They thought, like John Donne two centuries earlier, that 'to live in one land, is captivitie' and they sought the companionship of kindred spirits who had taken to the road of life: nomads were their ideal, and the deserts of the Middle East the place where such nomads – in the broadest sense – were to be found. Despite, or because of, the differences of sexual mores, society ladies like Hester Stanhope and Jane Digby braved the embraces (physical sometimes as well as symbolic) of itinerant Arab sheiks; adventurers like Burton, Lawrence and Thesiger braved the most extreme rigours of desert travel; Arab enthusiasts and scholars like Blunt, Thomas and Philby dedicated large parts of their lives to travelling with and like the nomadic bedouin. Theirs was a common obsession, but their individual stories were very different one from another.

LADY HESTER STANHOPE, who was born at Chevening in Kent (now the British Foreign Secretary's official country residence) on 12 March 1776, was not only to plant the seeds of an English preoccupation with nomads, but to prove something of a nomad herself. To understand why, it is necessary to be reminded of her remarkable background.

On the face of it, nothing could have been less predictable than Lady Hester's nomadic existence: she was born into the most elevated and distinguished stratum of English society. Her father was to become the 3rd Earl Stanhope and a huge landowner, while her mother was daughter of William Pitt the Elder, 1st Earl of Chatham, and sister of William Pitt the Younger. But there was a streak of the unconventional in the family on both sides, and it was to find its fulfilment in Lady Hester.

Her early life was unusual but gave little hint of what was to lie ahead. She quickly demonstrated her prowess as a rider, but because her father did not hold with the traditional way of bringing up a family, she was not given the usual launching in London society. However, she managed to infiltrate herself into a ball – or rather into a 'grand review' – given by Lord Romney to mark the occasion of King George III's visit to Kent. She was such a success at the party that the King enquired who she was, and thereafter always remembered her as a spirited and witty girl who, though no conventional beauty, was outstandingly fresh, lively and attractive. With this royal favour and the support of her uncle William Pitt, she made her own way in what was to become the dazzling society of Regency London. The oppressive regime of her father at Chevening drove her to leave home and first to seek a base with her grandmother – Lady Chatham – and later (after the latter's unexpected death) with her uncle, William Pitt.

She was to prove no quiet and submissive poor relation in either household. When she joined her uncle, he was a forty-four-year-old bachelor who had already served as Prime Minister for seventeen years, but who was temporarily out of office and living at Walmer Castle in Kent – his official residence as Lord Warden of the Cinque Ports (a position which – then as now – was more of an honour than a job). Lady Hester became his confidante and his hostess, and shared her uncle's concern about the prospect of a French invasion in the summer of 1803 – an invasion that almost certainly would have been in close proximity to Dover, opposite which Napoleon's forces were massing just across the English Channel. Lady Hester was able to observe at close range her uncle's calm and sang-froid in the face of threats – a characteristic she was to emulate herself to a remarkable degree later in life. Another characteristic of the great statesman, but a less practical one, which she was also to observe and later to emulate was his total disregard for prudence in his personal money matters: she learnt to give without counting the cost, whether she could afford it or not. Pitt was to die in straitened financial circumstances; so was she.

In 1804 Pitt returned to Downing Street as Prime Minister again. Lady Hester moved in with him. Her role as hostess now became both more demanding and more rewarding. She not only knew all the great and good in England, but she was flattered and courted by them. These were the most testing years of the Napoleonic Wars: the Battle of Trafalgar was won during Lady Hester's time at No. 10. But the strains of wartime leadership and parliamentary duties, not to mention a heavy consumption of port, were taking a toll on Pitt's health. Lady Hester did what she could to cherish him, taking him for brief breaks from London at their country house at Putney or at Walmer Castle. But before the end of January 1806 Pitt was dead, among his last words being a blessing to his beloved niece. Once more, Lady Hester was on her own in life.

A grateful British parliament not only settled Pitt's debts after his death but also bestowed a pension on Lady Hester of £1,200 a year – a substantial income at the time – which gave her financial independence. The fact of the pension, together with more than one unhappy love affair, turned her mind towards going abroad; she had already been greatly taken by the charms of France, and felt that England had little to offer her to fill the vacuum left by Pitt's death and the termination of her role as a young political hostess. Like George Herbert in his poem 'The Collar', she might have said: 'I struck the board, and cry'd, "No more. I will abroad." '

Her travels took her first to Gibraltar and then to Malta, but it was not until she reached Constantinople that she began to develop the passion for the East which was to dominate the rest of her life. Travelling as she did, with her lover, her doctor and a retinue of servants, bodyguards and porters, she was admired – by everyone from the Ottoman Sultan downwards – as a fine horsewoman, an obvious aristocrat (often treated as a princess) and an independent spirit of a sort that had never been seen in the Orient before. After an unfortunate shipwreck in which she lost all her clothes, she even adopted the dress of a bedouin prince and found it so practical and becoming that from then on she wore no other costume.

Constantinople had been only a staging post. She and her entourage went on to visit Alexandria, Jaffa, Jerusalem and Acre before arriving – in considerable state – in Damascus. The journeying through the Levantine and Syrian countryside had been spectacular rather than comfortable: Lady Hester rode a fine Arab horse with a crimson velvet saddle and a bridle embroidered with gold thread; her scarlet riding jacket was also embroidered with gold; two Mameluke body servants accompanied her everywhere; ten camels were needed to carry the tents alone; and all this splendour was paid for from her own private means and from the generous allowance paid by his father to her equally aristocratic Scottish lover, Michael Bruce. But alongside the luxury there were risks and rigours too: Syria was without roads (those which had existed in biblical times having fallen into decay under the deca-dent Ottoman rule); the bodyguards were a necessity and not a status symbol because disaffected tribes roamed the more mountainous and arid sections of the route; at one point Lady Hester placed herself voluntarily under the protection of the most notorious of the brigand leaders and so appealed to his sense of honour and hospitality (and incidentally won his permanent respect and admiration).

Lady Hester established herself in Damascus in the manner of visiting royalty. She was received by the Pasha – the Sultan's resident representative – and quickly started to plot her next move: she wished to visit Palmyra, the ancient classical ruined city that had been the home of the fabled Queen Zenobia whom Lady Hester appears to have viewed as a role-model for herself. No European woman had ever been to Palmyra, and hardly any European men. This in itself constituted a challenge and an attraction for her.

But the main appeal of the expedition was not the destination but the journey itself. Palmyra was divided from Damascus by a wide cordon of desert inhabited and dominated by nomadic bedouin tribes. These tribes had roamed the desert since pre-biblical times and viewed any intruder as a potential enemy and a threat to their traditional existence. To contact these nomad tribesmen was Lady Hester's prime objective: where others had always feared to tread, she would show the way; where others had been repulsed and often killed, she would establish a rapport based on mutual respect and a shared love of wandering in the desert. It was a romantic ideal after her own heart, and she persuaded the susceptible Michael Bruce and the subservient Dr Meryon to fall in with her plans.

Her first thought was to repeat the successful ploy she had tried on with previously encountered desert warriors: to place herself trustingly in their hands and hope to be treated as a guest where others had been treated as enemies. But the Pasha of Damascus would not hear of it; he said it was too dangerous; and (although he did not say it) he thought that it would be humiliating for him if this grand visitor were to make the journey to Palmyra under any auspices other than his own. The Pasha's prevarication delayed Lady Hester's adventure, but did not prevent it. In the event, the bedouin themselves took an initiative towards her to which she responded: their chief sent his eldest son to invite her to visit them in their desert camp. This was exactly the invitation she had been waiting for, and she accepted it in the face of all advice to the contrary. She thought that if her visit to the bedouin camp went well, she might risk making a longer desert journey under their auspices – despite anything the Pasha might say. Now at last, after all her travelling, she was to be among genuine nomads.

The trip to the bedouin did go well. It went very well indeed. Dr Meryon later recorded that when the bedouin chief – who was called Mahannah – saw 'a fair and elegant woman who had ventured upon those wastes where many a man has trembled to go, and where he knew she had been taught to expect nothing but brutality', he was lost in admiration for her. This was what Lady Hester had hoped to achieve and the reason why she had decked herself out with more than usual care in the dress of the son of a Bedu chief: a sheepskin pelisse picked out in gold and scarlet.

And the impression the Bedu made on her was equally favourable. She felt that at last she had found her true *métier*: she was treated like a queen and reported that when she raised a hand 'in one instant fifty lances spring to your defence'. Everything about the Bedu's nomadic way of life appealed to her: 'the space around me covered with living things . . . 12,000 camels coming to water . . . the women with their hands all over flowers and designs of different kinds.' This was the life of freedom and self-respect, of honour and influence spiced with danger, for which she had craved ever since the death of her uncle William Pitt and her decision to shake off the constraints of society in

Regency England. The Bedu romanticized about her and she in turn romanticized about them.

But even Mahannah, with all the warriors of his tribe at his command, could not guarantee a trouble-free crossing of the deserts around Palmyra. Other, lesser tribes, such as the feared Faydans, had heard tell of the fabulous wealth of the eccentric English aristocrat who was so determined to reach Palmyra. She and her treasure constituted a rich prize ripe for the taking. The risks added to the allure of the adventure, and Mahannah ensured that Lady Hester was mounted on a fast horse, had an adequate escort and was never far from one of his own friendly encampments. She finally arrived in triumph at Palmyra, to be greeted by the population, who had heard news of her impending arrival, as if she were in fact their legendary Queen Zenobia. It was the high point of her life. On her return journey across the desert, she again experienced the acclaim of the bedouin, and she subsequently wrote of them:

> They are the most singular and wonderfully clever people I ever saw, but require a great deal of management for they are more desperate and more deep than you can possibly have an idea of . . . for eloquence and beauty of ideas they undoubtedly are beyond any other people in the world.

In short, they were, she decided, her sort of people.

She abandoned all thought of ever returning to England, and in due course she settled in a former monastery on a remote hilltop at Djoun in the Druse Mountains, between Beirut and Acre. Here she received the tributes of the bedouin and held court.

Lady Hester's love affair with the Bedu was no passing whim: it was to become the main strand of her existence for the rest of her life. Michael Bruce was soon to return to England and marry a rich widow; Dr Meryon also eventually left her; her pension from the British government was suspended; her health gave way; every sort of material disaster overtook her. But still she stayed on at Djoun with a dwindling band of retainers.

Her absorption into the world of the nomadic desert peoples who surrounded her soon became well known far afield. English visitors to the Levant would make a point of calling on her, and reporting her obsession. Some were turned away, and often went home saying that she was not only obsessed but mad. Others were graciously received in her sparse surroundings and were kept up talking throughout the night about the preoccupations of her wandering neighbours. One such was Alexander Kinglake, who wrote of her in his widely read travel book *Eothen*. Another was the French poet Lamartine, who also wrote about her, in his *Souvenirs de l'Orient*. Such books, and the gossip which went with them, consolidated the legend of the strange recluse at Djoun. Lady Hester encapsulated in the popular imagination what was to become over the centuries that followed a very English obsession.

JANE DIGBY, although a generation younger than Lady Hester Stanhope, seemed on the face of it remarkably similar to her: both were true-born English aristocrats; both had a propensity to shock the society in which they were brought up; both emigrated at a fairly early age; and both developed an obsession with life in the deserts of the Levant. But a closer look at Jane Digby's life reveals a difference of emphasis and a very different set of achievements.

Unlike Lady Hester, Jane Digby, who was born in Dorset in 1807, was a celebrated beauty from the moment she appeared in London as a debutante, and at an early age (seventeen) married a highly eligible and ambitious politican, Lord Ellenborough. The fact that he was twice her age might not have mattered if he had been attentive to her; but he allowed his political career to dominate his activities and neglected his young and much-sought-after bride. The result was perhaps not altogether surprising: Jane first had an affair with her cousin George Anson, and then eloped with a dashing foreign diplomat, Prince Felix Schwarzenberg. The scandal that followed was sensational: Lord Ellenborough divorced her after a much-publicized case, and Jane became notorious where before she had been idolized. English society turned its back on her.

She went first to France with Schwarzenberg and, aided by a generous financial settlement, lived a slightly bohemian life on the fringe of Paris society. But Schwarzenberg (despite the fact that she had given birth to his son) declined to marry her and soon she moved on to Munich. Here she received numerous offers of marriage, notably from Baron Venningen, whom she eventually accepted (after giving birth to a child by him) and also embarked on a close and none-too-platonic relationship with King Ludwig I of Bavaria. A subsequent affair and marriage to a Greek count was followed by an affair with an Albanian general from the romantic mountainous regions of that country. No wonder that later in life she was to describe these years as 'a naughty version of the *Almanach de Gotha*'.

Finally, like Lady Hester, Jane found herself in Syria. She, too, was entranced by the desert life and found her way to Palmyra. The great difference between them was that whereas Lady Hester found the bedouin life fascinating for itself and persisted in her commitment to it even after her long-standing lover and companion, Michael Bruce, had abandoned her for home, Jane Digby's commitment to the bedouin was focused on one particular bedouin sheik whom she married (as her fourth husband) and who became the enduring love of the last thirty years of her life. In fact, she set herself the task of becoming a complete bedouin wife and a mainstay and support of her husband's tribe, while at the same time living an elegant European life in Damascus and elsewhere when not on prolonged expeditions to the desert. It would only be a slight oversimplification to say that while Lady Hester was primarily an enthusiast and adventurer in the nomadic world of the bedouin, Jane was primarily an enthusiastic lover of her sheik and an adventurer in the nomadic world of the bedouin in consequence of that love. But both ladies took to the life with a natural flair – aided by their prowess as horse-women and their total absorption in all aspects of the nomadic bedouin life which they found in the desert.

No European woman had visited Palmyra between Lady Hester and Jane Digby, and the latter found it almost as difficult as the former. The British consul in Damascus was determined to stop her making such a foolhardy journey, the precedents for which were hardly encouraging: Lord Dalkeith and some male companions had been forced a few years earlier to travel the desert route by night to avoid attacks, and had even then been captured by marauding tribesmen from whom they only escaped by good luck after a four-day captivity. Jane set out none the less accompanied by a good-looking young sheik called Medjuel, who flattered her about her riding and sketching abilities. More important, Medjuel defended her at the risk of his life when their caravan was attacked by horsemen from a hostile tribe brandishing lances. He enchanted her with his expertise as a hunter with his hawks and his Saluki dogs. He escorted her with gallantry at every step of the way, and – given her notorious susceptibility and remarkable beauty – it was hardly surprising that she fell in love with him and he with her. What was remarkable was that she remained constant in her affection for him. In due course Medjuel divorced his existing wife and married Jane, despite both the resistance of his tribe and of her aristocratic family. No one expected the relationship to last, but last it did.

Even more than Lady Hester, Jane became an authority on the bedouin, although most of her travelling was in fact done with caravans crossing the desert rather than with migratory tribes looking for pasture. On one such trip – a lengthy ride from Damascus to Baghdad – she was herself briefly captured and held hostage by marauders until the captain of the caravan managed to negotiate a price for her release. Although on that occasion her European maid became understandably hysterical – 'Oh, we shall all be sold as slaves' – Jane remained calmly aloof in the best traditions of her upbringing.

When after her return from Baghdad she eventually married Sheik Medjuel, she settled down to a life divided between her house in Damascus and long expeditions into the desert with her husband and his nomadic tribe. While in Damascus she put down roots, sending for seed catalogues from Carters in England and establishing a garden that combined features of an English country-house garden and of an Islamic-palace garden of terraces, herbs and water features. Her garden abounded in domesticated animals from the desert: tame gazelles (often rescued as young kids after their mothers had been shot) appeared to co-exist happily with her husband's hunting Salukis. She entertained both European visitors and distinguished local inhabitants in elegant rooms furnished with imported French and English furniture.

But the part of her life she enjoyed most were the long desert trips. She revelled in the whole migratory way of life – the movement from one pasture to another, the intimacy of living in a goatskin tent with her young sheik (he was seventeen years her junior), the wifely duties imposed by Islamic custom and practice. On the relatively rare occasions that Medjuel went to the desert without her, she felt frustrated by her inability to locate and catch up with him, because the tribe did not move in any predetermined direction but went wherever their outriders located grazing for the animals. When not tending to the needs of her husband or sketching desert scenes for her album, Jane devoted much time to helping other wives and tribesmen; although in no way a trained nurse, she tended to the ailments that developed on the march – most frequently eye infections caused by sand, sunburn and flies. She could turn her hand as readily to curing animals as to curing bedouin, her self-taught veterinary skills rivalling her self-taught medicine. She also adjudicated in inter-family quarrels, comforted the bereaved and counselled divorced wives. Instead of being an outsider and a foreigner among her husband's nomadic peoples, she established herself as a matriarch of the tribe. When her husband's tribe fell out with the Ottoman authorities, the tribe spent several months evading government troops and Jane (according to her biographer, Mary Lovell) 'revelled in the wild rides to hidden encampments in the mountains'.

As with Lady Hester Stanhope, Jane Digby's total commitment to a life that was – in large measure – a bedouin one was much noted by her contemporaries. Visitors never failed to be fascinated and impressed by her absorption in this very un-Victorian lifetstyle. And visitors came in plenty and included many of the most celebrated of her contemporaries. The Prince of Wales himself (the future King Edward VII) called on her in Damascus, undeterred it seems by her divorced and controversial social status (that would have excluded her for decades to come from the royal enclosure at Ascot). Emily Beaufort, who was later to become Lady Stangford and an important pioneer in the field of nursing, had visited Jane in Damascus and in the desert as an adventurous unmarried girl, and was to view her as a role-model ever afterwards. More significantly, Lady Anne Blunt (the grand-daughter of Lord Byron) visited Jane with her husband, the poet, diplomat and Orientalist Wilfred Scawen Blunt; the Blunts were intent on establishing themselves with the bedouin tribesmen as a step to acquiring breeding bloodstock from among the bedouin horses. Jane, and her way of life, made a great impression on the Blunts.

But probably the most influential of all Jane's acquaintances in Syria were Sir Richard Burton and his wife Isabel. Burton, who was already well established as an explorer and adventurer, had been appointed British consul in Damascus in 1869; he and his wife saw a great deal of Jane ('the only other English woman of note in Damascus'), and Isabel Burton was to write much about her on her return to England. The legend of an English obsession with the bedouin was gradually taking root.

SIR RICHARD BURTON and his wife Isabel did much more to foster English interest in the bedouin than merely to give wider currency to the remarkable experiences of Jane Digby. Burton was in his own person the lion among English Arabists. Long before he came as consul to Damascus he had made his reputation as a daring bucca-neer in other fields. As a young Indian army officer he had written a shocking report – based on personal observation while in disguise – about prostitution and pederasty in northern India. As an explorer sponsored by the Royal Geographical Society he had reconnoitred the sources of the White Nile. As consul at Santos in Brazil he had mapped the São Francisco river. He had won renown as a scholar and as a swordsman. But most memorably of all, in 1853 he had – again in disguise – made the pilgrimage to Mecca, a feat fraught with danger as discovery would have led almost certainly to a violent and horrible death – possibly by impaling. Only Burton's consummate mastery of Arabic and ruthless determination (he was widely believed to have killed an Arab who discovered him urinating in 'the European – standing – manner') ensured his survival.

In fact, Burton had done much to awaken British interest in the bedouin of the Levant and Arabia by his book about the illicit pilgrimage. He had taken notes about the life of the bedouin with whom he was travelling, even when doing so added considerably to the dangers of exposure, using a guide-wire attached to his notebook to help him write in the dark. When the supply of dried dates ran out, he lived partly off fried locusts, 'which tasted like stale shrimps'. He acquired a knowledge of bedouin lore and found much more to admire in the nomadic way of life, with its freedom and manliness, than in the more settled life of Arab craftsmen and traders, where he found 'a degradation, moral and physical, compared with the freedom of the desert'. This admiration was not dimmed – in fact, it was probably enhanced – by surviving a bedouin ambush in which a number of his fellow pilgrims were killed. For the last stage of the journey, from Medina to Mecca, Burton attached himself to a caravan taking the inland and largely waterless desert route. His account of horrific incidents on this leg of the journey only added a certain *frisson* to his tale, as when he describes how a Turk who had been stabbed in the stomach by an Arab was left to die of thirst and sunstroke 'and – worst of all, for they do not wait for death – the attacks of the jackal, the vulture, and the raven of the wild'. Burton's Arabia was no place for the squeamish, but it appealed to such architects of Victorian romanticism as his friend the poet Swinburne and the novelist Ouida, who wrote of Burton that 'he looked like Othello and lived like the Three Mousquetaires blended in one'.

This, then, was the man who arrived as British consul in Damascus in 1869. By then he was married to Isabel, who idolized him and shared his vision of the 'free' bedouin lifestyle. The Burtons took all permissible – and some impermissible – opportunities to absent themselves from the duties of city life in Damascus for the wider horizons of the desert. Isabel recorded in her journal:

> Jackals gambolling in the moonlight, sounding in a distant pack like the war cry of the Bedawin . . . big fires, the black tents, the picturesque figures in every garb, and the wild and fierce-looking men in wonderful costumes lying here and there.

Like Jane Digby, Isabel acquired a stable of fine Arab horses, and to these she added a menagerie of animals – five dogs, including a St Bernard, a camel, a Persian cat, three goats and a young panther (which slept by their bedside) among them. Much of her day was spent stopping her pets from eating each other.

Eventually Burton's consular mission ran into political difficulties. The local Pasha resented his denunciation of corruption (which was endemic in the Turkish administration); the British ambassador in Constantinople was jealous of Burton's reputation as an Arabist; the Jewish community reported to London that Burton and his wife were anti-Semitic (because already there was some Arab–Jewish friction and Burton always came down on the Arab side, and his wife was seen as a proselytizing Roman Catholic); there had been street fracas involving Burton which appeared unseemly; and his political supporter – Lord Stanley – in London was no longer Foreign Secretary. Burton was hastily recalled and replaced, prompting him to send the much-quoted instruction to his wife to 'pay, pack and follow'. It was the end of his active involvement in desert life.

But it was not the end of his influence on his compatriots. He continued to circulate in London society and to write for a wider public. Whereas other travellers in the East, such as the Swiss adventurer John Burckhardt, who had also penetrated to Mecca, wrote in academic terms about their experiences, Burton spiced his accounts not only with erudition but also with a measure of pornography (he had translated the *Arabian Nights* and the *Perfumed Garden*) and a great deal of somewhat suspect heroics. His books were best sellers, as he portrayed the world of desert nomads as being:

A haggard land infested with wild beasts and wilder men, a region whose very fountains murmur the warning words 'Drink and Away!' What can be more exciting? What more sublime?

Victorian England tended to agree with him.

WILLIAM GIFFARD PALGRAVE was born in 1826 into a family that was both distinguished academically and eccentric in its background and enthusiasms. His father had been born Jewish with the surname of Cohen; he had married an English girl of good family and – under some pressure from her relatives – not only converted to Christianity but adopted his wife's family name of Palgrave; he went on to be an archivist for the royal family and achieved a knighthood and a considerable reputation as a scholar; and he bred a number of equally successful sons. The eldest was to become a close friend of Lord Tennyson, to be Professor of Poetry at Oxford, and to establish a niche reputation in the field of English literature by editing *Palgrave's Golden Treasury of Songs and Lyrics*. The youngest became clerk to the House of Commons and also achieved a knighthood. But William Giffard Palgrave – as one of the middle sons – took a quite different line, and it is with this member of the family (who will be referred to hereafter simply as Palgrave) with which this story is concerned.

Palgrave shared the family's academic genes. He was captain of the

90

school at Charterhouse (at the same time as the author of *Tom Brown's Schooldays* was wrestling with the rigours of Rugby) and went on to take a first-class degree at Trinity College, Oxford, and proceeded from there to join the East India Company as a military ensign. He learnt Indian languages and went pig-sticking; in fact, he looked set to join his father and brothers in an honourable career of public service.

But Palgrave had a restless quality which singled him out from other members of his family. Not content with being a respectable second-generation member of the Church of England, he severed his connection with the Establishment and became a Roman Catholic at a time when 'popery' was a bar to most forms of public service in Victorian England. Not only did he become a Catholic, but he joined the storm-troopers of that Church as a Jesuit priest. His father was both baffled and impressed by a son who became – in his words – 'a scholar, soldier, hunter and priest' all in such rapid succession.

Having taken the plunge into the Jesuit fraternity, with all its political and proselytizing activities, Palgrave found himself by 1857 in the Lebanon, where he was busily engaged in converting the followers of Islam to Christianity and the followers of less acceptable (in his view) forms of Christianity to Catholicism. To do this controversial and dangerous work, he found it easier to adopt disguise and took to travelling throughout the Levant dressed in Arab robes. When the anti-Christian feeling became too strong, and massacres took place, he had to withdraw, first to Beirut and then to Hampstead – still wearing his Arab garb and claiming he had no other clothes.

It was while he was at a Jesuit college in France that Palgrave first became inspired with the idea of making a major journey across Arabia, starting not far from his old stamping grounds in the Levant, and eventually crossing the Arabian desert from west to east to end up on the coast of the Persian (or Arabian) Gulf. His motivation for the journey is – to say the least – somewhat mysterious, like his motivation for most of the changes of direction in his life. If, however, we are to believe his own declaration of his interests, then it appears that the

91

bedouin and nomadic peoples of Arabia had exerted their pull on him – probably ever since his earlier missionary travels in the Lebanon. He wrote in the preface to his subsequent two-volume *Personal Narrative of a Year's Journey through Central and Eastern Arabia*: 'the men of the land, rather than the land of the men, were my main object of research and principal study.'

But there are plenty of theories about why he made the journey. The most dramatic is that it was at the behest of the French Emperor – Napoleon III – who had ambitions to extend French commercial and colonial interests into the Gulf region and who, when he heard of Palgrave's enquiries from a French Jesuit, summoned Palgrave to an audience and pointed out to him the desirability of furthering French – and thus Christian – influence in the Arabian peninsula. It must also have been clear to Palgrave that French official backing, particularly in the early stages of mounting the expedition from the Levant, would be an immense help. But whatever the inducements, taking a brief from Napoleon III, who was well known to have ambi-tions in the Near East to emulate his celebrated predecessor, Napoleon Bonaparte, as master of Egypt, was a curious and dubious action by an Englishman who had not so long previously been a serving officer in the forces of the British Raj in India. Could it have been significant that shortly before his audience with Napoleon III Palgrave had renounced his English name (so carefully acquired by his father) and reverted to his Jewish one of Cohen? If espionage was his object, on whose behalf was he spying?

And there were other less sinister reasons for Palgrave's sudden urge to cross Arabia. Possibly his missionary work in the Levant had awoken his conscience to the possibilities of taking the Gospels further into alien territory. Possibly he was responding to the sheer call of adven-ture: the fact that he had to make the journey disguised as a Syrian doctor must have added to the thrill of the undertaking. As a scholar, he cannot have been unmoved by the opportunities his trip opened up for making new discoveries in the fields of geography and geology. No

European had crossed this fearsome desert before.

True to his interest in the men rather than the land, Palgrave hired a wizened bedouin guide called Salim who was a personality in his own right – possibly too much of a personality, because it transpired in mid-journey that he could not enter the desert settlement of Al Jawf because of a murder he had committed there on a previous visit. Palgrave also had a fellow Jesuit (of a conveniently swarthy appearance) as a travelling companion. Under their new identities, they set out from Gaza to Ma'an in what is now southern Jordan, and then plunged into the desert until reaching, after some hundred miles, the settlement of Al Jawf. Beyond this, 'the immense ocean of loose reddish sand' which constituted the Nafud Desert closed around them. Palgrave was later to describe it as enormous ridges of sand running parallel to each other and eventually stretching out to burning sand walls on every side. The heat was such that the whole region seemed to him 'a vast sea of fire'.

There were two major stopping points on his crossing. The first was the township of Ha'il. Here the Emir unwittingly helped the two European priests to establish their disguise by sending members of his family to seek medical advice from the two 'visiting Syrian doctors'. Despite this, they had one or two narrow escapes from exposure when former acquaintances from the Levant claimed to recognize them. They responded blankly and carried off their imposture. Palgrave – always on the lookout for itinerant tribesmen – noted with sympathy that the bedouin, who had come into Ha'il to unload and trade camels, 'looked anything but at home' in these comparatively urban surroundings. No doubt hoping to meet more such bedouin further into the desert, Palgrave and his companion pressed on towards Riyadh, the capital of the Wahhabi peoples.

Here the Emir was less helpful. He declared that Riyadh had no need of their medical skills and suggested they passed on their way – even offering them fresh camels as an inducement to do so. But Palgrave's curiosity had been aroused, and he was not satisfied with a fleeting glimpse of this great tribal centre. He managed to persuade a bedouin chief with whom he had struck up an acquaintance in the desert to intervene with the Emir on his behalf. The representations were successful, and Palgrave and his companion were – after all – allowed to practise their dubious medical activities in Riyadh, as they had been in Ha'il.

But there was an additional danger in Riyadh. The Emir's eldest son and heir – Abdullah – was conducting a feud against his more popular younger brother. Abdullah approached Palgrave about supplying him with strychnine poison, but Palgrave had a good idea of the likely victim, so he refused. After this, Abdullah became his enemy and, with singular percipience, accused him of being a Christian spy and threatened him with the death penalty, which was the rightful punishment for any such intruder. Palgrave declared that he was the Emir's guest and claimed protection as such, adding for the benefit of other listeners that 'if any mishap befalls us it is all Abdullah's doing'. It was clearly time to leave Riyadh while he could, and Palgrave and his companion managed – with the help of a dashing caravan leader who was a genuine Syrian – to make an escape during the evening hour of prayer when the town gates were unmanned. Once back in the enfolding hills, they 'drew a long breath, like men just let out of a dungeon'. He was the first European to spy out the land in Riyadh, which he described – not without justification – as 'the lion's den'.

Now clear of Riyadh, Palgrave could again pursue his nomadic links and join wandering bedouin or passing caravans to help him on the last stage of his journey towards the shores of the Persian Gulf. When he reached the Gulf, he was disappointed by its waters compared with the sparkling Mediterranean, finding his long-sought prize 'a leaden sheet, half ooze, half sedge'. But his real prize was the achievement of having survived the crossing, and encountered those people of the desert whom this scholar, soldier, hunter and priest had sought more keenly than any of the other objectives of his erratic life, and whose 'most distinctive good feature' he identified as 'their liberality'.

His book confirmed this passionate curiosity about the bedouin, but there were an embarrassing number of things it did not confirm. His estimates of the sizes of the settlements he had passed through did not tally either with later estimates or with the facts. Sir Lewis Pelly (a British political agent on the Persian Gulf from 1862 to 1871) was sceptical about his whole adventure. His account of the height of the sand-dunes and the nature of the Nafud seemed so exaggerated to some later travellers – like Philby – that they doubted if he had been there at all. The description of the Arab horses seemed to later experts – notably the Blunts – so wide of the mark as to arouse derision.

What can be said in defence of Palgrave's claims is the same argument that is put forward in defence of Marco Polo's account of his travels: although much is wrong, much remains true and almost inconceivably beyond the range of invention or imagination. It is also relevant that many of his sharpest critics were not unprejudiced: they were later explorers who resented the earlier achievements of an amateur.

But despite this, and despite the length and apparent detail of his two-volume published account of his travels, Palgrave still leaves the reader with uncomfortably many questions unanswered; he seemed aware of this when he wrote at the conclusion of his book 'Much, how much! is left untold'.

WHILE Lady Hester Stanhope, Jane Digby and Richard and Isabel Burton were all notable eccentrics who had flouted the conventions of their time, the Englishman who set out from Damascus to live with the bedouin in 1876 was – in his own way – probably more strange and odd than any of them. Charles Montagu Doughty (1843–1926) was ill-equipped by appearance, temperament and manner to integrate into bedouin nomadic life. He was tall, red-headed and full-bearded, and he had a cantankerous personality coupled with a bad stammer. While Burton was agnostic and relaxed on questions of religion, Doughty was militantly Christian. While Burton admired the Islamic world, Doughty described it as 'the most dangerous grown confederacy and secret conspiracy, surely, in the whole world'. Unlike Stanhope and Digby, he was not supported by extensive private means, but struggled on a scholar's stipend. But none of these disadvantages deterred him from going to Damascus, learning Arabic and setting out with a pilgrim caravan heading in the general direction of Mecca.

Relatively early on his pilgrimage, Doughty was deflected from his avowed purpose of reaching Mecca by his fascination for the nomadic way of life in the desert. This led him to travel for many months with bedouin graziers and later with other nomadic groups. His adventures were both arduous and frightening. At different times and in different places, he was robbed, he was abandoned in the desert, he nearly died of starvation, he was expelled from some regions by the Turkish authorities, he was taken prisoner and he was very nearly murdered. As he got deeper into Arabia, conditions worsened: 'I passed one good day in Arabia, and all the rest were evil,' he pronounced.

Typical of his misadventures was an occasion when, at an oasis called Taima which he revisited with a small group of bedouin, he found that he was blamed for the fact that the walls of their well had fallen in since his first visit – clearly as a consequence of his Christian 'evil eye'. He was charged with the task of using his diabolical powers to restore the well, which had proved impervious to all local efforts to repair it. Too exhausted to move on, he had stayed at Taima for a month supervising repair work and all too aware that if his efforts failed he would be held responsible and his life forfeited. Eventually his efforts prospered and he escaped from Taima.

He took to wearing a loaded pistol under his shirt but, on the one occasion when he was under such imminent threat of death that he felt obliged to draw the pistol, he could not bring himself to use it and handed it over to his assailant, who was about to shoot him with it when a black servant of the governor of Mecca unexpectedly intervened to save him. His journeyings lasted for two years, and it was a wonder that he survived to tell the tale.

When eventually he emerged from the deserts, he settled down to write his remarkable *Travels in Arabia Deserta*. The book is extra-ordinary in two respects. Firstly, it gives a more detailed account than any that had been written in English before about the minutiae of living with bedouin nomads. Doughty describes in elaborate detail the life in a bedouin tent, how they move camp, how the bedouin treat their women, how the camels are loaded and employed, and the whole intricate structure of nomadic social relationships. He observed these things partly from the inside and partly from the outside, because he was not always a welcome guest and frequently was exploiting as a para-site the traditional hospitality of the desert. He was more of an anthro-pologist and less of an adventurer than Burton; more of a hanger-on and less of a hero.

The second extraordinary feature of *Arabia Deserta* is the language in which it is written. In the ten years between his travels and the publi-cation of his book, Doughty developed not only his obsession with nomads but also an obsession with medieval and Renaissance English literature. His syntax becomes weird and his vocabulary larded with words and phrases that would have been more at home in the writings of Chaucer or Spenser than of a Victorian traveller and aspiring poet. The meaning of his sentences becomes oblique to the point of obfus-cation, and his judgements become clouded to the point of baffling rather than enlightening the reader. A general tone of disapproval permeates the whole. What – for instance – is one to make of remarks such as: 'The camel on which they rode was an oblation of the common charity; but what were their daily food only that God knoweth which feedeth all life's creatures'?

But dimly glimmering through all the obscure and antiquated verbiage are a few lasting impressions. Chief among these is that the 'pure' nomads of the desert are less corrupted by those Islamic practices he deplores and by the modalities of life than those living on the fringes of civilization or in the cities of the Levant: 'the Arabs of the wilderness are the justest of mortals . . . the nomad justice is mild where the Hebrew law, in this smelling of the settled countries, is crude.'

If other nineteenth-century travellers could be said to have fallen under the spell of bedouin nomadic life because they were attracted by it, Doughty could be said to be hypnotized by it as a bird might be hypnotized by a serpent – attraction and repulsion seemed to wrestle with each other in his approach. Richard Burton, who reviewed Doughty's book, had little time for his passive approach, writing:

> Doughty is bullied, threatened and reviled; he is stoned by the children and hustled by the very slaves . . . His life is everywhere in danger. He must go armed, not with a manly sword and dagger, but with a pen-knife and a secret revolver . . . I cannot, for the life of me, see how the honoured name of England can gain aught by the travel of an Englishman who at all times and in all places is compelled to stand the buffets from knaves who smell of sweat.

Lawrence of Arabia, on the other hand, found that when he went into the Arabian desert forty years later, Doughty was still remembered. Lawrence said:

> They tell tales of him, making something of a legend of the tall and impressive figure, very wise and gentle, who came to them like a herald of the outside world . . . They say that he seemed proud only of being a Christian . . . they found him honourable and good.

Lawrence was later to refer to Doughty's book as a bible for desert travellers: certainly, like the Old Testament, *Arabia Deserta* was a chronicle of bedouin tribes, and like the Old Testament it was to be read by future generations and accepted as received truth. Doughty – whether viewed as a timid pen-knife-wielding scrounger or as a high-minded Christian scholar – would not have asked more.

OF all the nineteenth-century British travellers in the Levant and Arabia, none were more genuinely motivated by a curiosity about nomadic life than Wilfred Scawen Blunt and his wife, Lady Anne Blunt. They were unabashed romantics, by birth, upbringing and inclination.

Blunt started his career as a diplomat, but was at heart a poet and never took his diplomatic duties too seriously. As an attaché at various fashionable embassies in Europe, he confessed that amusing himself and making friends were his main occupations. Good-looking and of independent means, he had innumerable affairs until in 1869 he married Lady Anne King Noel, a granddaughter of the poet Byron and a considerable heiress. Lady Anne had many striking personal qualities in addition to her inherited assets: she was a gifted linguist, an accomplished musician (she played the violin for many hours each day) and a talented artist. But, most important, she shared Blunt's determination to seek out a life of adventure in unexplored and colourful parts of the Orient.

It was partly by chance and partly for philosophical reasons that it was the bedouin life of the desert that established itself as their chosen milieu. After exploring on horseback parts of Asia Minor in 1873, they went on to winter in Algeria. It was here that two significant things happened: they journeyed into the Sahara and had their first contact with nomadic tribes, and they developed a strong aversion to colonial rule – whether from Constantinople, Paris or London. They saw the bedouin (half a century before Lawrence of Arabia) as deserving the freedom to which they aspired. Blunt's writings became full of such phrases as 'the noble pastoral life' and the 'high traditions of the bedouin', which he saw as based on a tribal memory of heroic deeds and upright principles.

The year 1875 saw the Blunts spreading their wings further. They travelled to Egypt and hired camels and bedouin guides and set off from Suez to Cairo by one of the established caravan routes across the desert. This inspired them to try something more ambitious: they set up another camel team and crossed the Sinai Peninsula eastwards towards the Levant. Despite running out of water at one stage, their taste for desert travel and their fascination with nomadic life were taking a hold on them. It was at this stage that Blunt and his wife resolved to undertake an even more ambitious project.

By now Blunt had inherited unexpectedly a large country estate in Sussex, Crabbet Park, and the sizeable fortune that went with it, from his brother, who had died prematurely. They could afford to travel wherever they liked in a style that established the Blunts as grandees – suitable to be entertained as equals by powerful sheiks and other princes of the desert.

In 1877 they headed for Mesopotamia and decided to explore the Euphrates valley. Although not as unknown as the Nile (which Richard Burton had been exploring a few years before), the Euphrates was at that period firmly off limits for European travellers. While in Aleppo they spent much time with the British consul there – James Skene, who turned out to be a cousin of Lady Anne's. Skene shared their enthusiasm for the desert, and he persuaded them to extend their plans to include the valley of the Tigris and to make the journey in truly bedouin fashion. Luxurious tents were ordered; retainers were hired; horses, mules and camels were purchased.

Once they left the desert-fringe habitations behind them, the reality did not disappoint. The valley was carpeted in lush vegetation, which had attracted numerous bedouin encampments and vast flocks of sheep. Wildlife also abounded, not least in the form of the maneless Babylonian lion, which stalked the pastures carrying off not only sheep but the occasional nomad. When the bedouin warned Blunt of these dangers, it confirmed his impression of a biblical terrain where the lion-slaying Sampson and the Israelites would have felt as much at home in the nineteenth century AD as in the centuries before Christ.

Not having the physical strength of Samson, Blunt and his wife compensated by being heavily armed. Blunt was a good sporting shot, and went hunting for the pot; his wife carried a revolver, but had little intention of using it if she could help it, as she was convinced that shooting at marauding bedouin would only increase the risks of death or injury (a view later to be confirmed by events). When she passed the graves of some earlier European travellers who had been killed for their horses, she assumed it would not have happened if they had not resisted.

The Blunts' attraction to the bedouin was enhanced by their dislike of the Turkish authorities, who appeared on the scene whenever they reached permanent settlements. In one of these - Deyr - Blunt was convinced that the Turkish Pasha assumed they were government agents come to spy out the land in advance of some European invasion. Baghdad they particularly disliked, and they felt 'free' again only when - having exchanged their horses for camels - they pressed on into the deserts flanking the valley of the Tigris.

If they disliked Turkish Pashas, they compensated for this by being almost exaggeratedly impressed by 'aristocratic' bedouin sheiks. Blunt was very conscious of his own aristocratic forebears - his family had come to England with the Norman Conquest - and Lady Anne was similarly aware of her own distinguished ancestry. They unhesitatingly described themselves to their hosts in Arabia as being 'persons of distinction', and in the books that both of them wrote after their travels (Blunt wrote the prefaces to his wife's travelogues) there are frequent references to the importance of good breeding and good birth, whether among the English gentry or among the bedouin. So it was with particular pleasure that they encountered Sheik Faris of the Shammar tribe, who was immediately declared by them - on the basis of his good looks, obvious power and generous hospitality - to be 'a gentleman of the desert'. Their pleasure was turned to childish delight when the Sheik (who appears to have been impressed with Blunt's sporting prowess) declared that they were to become blood brothers and performed an elaborate ceremony with Blunt, culminating in a declaration that 'our tribe is your tribe and our tents are your tents'. This was social acceptance of the sort that was dear to both of them. It was very different from the deprived and outsider attitude that characterized much of Charles Doughty's time in Arabia.

Another high point of their desert travels was south of Palmyra, where they managed to locate the Rowalla bedouins. This was nomadic life on the grand scale, with some 150,000 camels and more than 20,000 tents at the one encampment. But what impressed the Blunts most of all was the size and grandeur of the sheik's own tent. Once again they were accepted as 'persons of distinction' and given the treatment they had come to expect. In this mood, everything was pleasing. They even rhapsodized over the taste and cooking of locusts: 'an excellent article of diet . . . would hold its own among the *hors d'oeuvre* at a Paris restaurant.'

But the Blunts' love affair with the bedouin nearly had a disastrous end. While they had noted with approval, and indeed as evidence of how well bred the desert bedouin were, that instances of petty pilfering were unknown among the tribes with whom they had been living, they were also aware that more large-scale highway robbery was a distinct feature of bedouin life. Indeed, the 'raids' inflicted by one tribe and group on another, or more frequently on desert travellers who belonged to no recognized tribe, were considered evidence of virility and part of the rich pattern of desert life. The Blunts saw nothing to criticize in this, viewing raids as part of the free-ranging existence they had come to admire and almost envy.

All that nearly changed when, after returning to the Levant in 1878 to penetrate northern Arabia and the Najd, Blunt and his wife were travelling southwards from Damascus across an apparently empty stretch of desert. They had allowed their usual precautions to lapse: they were riding ahead of the rest of their group and without their accustomed firearms, and their concentration was on watching their dogs (they took greyhounds with them for coursing hares and other game) playing among the dunes. Suddenly from among these dunes came not their dogs but a posse of galloping horsemen with lances lowered and grimly intent on rounding them up at sword and lance point as captives. Lady Anne, dressed, as was her custom, in Arab robes and riding astride, was indistinguishable from a man. She quickly called out the Arabic phrase for surrendering; Blunt did the same and dismounted to emphasize his passive intentions. Their horses and all their personal possessions were seized and they were led off to the raiders' camp as hostages. Things looked black indeed for them.

The way in which the situation was saved seemed to the Blunts to justify, in fact to glorify, all their attention to bedouin social standing. Their one Arab attendant explained to their assailants that the Blunts were friends of another bedouin chief – one of their erstwhile hosts and a 'gentleman' in the Blunts' eyes – with whom these robbers had a tribal link. Blood was thicker than water: honour was stronger than greed. The prized horses and all the personal possessions (including Blunt's tobacco pouch) were returned with apologies. Particular mortification was expressed by the robbers that they had threatened Lady Blunt with their lances: they declared (probably quite truthfully) that they had not realized that she was a woman. Instead of being a sad end to the Blunts' romantic sentiments about the bedouin, the whole incident merely tended to confirm their admiration and respect for them and their code of conduct.

Apart from their (much traded upon) social standing and wealth, the Blunts had one other great asset in communicating with the bedouin. They were passionate about horses. Not only did they both ride well (as of course did those other favourites of the bedouin, Lady Hester Stanhope and Jane Digby) but the pursuit of pedigree Arab horseflesh had been one of their motives in coming into Arabia in the first place – second only as a motive to their attraction to the nomadic lifestyle. The enthusiasm for bloodstock was not a merely academic interest. Blunt was set upon introducing Arab brood-mares into England and establishing a stud at Crabbet Park in Sussex. It was a measure of the confidence that he established with his bedouin hosts that he succeeded in this; they recognized in him one who not only shared their commitment to excellence in horse breeding, but who had the eye to identify the qualities that constituted an exceptional horse.

When eventually the Blunts retired from their Arabian travels to enjoy the more conventional pleasures of squirearchical life in rural England, Wilfred Scawen Blunt did not forget the political philosophy he had developed in his nomadic years. He became an active critic of British imperialist policy in India, Egypt and elsewhere. He thought that the bedouin had unlocked a secret of life and society. Their tents were their castles. They did not pay taxes or tribute to anyone. They lived in a social structure of their own choosing, and which they could leave should they so wish (at least theoretically – life in the desert outside the tribe was scarcely supportable in practice). He admired the morality of the bedouin and their ingrained wisdom, which he contrasted with more sophisticated societies, to the disadvantage of the latter. In short, he wrote: 'They had solved the riddle of life by refusing to consider it, or even understand that there was a riddle at all.'

IT is ironic that the man who, above all others, turned the English-speaking peoples' attention towards the Arabian desert and its inhabitants was not really interested in nomads for their own sake. Colonel T. E. Lawrence, who did so much to organize and lead the revolt of the Arabs against their Turkish overlords in the First World War, was dealing principally with the family of the Sherif of Mecca and the Emirs who led the Arab independence movement. When he was operating with them and their supporters, they were moving as army or at least as military units; they were never moving as small bands of bedouin grazing their flocks as they passed on migration across the mountains and deserts, but rather as 200-strong 'raiding parties'. The world of *Seven Pillars of Wisdom* (his account of the campaign first printed privately in 1926) was far removed from the world of Doughty's faltering footsteps through the sands.

But this did not mean that Lawrence was unaware of the simpler nomadic life of the Levant. He had travelled through the region before 1914 researching a thesis on Crusader castles. Indeed, he was later to write:

I had been many years going up and down the Semitic East before the war, learning the manners of the villagers and tribesmen . . . my poverty had constrained me to mix with the humbler classes, those seldom met by European travellers.

Lawrence had in fact made a close study of the migratory patterns of the nomadic tribes, and explained in the opening chapters of his *Seven Pillars* how the weaker tribes had been squeezed out of the fertile coastal strips and the oases of the Arabian peninsula to 'poorer springs and scantier palms' until they were forced 'to eke out their precarious husbandry by breeding sheep and camels', being finally 'flung out of the furthest crazy oasis into the untrodden wilderness of nomads'. For Lawrence, the nomadic state was something forced on reluctant refugees from more settled pastures; but equally he felt that the nomadic tribes were eventually forced by the pressures of 'the well-roads of the wilderness' into rejecting their wandering status and once more putting down roots and planting crops. The cycle, he maintained, repeated itself until there were few, if any, Semite tribes who had not – like the Children of Israel in Old Testament times – undergone their years in the wilderness: 'the mark of nomadism, that most deep and biting social discipline, was on each of them in his degree.'

Although Lawrence saw the nomadic state as imposed rather than chosen, he none the less appreciated and conveyed its romantic aspect. The bedouin had 'embraced with all his soul' the harshness of the desert life because by doing so he felt himself 'indubitably free'. Part of that freedom was, of course, a disregard of discipline: the bedouin felt free to leave a campaign – with their camels and their rifles – at any moment, and return to their own tents and tribe. What in a western army would have been viewed as desertion, with them was a mere assertion of independence. What kept them together as a military unit was often no more than the prospect of booty. But to Lawrence these shortcomings were compensated for by the bedouin skills as sharpshooters – skills developed by the hunting of gazelle and other wild game in the desert.

Individual bedouin leaders evoked particular romantic images for

Lawrence. Auda, the sheik of the Howeitat bedouin, was one such: according to Lawrence, 'he had been married twenty-eight times, had been wounded thirteen times, had slain seventy-five Arabs with his own hand in battle . . . of the number of dead Turks he could give no account . . . they did not even enter the register'. The bedouin, he concluded, saw things in primary colours; they were free from those doubts that he described as 'our modern crown of thorns'.

Lawrence goes on to philosophize about how the bedouin bring Allah into all their activities – 'their eating and their fighting and their lusting' – in marked contrast to Christians, whose God, he feels, is 'wistfully veiled from them . . . by the decorum of formal worship'. Like Lawrence, the bedouin had the capacity to accept pain without resentment or whingeing. Lawrence felt that to be accepted by the bedouin, as a comrade and, more important, as a leader, he had to emulate their manners and their characteristics. The easier part of this was dressing as a bedouin sheik ('wear the best – clothes are significant among the tribes,' he stressed); the difficult part was living up to the expected standard of commitment to his followers. When one of his men (the most useless and unappealing of them, as it happened) fell behind and got lost in the desert, Lawrence rode back alone through a sandstorm to find and rescue him. He knew that, as a foreigner, the Arabs did not expect this of him; but equally he knew that if he were to establish himself truly as their leader he had to live up to their highest self-imposed standards of behaviour. It was, he wrote, 'doubly hard for a Christian and a sedentary person to sway Moslem nomads'; so he had to act the part in the tough as well as the easy ways.

It is not, of course, for his philosophizing about the bedouin that Lawrence is remembered. His contribution to their legendary appeal for his compatriots was based on what he did rather than on what he thought: his two-month crossing of a thousand miles of desert that culminated in the attack on the Turkish-held fortress of Akaba; his crossing of Sinai in a forty-nine-hour camel ride; his lyrical entry into the defile of Wadi Rum; his survival of the shifting quicksands . . .

these were the incidents that inspired his contemporaries and successors with a desire to seek out the bedouin for themselves.

In short, Lawrence of Arabia (as he was to be remembered) was not in reality a case of an Englishmsn being attracted to the nomad way of life; it was other aspects of his time in Arabia that most attracted him – the glamour of an independent command, the comradeship of the desert, and the exhilaration of living dangerously. But he was a case – perhaps the supreme case – of an Englishman attracting others to what they saw as the romance of bedouin life. Not all the visitors to Lady Hester Stanhope and Jane Digby, nor all the readers of Doughty's *Arabia Deserta* and Burton's reminiscences, had a fraction of the influence that Lawrence exercised by his life and his myth.

IN a book about Englishmen, Scotsmen and Americans who have been obsessed by their interest in nomads, it may seem strange to include an adventurer of German origin called Carl Raswan. But when Raswan came to the deserts of Arabia to live among the bedouin he was totally under the influence of English traditions and English writers: 'Colonel Lawrence of Arabia has been my constant companion through the pages of this book,' he writes in the foreword to *The Black Tents of Arabia*. 'To Charles Doughty I owe the fact that . . . I had lived in peace under the goat-hair tents of the Ishmaelites,' he writes on the same page. 'The work and ideals of Lady Anne Blunt sustained me in my quest for the true Arab horse,' he claims, and he even persuaded that great British pro-consular figure in the Levant – Sir Ronald Storrs – to open an exhibition of his bedouin photographs. Although – admittedly – in the First World War he returned to 'the land of my birth and offered my services as a volunteer in the German cavalry', and although there were those in the Second World War who had doubts about where his patriotism lay, the fact was that he made America his home (for the periods when he was not in Arabia) and seems to have felt himself an American nurtured on the British traditions of Arabia.

So if he is eligible for inclusion, the next question has to be why is he worth including? This is easier to answer. His passion was 'to enquire into the wanderings of the bedouin tribes', and he devoted most of the inter-war years to doing just that. But whereas other travellers in Arabia during those years came as explorers, as students, as anthropologists, as administrators or as collectors of carpets and other artefacts, Raswan came as a full-blown participant in bedouin life, with all its passions, blood feuds, raids and casualties. He was a player rather than an observer.

Early on in his time in Arabia, Raswan became – by dint of a curious accident – the blood brother of a bedouin boy who was to become a prince of the Ruala tribe. The relationship arose from the fact that the bedouin boy had hit Raswan between the eyes with a pebble thrown from a powerful sling and had felled him – bleeding from the head – like Goliath; when solemnly invited by the boy to name the due retribution for having wounded a guest, Raswan wisely replied: 'This had happened according to the will of Allah. I know no other price than thy friendship.' The friendship was to involve a total commitment to the wild, wayward, raiding practices of the Ruala tribe, which was to give an alarming pattern of continuity to eleven visits spread over a period of twenty-two years.

During these long and frequent visits, Raswan wandered, hunted and fought with the Ruala; on horseback and on camel-back he crossed and recrossed their grazing grounds year in and year out: 'they knew and loved me as I knew and loved them,' he wrote. Always it seems the bedouin with whom he lived were on the move. He describes how every day the whole tribe had to shift camp, how the camels were made to kneel while the women and girls mounted them, how a camel calf – too unsteady as yet to travel on its feet – hung in a hamper suspended from its mother's hump, and how 'the wistful faces of two little girls peeped from the saddle-bag'.

But what makes Raswan's experiences distinct from those of other travellers who joined the migrations of bedouin across the Arabian peninsula was that so often his migrations are not peaceful ones but either savage raids on other tribes or subject to attack from other raiders. Sometimes these raids take place on camels, but – with the advance into the twentieth century – often they are made in motor vehicles. There is a flavour of the Libyan desert in the Second World War, of the Long Range Desert Groups that preceded the SAS, about some of Raswan's exploits.

On one occasion, driving back to a Ruala camp, Raswan and his companions were ambushed by Saba tribesmen. The bedouin sitting immediately behind him in the car was fatally wounded by a bullet in the stomach and ordered his slave to shoot him through the head to end his agony. This was done, and, while some of the party buried the dead man in a shallow grave, they set to work to change the tyres on the vehicle, which had also been riddled with bullets. When the attackers renewed their assault, others in the car were killed and Raswan's closest friend among the bedouin – Faris ibn Naif es-Sabi – was shot twice in the chest. When the shooting finally stopped, Faris – by now clearly unlikely to survive – insisted on being taken not to hospital in Damascus but back to the tribal tents to see his fiancée. According to Raswan, the bride-to-be then decked herself out in all the finery of an Arab wedding feast and the marriage ceremony ensued, after which it was apparently consummated by the dying man and resulted nine months later in the birth of a fatherless child who was accepted as a valuable addition to the tribe. The whole story, as with a number of others in Raswan's book, has an improbability that stretches the reader's credulity quite considerably. When later an Arab girl is described as riding 'Ishmael's camel-throne' (a sort of Ark of the Covenant) bare-breasted, credulity is further strained.

What is one to make of all this drama? Raswan's book was published both in New York and in London. In the latter city, it was well received in 1935 (taking its place, incidentally, in the Paternoster Library series alongside such other best sellers as a translation of Hitler's *Mein Kampf* and of Mussolini's autobiography) and was described by the *Spectator* as 'an account as authoritative as it is absorbing'. Certainly parts of it are authoritative: his descriptions of falconry in the desert and of hunting down wolves on horseback with lances are totally convincing and compelling reading. But the vivid and personal dialogue between himself and his bedouin hosts sits strangely beside the less extrovert exchanges recorded by Doughty and Blunt, Lawrence and (later) Thesiger. *The Black Tents of Arabia* reveals Raswan's absorption into the nomadic life of the bedouin for which he shares the enthusiasm of his fellow (adopted) countrymen, but it also reveals how far he was from sharing the detached, self-deprecating attitude of so many of those countrymen. Even the rumbustious and at times self-glorifying Burton would surely have quibbled at 'as the death-car thundered past . . . my last shots spat venomously after the swiftly retreating [vehicle]'. Raswan may or may not deserve a place in this book, but one feels he would not have achieved a place in the counsels of the Royal Geographical Society.

WHEN the young Captain Glubb arrived in Mesopotamia in 1919 he was already a hardened soldier with a distinguished war record (including the award of a Military Cross in France) behind him. He was to be different from all other English-speaking travellers and settlers in Arabia and the Levant, because he set himself a different task. Lawrence had worked with the bedouin to win a war against their Ottoman overlords, but he had never more than temporarily harnessed them to his war machine. Glubb set out to do something more permanent: to disprove Doughty's statement in *Arabia Deserta* that 'like herdsmen and wolves, soldiers and bedouins may never agree together'. He was to make not just irregular guerillas but regular soldiers out of bedouin tribesmen. It was a formidable and unprecedented task, and when he arrived in the region he had no idea that this was to be his life's work.

John Bagot Glubb (to be known as Jack to his friends) was born in 1897 into a military tradition. His father was a major in the Royal Engineers and was to rise to become a major-general. Young Jack

Sir Henry Layard, who became deeply involved with the nomadic tribes of southern Persia during his travels in the 1840s, in Bakhtiari dress. The weapons were for use and not for show.

Bakhtiari crossing the Zagros Mountains on their annual migration to summer pastures.

The Bakhtiari hosts to the Americans who made the film *Grass* in the 1920s, in their black sheep-skin tents in the foothills of the Zagros.

A Bakhtiari tribesman is never too young to learn to use a rifle.

(Left) Vita Sackville-West, the poet and creator of Sissinghurst garden, travelled with the Bakhtiari in 1927 – the year this photograph was taken.

(Right) Bruce Chatwin who spent three years struggling with a book about nomads and who travelled with the Qashqai and others.

(Left) Lady Hester Stanhope who impressed the Bedouin with her horsemanship and with her stylish mode of travelling.

(Right) Jane Digby whose beauty and feckless character finally led her to an Arabian Nights existence and marriage to a Bedouin sheik.

Sir Richard Burton, who 'looked like Othello and lived like the Three Musketeers blended in one', was a swashbuckling adventurer among the Bedouin.

Camel caravans across the desert, unchanged since the days of Burton, Doughty, Palgrave and others.

(Left) Carl Raswan, an American by adoption, became a blood brother of the Bedouin and got involved in tribal fights in the desert.

(Right) Wilfred Thesiger in Arab dress. He believed – like Lawrence of Arabia – that 'the harder the life, the finer the person'.

Beatrix Bulstrode was an intrepid traveller in Mongolia but 'the sort of woman of whom consuls' nightmares are made'.

Yurts, the preferred dwelling of most Mongol-descended nomads in Central Asia, photographed by the author in Kirgizstan.

Horses and Bactrian camels are both being loaded by these Mongolian nomads.

Young Tuareg tribesmen prepare for a Saharan camel race.

Freya Stark as the author remembers her in the late 1960s, when she visited the Minaret of Djam and philosophized about nomads.

Contemporary travellers encountered by the author on the Karakoram highway between Pakistan and China continue nomadic traditions.

Alexander Laing (left) and Hugh Clapperton (right) were both travelling with the Tuareg nomads in the northern Sahara at the beginning of the nineteenth century; Clapperton was threatened by them and Laing was murdered by them at Timbuctoo. The author was more fortunate with his own guide (below).

Sir Harry 'the Caid' Maclean, who tried to recruit nomads to the Moroccan army and was kidnapped, wearing his Moroccan/Scottish attire.

The Hoggar Mountains in mid-Sahara: haunt of the Tuareg, their racing camels and their Foreign Legion opponents.

Glubb followed his father into the Sappers, and they both served throughout the First World War, keeping in close contact. Jack Glubb was badly wounded in 1917, his jaw being smashed in a way that for the rest of his life affected his appearance and resulted in his later being given the Arab nickname of *Abu Hunaik* – him of the little jaw. As soon as he was sufficiently recovered from his wounds, he returned to the front line. He had already demonstrated a talent for horsemanship, and was to develop a flair for languages.

Glubb's arrival in 1919 in Mesopotamia (as Iraq was still called) was in response to a requirement for British officers to help quell protests against the temporary British administration there after the war. His biographer, James Lunt, dates his commitment to the bedouin to one particular incident during his early travels when Glubb witnessed the Shammar tribe crossing the Euphrates; Glubb himself described the scene in detail in his book *The Story of the Arab Legion*:

> For five days the Shammar flowed in a constant stream across the bridge – five of the most strenuous but absorbing days of my life. Before my eyes passed in review a complete pageant of that nomad life which had not changed in its essentials since the days of Abraham . . . They looked unkempt and ragged to English eyes, but they managed their horses with unconscious ease . . . some carried long lances decorated with ostrich feathers . . . At other times came great camel litters, wooden crescent-shaped frameworks hung all over with carpets, tassels, white shells and blue beads . . . Then the last flock was over, the last of the swaying litters and lean horsemen disappeared once more into the shimmering mirage of the desert.

It was an image that stayed sharply in focus with him all his life.

Glubb's early responsibilities in Iraq were considerable. He was in charge of some hundreds of miles of desert country along the banks of the Euphrates, and while other young officers spent their time at country clubs playing tennis and drinking, Glubb cultivated his contact with the Arabs. He travelled ceaselessly. In 1924 he took two months' leave and set out for Transjordan on a camel accompanied by only one Arab servant. In four weeks he crossed nearly five hundred miles of wild country and desert, much infested with marauding bedouin. On arrival in Transjordan, the Emir Abdullah and his father were so impressed with Glubb's achievement that they declared 'this man is a true bedouin'. From then on, he was to carry (in Thesiger's words) 'the imprint of the desert, the brand that marks the nomad'.

When he returned from Transjordan, Glubb found that the Ikhwan (or the 'brotherhood', as they were known – a militant branch of the Islamic fundamentalist Wahabi movement) had been raiding and terrifying the migratory tribes in Iraq. Glubb was appointed a special service officer to help defend these vulnerable nomadic people. He developed his own definition of a genuine bedouin: 'the first requisite is that the bedouin must be a nomad who breeds and keeps camels', as distinct from any form of *fellahin*, who cultivates the fields. And he recognized that breeding was important to the bedouin, both their own breeding and that of their horses, camels, Saluki dogs or falcons. Whatever the Emir Abdullah might say as a compliment about Glubb's bedouin status, the fact of the matter was that bedouin were born as such and not recruited into the tribal life.

Glubb was promoted to be 'administrative inspector of the southern desert' in Iraq and was to work closely with the air force, which was inclined to think that all problems could be solved from the air without intervention on the ground. Despite the scepticism of his compatriots in the police and air force, he recruited mobile detachments of bedouin to protect the migratory grazing tribes from raiding Ikhwan. He was everywhere at once: driving or riding out to shepherds' tents, always reassuring them and – even more important – always listening to them. But successful as he was, his job was coming to an end. In 1930 a treaty terminated the British mandate in Iraq, and it became clear that Iraq was not to be Glubb's long-term home. He had developed his affection and commitment to the bedouin there, but now he brought these qualities to the service of a smaller and embry-onic state: the Emirate of Transjordan, which was shortly to become the Hashemite Kingdom of Jordan.

From the start, Glubb enjoyed the confidence of the Emir Abdullah. There was already a Transjordan Frontier Force in existence to supple-ment the work of the military Arab Legion. But Glubb had reservations about the lines on which these were run: the rank and file were of multi-racial extraction and mostly recruited from settled areas, and there was a formal hierarchy of British officers which made the whole set-up resemble in many ways the British army in India. Added to which, neither unit was very effective either at controlling or protecting the bedouin. Glubb's ideas were different. He wanted to create a force that was primarily recruited from among the bedouin themselves. As in Iraq, there were many sceptics: the bedouin – it was generally declared – could not be brought under any enduring form of good order and military discipline. Glubb set about forming a Desert Patrol made up of bedouin who were to disprove the sceptics. The Desert Patrol was to work with and within the broader Arab Legion and demarcation lines were never very clearly defined.

The immediate problem was the Howeitat tribe, which had featured largely in Lawrence's march on Aqaba. They now felt vulnerable to attacks by the more numerous Ikhwan and inclined to respond by indulging in raids into Ikhwan territory themselves, which in turn provoked massive retaliation. It was Glubb's great achievement that he purveyed both reassurance and restraint. He even persuaded increasing numbers of Howeitat and other bedouin tribesmen to join the ranks of his Desert Patrol. Soon it became the case that those who wanted to bear arms – 'the bedouin's chief pleasure in life', according to Glubb – found that the Patrol or the Legion provided the only outlet for so doing. The life in the Desert Patrol was less stratified and conventional than in other European-led forces: the men and their officers ate out of the same dishes; there was an informality later to be associated in the British army with the SAS; expulsion from the unit was the ultimate

113

disgrace and therefore the ultimate sanction. In speaking to the Royal Central Asian Society in 1937, Glubb maintained that 'mental and moral training . . . does not necessitate the introduction of either foreign social distinctions or of foreign dress'. Glubb himself – unlike Lawrence – continued to wear a modified version of British service dress, topped by the red and white chequered headcloth (or *shamagh*) now so generally associated with Jordanians and Palestinians.

A further radical and key element in Glubb's organization was the mixing of the bedouin tribes within the Desert Patrol and ultimately within the Arab Legion. Traditionally, the Howeitat and the Beni Sakr had been at loggerheads; but now they drilled, lived and fought side by side. The Desert Patrol did not only undertake patrols; it also established permanent forts at points in the desert where there was an adequate well to sustain a small garrison – usually some dozen men. With their towers, whitewashed walls, camel lines and national flag flying from the masthead, these forts resembled smaller versions of the French Foreign Legion ones in the Sahara. But Glubb added one feature that had both a social and a practical aspect: he included in the design of his forts a small council chamber or coffee room, where passing bedouin who called at the fort were encouraged to stay for refreshments and to exchange gossip and news. In this way the Desert Patrol's officers often got early intelligence of tribal movements – particularly by the dreaded Ikhwan. The Howeitat had always been prepared to risk death to secure grazing for their camels; now the grazing was better and the risk was less acute. Not for nothing had Abdullah identified the characteristics of a bedouin in Glubb.

And it was not only Abdullah who saw Glubb in this light. He had been granted the title of Pasha (and indeed was to be known as Glubb Pasha for the rest of his life) and it seemed natural to Jordanians, even those who were no part of the Desert Patrol or the Arab Legion, to address him as such. He lived as they did, in a tent and without luxury, speaking their language and respecting their customs. He also learnt that hardest of lessons for Europeans – to take life at the pace of bedouin, never to be too rushed or stressed to find time to listen and talk and drink coffee and meditate.

It was not until 1939 that Glubb formally assumed overall command of the Arab Legion, on the retirement of General Peake, the British officer who had founded the Legion nearly twenty years earlier. By then, Glubb had been in action with the bedouin of the Desert Patrol and the Legion on more than one occasion when they had come under attack from marauding tribes. They had come to respect him not only as a kindred spirit, as an administrator and as a negotiator, but as a fighting man too. The Emir Abdullah extracted a solemn promise from Glubb, at his audience on taking command, that he would 'act always as if born a Transjordanian', although the Emir sensibly agreed that if ever Transjordan and Britain found themselves on different sides, Glubb would be free to 'stand aside'.

With the outbreak of the Second World War, the Arab Legion increased in size and scope. By now, about thirty per cent of the whole force was of bedouin extraction, and Glubb tended to equip his bedouin units to a higher standard (the most modern armoured cars) than the rest of the force and to use them for the most demanding tasks. He discovered unlikely aptitudes among his bedouin recruits: they were, for instance, particularly adept as Morse code operators. They also were less inclined to involve themselves in politics than units recruited from settled areas with urban or regional affiliations: Glubb saw them as a praetorian guard – at the same time fiercely loyal to the Emir (or King) and prepared for action as a modern strike force.

During the Second World War campaign in Iraq, when the British managed to overthrow the Vichy French regime there and deny the Germans the use of Syrian airfields, the Arab Legion distinguished itself under Glubb's leadership; it was accepted for the first time internationally as a serious military fighting unit. The French officers and officials who were involved in Syria viewed Glubb with grave suspicion and resented the rapport that he had managed to set up with the bedouin – a feat they had never achieved themselves.

After the Second World War, Glubb was to lead his Arab Legion into action against the Israelis. He proved himself capable of identifying political priorities amid the turbulent fighting and, although he had had none of the staff training and education in military theory which most other generals had received (he now had the local rank of lieutenant-general), he managed to keep control of a fast-moving situation. Even after a truce was agreed, raiding continued in the mountainous border regions between Israel and Jordan, and Glubb was in constant touch with his forward units, ringing up local commanders on field telephones at all hours of the night to get the latest reports, and giving comfort, advice and instructions. Similarly, as the Legion expanded in size, so Glubb continued to take a detailed interest in promotions and appointments. He was an intensely 'hands-on' commander, and kept the tight control he had exercised over the 300-strong Desert Patrol now that he was commanding a 20,000-strong Arab Legion. This did not always endear him to other Britsh officers seconded to the Legion – Glubb regretted that there were so many of them – who sometimes felt he bypassed them or interfered in their commands. But it certainly did endear him to the Legion's bedouin element, who were used to the close relationship between leader and led which had always typified the atmosphere of tribal raids and activities.

But eventually Glubb's position became undermined by forces beyond his control. When one particular Israeli reprisal raid resulted in the destruction of a Jordanian village and the reported virtual massacre of its inhabitants, Glubb was openly criticized. It was felt that Glubb had not taken sufficient trouble to set up a proper intelligence service, but had been too content to continue to rely on gossip and news from nomads and cross-border travellers, as he had done in the early days of his Desert Patrol. When there were riots in the capital, the Arab Legion at one moment had to fire on the crowd. Glubb's relations with the young King Hussein were never as good as they had been with King Abdullah. Hussein was inclined to innovation, and Glubb had become entrenched in the system he had built up and which he

116

had served so long and well. Sandhurst-trained himself, Hussein was anxious to see more Jordanian officers in the top positions in the Arab Legion. Many people saw the writing on the wall before Glubb himself did, and it came as a total shock to him when Hussein dismissed him summarily on 1 March 1956: he was asked to leave the country by 7 a.m. the following morning after more than a quarter of a century's loyal service to Jordan.

One of the many legacies which Glubb left behind was the intense and personal loyalty of the bedouin elements in the Arab Legion to their king. Whenever in subsequent years King Hussein felt that his throne was under threat and found himself insecure or exposed, he would move out of his palaces and seek reassurance in the tented camps of his own bedouin units in the Arab Legion. This was indeed to prove to be a praetorian guard of the best and most reliable sort. Without the discipline and *esprit de corps* which Glubb had instilled, such a role would have been unthinkable for the wild and nomadic men of the desert.

Other Englishmen both before and after him were to seek in the bedouin an answer to their own romantic cravings; Glubb Pasha was following in their tradition in succumbing to the appeal of the desert nomads; but he was unique in moulding out of the bedouin an entity of his own creation, without destroying their integrity or spirit.

THOSE Englishmen who first crossed the Empty Quarter of Arabia were all heavily dependent on the nomadic tribes – usually the Rashid – to realize their objectives. This is in equal measure true of the three men whose names will always be associated with this most challenging of journeys: Bertram Thomas, Harry St John Philby and Wilfred Thesiger. For the first two of these – Thomas and Philby – the overriding consideration was the achievement of the crossing itself; both wanted to be the first, and in the event Thomas managed to do a south–north crossing in 1930, and Philby had to be content with a more prolonged and difficult crossing from the north a year later.

117

Thomas was a British official (he had started as a Post Office clerk) working as *wazir* (first minister) to the Sultan of Oman. He had long held the secret ambition of crossing the Empty Quarter, but – knowing the official mind – was convinced that if he disclosed his objective, obstructions would be put in his way. Merely to be aware of such a plan and not to forbid it could – Thomas calculated – make Arabian officials feel that they had connived at such a venture and would bear blame and responsibility if it ended in disaster. He therefore slipped away from Muscat in the night, hitching a lift on a passing British warship, to Salala on the Indian Ocean coast of Arabia. There he awaited the Rashid tribesmen with whom he had made a secret rendezvous. He had to wait several months, as his potential guides were involved in hostilities with other tribes in the interior. When he did manage to set out, it was a perilous undertaking on two counts: first, of course, was the sheer length of the camel rides between wells whose position and viability were in question; and second was the danger from the Murrah – a warlike and hostile nomadic tribe who were no friends of his escorting Rashid.

It would be tempting to imagine that Thomas made his journey to the heart of the Empty Quarter out of curiosity about the Rashid – that he was essentially 'in search of nomads'. He was not. His personal agenda was to be the first to cross this most inhospitable of deserts by whatever means and in whatever company he could. But, that granted, Thomas became a memorable, respected and admired figure among the Rashid. When Thesiger was making his crossing of this desert over fifteen years later, he found that the Rashid recalled Thomas's good nature, generosity and determination. To these most demanding of desert travellers, who expected others to share their standards of self-lessness, courage and endurance, Thomas had passed the test: he was declared 'a good travelling companion'. So although it might be fanciful to imagine that Thomas set out to study the Rashid nomads, they certainly studied him and did not find him wanting.

Harry St John Philby was a different and in many ways a less likeable character. He, too, was a British official and one with less humble origins than Thomas. He worked as an administrator at the court of Ibn Saud, King of Saudi Arabia, and it was the King's procrastination that had been responsible for delaying Philby's expedition across the Empty Quarter until – to his surprise and chagrin – he found that Thomas had done it first. When Philby set out on his own trip in 1931, he had certain advantages Thomas did not. To start with, he had the (albeit belated) blessing of the King on his venture. This was more than a gesture of goodwill: it meant that even the tribes of the interior, such as the Murra, would be afraid to molest one who had royal protection. He also did not have Thomas's local disadvantage of being a Christian and thus an 'infidel'; he had earlier converted to Islam with (one cannot help feeling) considerations of self-interest in mind, and so he was able to join in the all-important rituals of the faithful.

Philby, even more than Thomas, was a celebrated Arab scholar, but his heart was not with the nomads of the desert so much as with the politicians and courtiers of the capital. He became deeply involved in resistance to Jewish settlement in Arab lands and highly critical of many aspects of British imperial policy. With the advent of the Second World War, these criticisms of his own country, coupled with a militant pacifism (which appeared to condemn all wars except those of King Ibn Saud), resulted in his arrest by the British authorities in India and his detention under Section 18B of the Defence of the Realm Act (the same section under which Oswald Mosley was imprisoned). He was not detained very long and before the end of the war was once more seeking British government employment. He had written several authoritative tomes on his travels and on the history of the region, notably *Sheba's Daughters* and *Arabian Highlands*. In these he displays his knowledge of all matters Arabian, and he narrates in detail the stages of his journeys; but he does not analyse the character of his nomadic guides, nor does he show any enduring interest in their mode of life. An intensely egocentric man himself, he passes through the Empty Quarter, as he passes through life itself, somewhat detached from his surroundings and from the normal loyalties which shared dangers inspire. It is tempting – but probably misguided – to see in him that lack of commitment to his own faith, to his own countrymen and to a wider humanity which was to surface in his son Kim Philby – the notorious Communist spy and traitor.

It is therefore to the third of the great English explorers of the Empty Quarter that one must look for a real in-depth fascination with, and comprehension of, nomadic life. Wilfred Thesiger had a long track record in this direction even before he came to Arabia. Born the son of the British minister to the court of Haile Selassie, Emperor of Ethiopia, his childhood memories were of Abyssinia (as Ethiopia was then more generally known), of hunting trips with his father, of the clamour of tribal wars, and of travels beyond the reach of government or embassy support; all combined to confirm in him a 'perverse necessity which drives me from my own land to the deserts of the East'.

He had scarcely left Oxford before he was notching up remarkable journeys among the Danakil of northern Ethiopia – a nomadic people who owned camels, sheep, goats and cattle and among whom the richer tribes had some horses, which (Thesiger noted) they kept exclusively for raiding other tribes. In the Second World War, while Philby was displaying doubtful patriotism, Thesiger was being awarded a DSO and becoming a founder member of the Long Range Desert Group in North Africa, penetrating far behind Rommel's lines in military forays that were to become the inspiration for the foundation of the Special Air Service (SAS). After the war, an attachment to the Middle East locust control body, which was an offshoot of the food and agricultural organization of the United Nations, gave him a mandate to live and travel in Arabia. This was the ideal springboard for his own crossing of the Empty Quarter and for developing a rapport with the Rashid and other bedouin of the Arabian peninsula. In distinction from Thomas and Philby, his relationship with these nomadic people was the central inspiration of his travels, and in *Arabian Sands* (first published in 1959) he was able to share his findings with a wide readership.

Thesiger found a series of paradoxes about the bedouin when he was living with them. For instance, they assumed a natural superiority over the settled peoples on the fringes of the desert, and yet they never found it inconsistent with this superiority to scrounge for anything they wanted. They would cadge meals and hospitality. They would cadge 'servings' from male camels for their own female camels, without it ever occurring to them that they should have their own males. They found it more convenient to ride female camels, which were more biddable (enraged males would bite, where enraged females would only spit), which provided milk and which were capable of increasing the herd; so it was females they had. But despite the scrounging and the cadging, the bedouin had a real and deeply felt admiration for generosity: Thesiger quotes the case of an elderly bedouin who was positively envied because he had given away everything he had out of liberality of spirit, slaughtering his last camels to provide hospitality for his guests.

The bedouin had a peculiar and ambivalent attitude towards violence and pain. They appeared indifferent to death – and even to inflicting death – if one of their own tribe was not involved. Yet they were never gratuitously cruel, and would rather see a man killed than humiliated. Their anger was quickly aroused and, if their honour was impugned, slow to subside; they could be vindictive if slighted.

Another paradox recorded by Thesiger was the bedouin attitude towards space and privacy. They lived by choice far from other people, indeed as far from the madding crowd as could be achieved, in an infinity of space and silence. And yet when together they were always right on top of each other: their tents or sleeping rolls practically touching, their faces thrust in front of each other while speaking, their voices raised loudly even when at the closest proximity.

Thesiger pointed out what many others (including myself) had found when travelling with bedouin in the desert: firearms were an important preoccupation and part of their lives, never far from their persons and seldom absent for long from their conversation. But they handled their firearms (usually ancient rifles and sometimes museum pieces) with a familiarity which was quite divorced from safe practice. When walking beside their camels, the normal way of carrying a rifle would be over their shoulder, loaded, muzzle to the front and pointing straight at the back of the man in front. The bedouin saw nothing unnerving or bad mannered in habits that would have resulted in instant ostracization from an English pheasant shoot or an American quail hunt.

A further paradox was their attitude to money. Thesiger found them at once fascinated by money but uninterested in either earning or stealing it. He says they would talk intermittently for days about the price of a cartridge belt or some other object they had seen in the market; even handling coins seemed to give them a thrill. But during all the time he travelled with them – loading and unloading bags of silver coins daily on to the camels – he never lost a single coin or a single round of ammunition.

Being as observant as he was, Thesiger was also struck by the contrasting attitude of the bedouin towards different forms of beauty. They would often break into verse when talking among themselves and had a keen ear for poetry. On the other hand, they seemed to have no eye for visual beauty, whether of landscape or of architecture. (Bruce Chatwin also observed this with the Qashqai in Iran.) The play of light on the sand-dunes or the glories of a desert sunset left them equally unmoved.

Another contrast was that between a form of democracy and a resolute authoritarianism. Decisions would be taken by consensus, but once taken were absolute and binding. The ultimate sanction was always sensed as an unspoken threat hanging in the air: if a man could not abide by the decision of the group, then he would have to leave it, and to attempt to survive alone in the desert was to court certain death. When disputes arose, they would usually be settled by arbitration, the arbitrator sometimes insisting that a man should confirm his good faith by swearing an oath on a sacred tomb – even if that tomb was several days' ride away.

One paradox was the bedouin attitude to the weather. Sandstorms and other natural occurences were of overriding importance for their effects on travel and safety, but the bedouin would never speculate about or attempt to forecast the weather: it was the prerogative of Allah and to anticipate His will was a form of blasphemy.

Thesiger, like Lawrence of Arabia before him, was determined that no allowances should be made for him however arduous the conditions of travel. Even when most thirsty, he would restrain himself on arrival at a well until the last of his party had arrived. Like his companions, he would walk for the first two or three hours of a day's march, to rest the camels, and would walk rather than ride in mountainous terrain for the same reason. The one thing he did not attempt was to follow the bedouin practice of riding a camel perched on the saddle in a kneeling position: unsteadiness and the prospect of cramp made this an impossible feat for a European, particularly if he might need to shoot at game while on the move. Possibly more than any European traveller with the bedouin, Thesiger became absorbed in their ways, and by his writings acted as an interpreter between them and the Western world.

He entitled his book of photographs about travel in Arabia, Morocco, Afghanistan, Ethiopia and elsewhere *Visions of a Nomad*, and it was this aspect of travel that most firmly gripped him. Like Bruce Chatwin and other compatriots, he saw nomadism as a norm and not as an aberration. Thesiger reminds his readers that the domination of the desert by the itinerant bedouin had lasted longer than all the ancient civilizations. Until the advent of the car and the light aircraft, the bedouin had always had the capacity – like Norsemen at sea – to disappear to safety over the horizon. It was a horizon that beckoned him and all who went in search of nomads.

But Thesiger had developed his own particular philosophy regarding the nomadic bedouin. It could be summed up in a belief that the harder the life, the finer the person. This is a leitmotiv running through his *Arabian Sands*: nobility of spirit and mind was to be achieved by forgoing the corrupting comforts of urban life or even settled life on the fringe of the desert. The qualities that Thesiger so much admired in the bedouin – courage, generosity and loyalty – were refined in the fire of danger and hardship.

Taking this a step further, Thesiger distinguishes between various tribes and sub-tribes in and around the Empty Quarter of Arabia. The Bayt Kathir tribe were migratory, moving north along the wadis until they came to the rim of the Sands (as the Rub al Khali or Empty Quarter was often referred to); they would follow the rains but seldom venture far into the Sands themselves. Thesiger made some of his early journeys in Arabia with them, but he mistrusted their knowledge of the desert and their commitment to true bedouin standards. He preferred to travel with the Rashid (or Rawashid) tribe, who were the only people in Dhofar who had a real familiarity and intimacy with the Sands. His overt preference for the Rashid – amounting to favouritism among his guides and companions – often caused frictions amounting to desertion or threats of desertion, and upset those from other tribes; he found the Rashid not only better at desert-craft, but less grasping and more congenial as companions.

Thesiger was not entirely original in holding this concept. The Swiss traveller Burckhardt, who rediscovered Petra in the early nineteenth century, believed that the bedouin of the remotest desert had kept certain national characteristics over several millennia which 'gave them a special claim on the admiration of Europe . . . the remoter bedouin of the peninsula, the ones, so to speak, over the next sand-dune, were paragons of bravery, patriotism and honour . . . the true bedouin was a mirage that danced tantalizingly before his eyes' (according to Kathryn Tidrick). This view was commmoner in the early nineteenth century – at the height of the Romantic movement when concepts of 'the noble savage' were widely held – than it was in the more disillusioned mid-twentieth century. This was not the only respect in which Thesiger appeared to many as a figure from an earlier age.

The American anthropologist Professor Donald Powell-Cole, who lived with the Murrah bedouin (known as 'the nomads of the nomads') in the northern part of the Empty Quarter in the 1960s, also felt that Thesiger's view of them was over-romantic. He pointed out that although attracted by the nomadic aspects of bedouin life, Thesiger never experienced these in their normal way, because most of his journeys were special expeditions undertaken to fulfil his ambitions to travel in uncharted sands, rather than as part of a normal annual search for pastures. In this, Thesiger was typical of so many of his fellow countrymen: it was the romance of the nomadic life that attracted him, rather than any desire to analyse it.

And of course this in itself presented problems for him, just as it had for the Arabian travellers of earlier times: his motives were always somewhat suspect in the eyes of his companions and hosts. He himself might feel that subjugating the flesh to advance the spirit was a worthy objective, but it was an incomprehensible one to his hosts. Nor was the study of locusts much more convincing; even his closest companion and protégé – Salim bin Kabina – later told Michael Asher that he never really believed Thesiger was much interested in locusts: 'he said he came to destroy them . . . well, the locusts came before him and they came after him . . . I think he had some reason for coming he didn't tell us.' Many attributed his curiosity to oil prospecting (which was ironic in view of Thesiger's own abhorrence of the effects of oil discoveries on the bedouin way of life) and others thought he was secretly mapping for the British government or army. Part of the difficulty that he and his immediate predecessors experienced with the authorities was that they, too, shared these suspicions. The king of Saudi Arabia was furious when he found that Thesiger had penetrated his kingdom without prior consent. Like the Shahs of Persia, who resented any British contact with the Bakhtiari or the Qashqai tribes, Arabian potentates simply could not believe that Englishmen did this sort of thing for fun.

Indeed, 'fun' was not among the qualities they recognized either in themselves or in others. For all his admiration for the bedouin, Thesiger never claimed they had much sense of humour. In fact, on one occasion he told an interlocutor that he thought the bedouin had lost any sense of humour they once might have had, and now were left with no more than himself – 'and I always think that I've got none,' he added with typical English self-deprecation.

To Thesiger, unlike to Thomas and Philby, getting to know the bedouin was as much an attraction as getting to know the Empty Quarter, and he needed the former to explore the latter. Even the Rashid were disconcerted by the magnitude of the problems that the crossings entailed. The sand-dunes were an even greater obstacle than the search for grazing for the camels: although never steeper than thirty-three degrees (any sharper angle would result in a landslide), the sand grains were packed loosely and therefore camels' feet would sink deeply into them and virtually halt progress. Only where the grains were smaller and therefore more tightly packed would progress be possible at at all – and finding such patches of sand on a range of dunes that might stretch over many miles was a challenging task even for the most skilled Rashid guide.

Such challenges might have been expected to bring Thesiger ever closer in spirit to his bedouin guides and protectors. Up to a point they did. But beyond a certain point Thesiger was always aware that – as a Christian and an outsider – he was a potential liability to his travelling companions. At one stage it was suggested that he described himself as a Syrian if he became the subject of hostile questioning by other tribes or by the authorities. And whenever contact was made with other friendly bedouin, Thesiger became immediately aware of being excluded from their intimate exchanges of news, gossip and affection.

Thesiger best summed up his relationship with the bedouin in his paper to the Royal Geographical Society in 1948, when he wrote: 'Between us was the bond of hardships endured together and the comradeship of the desert life . . . I also know that amongst them in the desert I have found a freedom of spirit which may not survive their passing.' In truth, he succeeded in his quest to find, travel with and get to know the nomads of the Sands, but he never succeeded in his quest to become one of them.

126

# BOOK III

# THE MONGOL HORSEMEN
# OF CENTRAL ASIA

'The connection between the people and their territory is so frail a texture that it may be broken by the slightest accident. The camp, and not the soil, is the native country of the genuine Tartar.'

Edward Gibbon, in
*The Decline and Fall of the Roman Empire* (1788)

'The "unharvested steppe" forms a continuous strip of grazing from Hungary to Manchuria . . . it was a reservoir of nomad Peoples.'

Bruce Chatwin, in *What Am I Doing Here?*

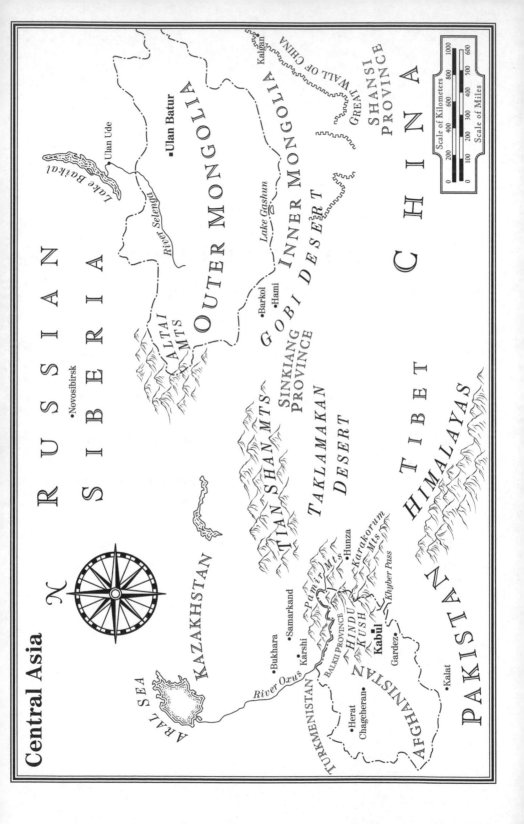

Central Asia

RUSSIAN
SIBERIA

• Novosibirsk

Lake Baikal
• Ulan Ude

River Selenga

■ Ulan Batur

OUTER MONGOLIA

Kalgan

GREAT WALL OF CHINA

SHANSI PROVINCE

CHINA

Scale of Kilometers
0  200  400  600  800  1000
Scale of Miles
0  100  200  300  400  500  600

ALTAI MTS

Lake Gashun

• Barkol
• Hami

GOBI DESERT

INNER MONGOLIA

SINKIANG PROVINCE

TIAN SHAN MTS

TAKLAMAKAN DESERT

TIBET

HIMALAYAS

ARAL SEA

KAZAKHSTAN

Pamir Mts

Karakorum Mts

• Hunza

Khyber Pass

• Samarkand

Bukhara •

Karshi •

River Oxus

BALKH PROVINCE

HINDU KUSH

• Kabul

• Gardez

TURKMENISTAN

• Herat

Chagcheran •

AFGHANISTAN

• Kalat

PAKISTAN

# 4

# Mongolia

—=>·◇·⊂=—

His contempt for pedestrians is so great that he considers it beneath his
dignity to walk even as far as the next yurt.
Colonel Przhevalsky (1867–85) on the Kalmuck nomads

HOWEVER fascinated by nomads many people in the English-
speaking world might be, the country that was most typical of a
nomadic lifestyle was almost inaccessible to such people until the very
end of the twentieth century. Mongolia is remembered as the home –
or perhaps more accurately the base camp – of Genghis Khan. It was
from here that he set out to conquer all the world, and succeeded in
conquering most of it – or most of what was known of it – in the
thirteenth century. His armies of steppe horsemen swept like a forest
fire or a plague of locusts across Central Asia, Russia, China and alarmingly large parts of Europe. It was said that you could hear them before
you could see them, and that you could smell them before you could
hear them.

But although the Mongol sway held good to a greater or lesser degree
for a considerable while, aided by a network of horse-borne messengers
that put the North American pony express in the shade, the Mongols
did not settle down to be long-term world rulers in the sense that the

Romans had achieved earlier and the British were to achieve later. Eventually their formidable neighbours – Russia and China – not only freed themselves from Mongol supremacy, but imposed their own cultures and regimes. Indeed, Inner Mongolia was permanently absorbed into China, and until 1911 Outer Mongolia was under Chinese domination too.

When the Mongolians were left to their own devices after the Chinese withdrawal in 1911, they did not make notable use of their new-found freedoms. Buddhism had been introduced into China before the time of Genghis Khan, but it was only in the sixteenth century that the Chinese actively propagated the faith in the hope of pacifying their belligerent neighbours. By the beginning of the twentieth century, Mongolia had succumbed to Buddhism in a somewhat excessive manner: there were nearly 2,000 lamaseries or monasteries (the only permanent settlements in the country) and over 100,000 lamas, a third of the whole male population of the country being in Holy Orders. This would have been an economic aberration even if the monks had been upstanding citizens, but unhappily they were not. They milked the pastoral communities dry with their insistence on ecclesiastical tithes; they exploited the ignorance of the lay population by widespread sale of indulgences; they lived decadent and corrupt lives in their lamaseries, steeped in vice and spreading syphilis. In fact, they were a throwback to the worst of medievalism.

It was into this society that many of those escaping the Russian Revolution of 1917 fled. Mongolia was unlucky in its refugees. Most prominent among them was the notorious Baron von Ungern-Sternberg. This White Russian adventurer was supported by a motley band of Cossacks and reactionaries who established a bizarre regime in Urga (the former name of Ulan Batur); on the one hand, he set about turning what had been a monastic settlement into the semblance of a modern town; on the other hand, he fed his opponents and prisoners to a private pack of wolves. When the Bolsheviks finally arrived in 1921, they confronted the Baron in a series of bloody engagements from which they eventually emerged appearing as the forces of light and right. Mongolia was to become the first and most subservient of Soviet satellite states.

This remained the position throughout the seventy years of Communism in Russia. Indeed, at one moment Stalin proposed absorbing Mongolia terminally into the Soviet Union, along with Kazakhstan and so much of the rest of Central Asia. When Molotov fell from grace (after his decades as Soviet Foreign Minister) in the 1950s, he was exiled as ambassador to Outer Mongolia, somewhat in the spirit in which the Duke of Windsor had been sent as governor to the Bahamas during the Second World War – a faraway place where not much harm could be done. It was little wonder that during these long years few English or American visitors were permitted to come to Mongolia: collectivization did not fit comfortably on a nomad society, and the fewer outsiders who witnessed the stresses and strains the better.

But there was always a trickle of intrepid travellers who braved the distances, the rigorous climate and the frigid nature of the official reception in order to see for themselves a land where nomadism was the norm rather than the exception, where horses were tethered outside yurts rather than cars parked in front of houses, and where wealth was reckoned in heads of sheep rather than in bank balances or real estate.

One such was Beatrix Bulstrode, a determined English lady who managed to penetrate the fastnesses of Inner and Outer Mongolia in 1913 and who believed in the truth of the Chinese proverb 'With coarse food to eat, water to drink, and the bended arm as a pillow, happiness may still exist'. Another was the American professor Owen Lattimore who succeeded in travelling throughout the length of Mongolia and over wide areas of the surrounding steppes between the 1920s and the 1960s, and who in consequence attracted unwelcome attention from Senator McCarthy and the Un-American Activities activists in the United States, who felt that he could not possibly have

131

achieved what he did without actively collaborating with the Soviet KGB. While Lattimore was studying these people from his academic viewpoint, two modest missionary ladies – Miss Cable and Miss French – were studying them from a more spiritual standpoint – with a view to saving their souls. The compulsion to seek out such nomads was equal in all these disparate visitors, but the reasons behind that compulsion could hardly have been more different.

B EATRIX BULSTRODE was the sort of woman of whom diplomats' and consuls' nightmares are made. Determined to the point of wilfulness, brave to the point of rashness, and self-confident to the point of brazenness, she was impervious to all advice and hell-bent on doing her own thing. Her 'own thing', as it turned out, was visiting and travelling among the nomads of Inner and Outer Mongolia at a time (1913) when both states – particularly the latter – were in the throes of banditry verging on civil war, and when the Chinese army was poised to wrest Mongolia back from Russian influence.

Having been told that she would not be given a visa (or a passport, as she called it), she decided to leave Peking for Inner Mongolia anyway. She concluded: 'The less that I discussed my projected plans the better . . . merely informing a couple of friends who happened to be dining with me the previous evening . . . I set forth.'

She slipped away on her own by train to the end of the line at Kalgan, which she found heaving with soldiery and where she – predictably – failed to manage to attach herself to any caravan leaving to cross the Gobi desert in the direction of Urga (now named Ulan Batur). In the end she teamed up with a Finnish missionary who had plans to travel in the same direction. In her subsequent book, A Tour in Mongolia, she says: 'The caravan consisted of the Finnish missionary, his two open carts drawn by two horses each, myself in my Peking cart drawn by a mule and pony, a saddle pony, three Mongols, two of whom were mounted – nine of us in all.' Her supplies included such essentials as Bovril and oatmeal.

Bulstrode had some doubts about whether she would be able to get out of Kalgan by road without any passport, but in the event the Chinese officials took so 'little account of a woman' that they let her through without enquiry. She packed a revolver and slept with it under her pillow, and was amused to note that the missionary, despite abjuring her to 'put her trust in God rather than firearms', surreptitiously kept a revolver in his own pocket also.

The Mongol escort, having discovered that the English lady traveller packed a gun, decided that this was a good excuse to organize a wolf hunt. In the region through which she was travelling, the wolves were particularly troublesome, having not only ravaged the flocks and herds but having pulled down and killed a colt on the edge of a settlement. The Mongols did not fear for themselves on account of wolves because they faced them down, yelling and shouting and so drove them off, whereas they maintained that the Russians and Chinese ran away from wolves and so encouraged them to attack.

Bulstrode became an eager participant in a somewhat absurd wolf hunt: as neither she, her companion, nor her guides had a rifle, they set off to flush out the offending she-wolf with their revolvers. Not surprisingly, the nearest they got to success was 'scuffing up the dust after her retreating form'. So they then settled down to dig out the wolf lair for a whole exhausting day, which Bulstrode joined in enthusiastically because she had a secret ambition to 'become the owner of a couple of wolf cubs and take them back to Peking or possibly ship them home alive'. When the digging proved no more successful than the revolver shots, the Mongols (who seemed to be a thoroughly inept bunch) decided to smoke them out of their lair, and lit a fire which quickly turned into a prairie blaze, flushing out not only wolves but golden eagles and harrier hawks which proceeded to swoop on the fleeing ground game. Bulstrode found it all vastly amusing, despite the fact that at one stage the fire nearly engulfed the nearby Mongol yurts.

On the following day she was eventually rewarded with a 'pretty, soft little wolf cub', but only after one of the missionaries – encouraged by

Miss Bulstrode – had burrowed into its hole, at considerable danger to himself as a parent wolf might still have been lurking within, 'until nothing but his feet could be seen outside'. Having taken charge of the unearthed cub, Bulstrode then fed it from a bottle, made of a pierced cow-horn with a teat cut from the udder of a sheep, until it died a day or two later. Nothing and no one was allowed to get in the way of Miss Bulstrode's adventures and ambitions.

Tough as she was, however, she was not immune to being disconcerted by some of the Mongols' habits. In particular she found their practice of intruding on her privacy in her yurt and fingering her possessions with curiosity – rubbing their grubby fingers up and down her toothbrush, for instance – was mildly perturbing.

Bulstrode herself was as intrigued with the Mongols' possessions as they were with hers. She shamelessly admired the men's shaggy fur hats, their silver-mounted hunting knives, their ivory chopsticks, and their flint and tinder purses hanging from silver chains around their waists. But these handsome and elaborate ornaments did little to disguise their owners' lack of cleanliness. Bulstrode found that 'Mongols, generally speaking, are an extraordinarily dirty people', part of the trouble being that one of their superstitions was that if they had too much to do with water in this life they will become a fish in the next incarnation.

Being fascinated by the concept of nomadic movement, Bulstrode became somewhat disillusioned by the Chakhar people of Inner Mongolia who, even if the need for fresh pasture did not oblige them to move on, none the less transported their yurts a short distance periodically to satisfy their need to demonstrate their nomadic nature. She was still determined to find truly nomadic Mongols.

Feeling frustrated by this, and realizing that no amount of pushing on her part would enable her to penetrate to Urga through Inner Mongolia, Bulstrode returned to Peking and set about reaching her objective from another direction. This time she decided to go by train through Manchuria and Siberia to Verkne-Oudinsk (later called Ulan

Ude) on the eastern side of Lake Baikal and to attack her objective from the north. On this attempt, Bulstrode again recruited a travelling companion, not a missionary this time but a Mr Gull of the Chinese Maritime Customs Service, whom she described as 'a peppery little man' (and whom she later married).

The first major problem occurred on the Chinese-Russian frontier – 'the scene of all that is exasperating in connection with customs'. When she reveals in her book that what she wanted to take across this tense frontier was 'our guns, revolvers and ammunition' one begins to see why customs formalities might tend to be 'exasperating'. She had been warned that if she was caught trying to smuggle firearms into Russia (it was only a year or two before the Russian Revolution, when anarchists and assassins were much in evidence) she would not be let off with a fine but would be committed to prison. Despite this, and despite having heard stories of the awful dungeons on the Volga, she was not deterred from her own peculiar blend of headstrong determination and contempt for authority: she promptly set about dismantling her larger weapons and hiding parts in her underwear; the ammunition for the weapons – over a hundred rounds – was packed away in a tin jug and basin, and walnuts placed on top; under her Burberry she slung her Mauser pistol and a large Colt revolver, and 'my smaller weapon' she carried in a pocket with more ammunition distributed about her person. She was indeed a customs man or consul's nightmare. What Mr Gull of the Chinese Customs Service must have thought is not related; perhaps this was when he showed his peppery side.

Verkne-Oudinsk turned out to be a former Russian penal settlement which had latterly become a garrison town. It was still conspicuous for its overcrowded prison, where hundreds of prisoners were fettered and confined in dungeons, and was decreed by Miss Bulstrode to be 'not a place of many attractions'. She was pleased to get away (perhaps the talk of dungeons was bad for the morale) and took passage on a paddle-steamer down the Selenga river. The cabins were sweltering and the deck space subjected to 'a continual rain of red hot charcoal' from the funnel.

As soon as she could, Bulstrode (with Mr Gull still in tow) changed the paddle-steamer for a *tarantass*, a springless horse-drawn carriage, and set off across the steppe in the direction of the Mongolian frontier. She found that this part of Siberia 'bristled with Russian bayonets' and that the small towns they passed were dominated by churches and barracks. At one such settlement they hired another *tarantass* and *jamschik*, or coachman, who for sixty roubles (some £7) undertook to take them on the week-long drive to Urga, the Mongol capital. The coachman's indulgent attitude towards their excess baggage which sorely overloaded his *tarantass*, made Bulstrode wonder whether he was in league with the local Hung-hu-Tzes bandits, and therefore felt that the more booty loaded up the better. Her battery of weapons, she noted, 'had to be arranged so as to be immediately available'.

The border between Russia and Mongolia provided no obstacle, but swollen rivers held them up. As they penetrated more deeply into Outer Mongolia, they spied what appeared from a distance to be ant-hills with ants swarming around them, but which as they approached closer turned out to be yurts surrounded by cattle and flocks. They had at last reached their objective: Mongol nomads on the move, or – as Bulstrode in her somewhat egocentric and patronizing way put it – 'I had attained the desire of my heart . . . primitive life among an unmistakably primitive people'.

Bulstrode came to admire some aspects of the Mongol nomads, in particular their devotion to their hunting dogs. She tells long stories in her book of one hunter who was inconsolable after he had accidentally shot one of his own dogs while it was chasing a wild boar; and of another who spent days tracking down and killing an elk because it had kicked and mortally wounded his dog – and so had merited revenge. But on finally reaching Urga she had a narrow escape from a pack of wild dogs while returning at night from a dinner party, and in general she found more to revolt than to attract her. In particular she was appalled by the brutal practice of locking prisoners (possibly arms smugglers?) into coffin-like boxes through which they could only protrude their head or a hand to receive food. Her book has a horrendous photograph of these chests and their permanent incumbents. Altogether, as with Verkne-Oudinsk, she did not much care for Urga and, with a good deal of encouragement from the Russian consul who clearly could not quite make out what she and Mr Gull were up to, and after a final evening spent 'with the whitened skull of a camel for a target trying to improve our marksmanship with the Mauser in the twilight', she eventually headed for home. Even then, her adventures were not over: broken *tarantasses* and predatory guides – who were inclined to abandon her when their outrageous demands were refused – enlivened the return trip.

Bulstrode's description of the nomadic Mongols is disappointingly brief and superficial. She comments, for instance, on 'their small and well-shaped feet' and the fact that their boots always looked several sizes too large for them and had 'toes that turn skywards'. She admires the silver ornaments of the women and, as we have seen, the silver-mounted weapons of the men; and she deplores the squalor of many of the yurts and the personal hygiene of some of the Mongols. But she tells us little of how or why they moved or of how their society was organized. For one who travelled so far at such risk, she is remarkably uncurious about the source of her inspiration.

Be that as it may, her courage and determination were of a very high order and seemed to infuse the Finnish missionaries and even the peppery little man whom she co-opted for her second journey with something of her own pugnacious spirit. One has only to read her account of the fate of a certain Mr Grant ('a young Scotsman engaged in the Chinese telegraph service'), who was murdered by Mongol brigands because he refused to hand over his Chinese companions to them, to realize that the dangers were real enough. Perhaps her extensive armoury was justified after all – even if her method of smuggling it across international frontiers would have landed her in trouble beyond consular help. One wonders what the Mongol nomads made of this tiresomely bossy lady. We know at least what one of the younger Mongol girls thought: 'she obviously mistook me for a man,' Bulstrode records with some chagrin.

IT would be hard to find a greater contrast to Beatrix Bulstrode than the other British lady travellers who set off for a journey of several years across Central Asia and the Gobi Desert in the 1930s.

Mildred Cable and Francesca French were missionaries – and definitely not the gun-toting variety. They had lived and worked for more than twenty years in the province of Shansi in northern China, and then were encouraged by their spiritual mentors to set off beyond the Great Wall of China into the heart of the Gobi as itinerant gospel preachers. They wanted to bring the Christian message to the oasis dwellers, the caravan traders and – above all – to the nomadic peoples who roamed the Chinese–Mongolian frontier on the fringes of the Gobi. They eventually published an account of their travels, simply entitled *The Gobi Desert*, in 1942.

The oasis dwellers and the caravan traders proved easier to find than the nomads. The ladies had been on the road for many months before they left a main caravan route and found themselves heading through a chain of hills between Hami and Barkol, just south of the frontier between China and western Mongolia. The going was rough, and a young girl who had offered to lead them through 'a defile blocked with boulders' had turned back, telling them that 'the way was long and the water still distant'. It must have seemed to these pious and courageous travellers (much more strongly than it did to us in Morocco on the occasion described earlier) that they were indeed passing through Bunyan's pilgrim's Slough of Despond. At sunset they had not found water, but eventually came across a 'scummy pool' where they camped for the night using as fuel some leftover camel-droppings from earlier passers-by.

Imagine their delight when the next day they heard a dog barking and finally came upon a family of Kazak nomads from the steppes of northern Turkestan who, once they were satisfied that the strangers were unarmed and came in peace, received them into their yurts and gave them milk to drink. The Kazak yurts, then as now, were far better furnished with good-quality rugs and lacquered chests than those of the Mongol nomads; indeed, they 'conveyed a real sense of comfort' to the visitors. When later the missionaries visited Mongol yurts, they noted that not only were the comforts less but a part of the interior of the yurt would frequently be screened off for the use of delicate kids or lambs that needed to share the shelter of the nomadic home.

The ladies found that their new hosts' riches consisted of sheep, horses and cattle 'to which they steadily added by stealing from the flocks and herds of Chinese in the neighbourhood'. The missionaries were not judgemental about such practices but, when they moved on and came into view of larger Kazak encampments, they took care to secure their own horses overnight with iron hobbling-padlocks, as 'nothing except the strongest measures can make an animal safe against the clever wiles of a Kazak horse-stealer'. They noted that the oasis dwellers considered the Kazak nomads as a continual source of danger to the trade and traffic of a locality, and were consequently always trying to encourage them to move on.

Miss Cable and Miss French found that, while the Kazak nomads preferred horses, the Mongol whom they subsequently visited often preferred camels – 'the bulky Batrian species . . . a very different creature from the fleet dromedary of the Arabian desert'. The caravan men always employed these efficient beasts of burden. Indeed, the ladies became considerable experts on Bactrian camels. They describe how, when loading such a camel, the beast will 'grumble, growl and show resentment' and that no notice need be taken of such behaviour; but the moment the camel becomes silent, it is an indication that the load has reached the maximum acceptable weight. They describe the placid temperament of most Bactrian camels, but explain that an occasional rogue one can break up the discipline of a whole train. Many peoples, notably the Turkis, lack the temperament required, but the Mongols were reported to have a particular facility for being at one with their camels whether among the dunes or in the wide-open expanses of the desert.

In other ways, too, the missionaries found that the Mongol nomads had a special rapport with nature. On one occasion, Miss Cable recounts how they met a man blind since birth who could reproduce to perfection the calls of the steppe birds – a male eagle, eagle chicks in their nest, pheasant, hoopoe and many others. He could even reproduce the travel-call of wild geese migrating to the southern marshes. Impressed by this, and doubtless mindful of their Master's help to the blind, they rewarded him for his efforts generously with food and money.

Not all the encounters along the Gobi caravan routes were as innocent. The missionaries met one caravan of young Chinese girls – still children – who had been bought or kidnapped in a brigand-infested region and who were now being transported to the Muslim cities of Central Asia for sale; elsewhere, they encountered a troupe of young Chinese prostitutes on their way to satisfy military requirements further along the Silk Route. In both cases they comforted the girls, whose language they spoke and whose misfortunes seemed to evoke sympathy rather than censure.

Not only was corruption to be found: there was an undercurrent of violent revolt among many Muslims in parts of the Chinese-dominated regions of the Gobi. The missionaries were detained 'for a considerable time' in the camp of one brigand chief, but even he seems to have been won over by the palpable goodwill of these eccentric English ladies. On another occasion while in the garden of a local khan, they met a party of gunrunners whose camels were so exhausted by the weight of their metallic loads that they were unable to move on and risked capture; the gunrunners took flour from the missionaries bins and made it into a paste with which they fed the reluctant beasts, then forced them on. At other times they reported that 'in the cold grey dawn the firing squads were kept busy with executions', and although as foreigners and missionaries they managed to stay largely outside the conflict, they periodically became victims of it: 'the brigands,' Miss Cable records, 'did not hesitate to turn us out of our quarters in midwinter, to take our best mules and to rifle our medicine chest.' When finally confronted with General Ma – the brigand leader – in his hideaway hung with weapons and surrounded by a bodyguard of turbaned murderers, Miss Cable responded by giving him a copy of the New Testament in Chinese – 'a book which would rebuke him'. The doughty warrior saluted and withdrew: he knew when he had met his match.

It was in the eastern Gobi, along the banks of the Etzingol (or Shui) river and near the lakes of Gashun and Soco, that the missionaries had their longest and most rewarding sojourn among nomads whose tradition, they describe, was that of 'hunting, herding and flitting'. This had always been a harsh stretch of desert: Marco Polo described how at Etzina 'you must lay in victuals for forty days because when you quit it you enter on a desert . . . on which you meet with no habitation or baiting [feeding] place'. The nomads whom the missionaries encountered here were Mongols who proved hospitable; they were said to leave their tents unguarded while they ranged over the desert, leaving a box of parched corn and a skin of milk at the door for the sustenance of any passing traveller; but any passer-by who abused this hospitality by helping himself to other contents of the tents would be relentlessly tracked across the desert and ruthlessly hunted down and killed.

The English ladies entered this region at the invitation of its 'Prince', who was – not surprisingly – intrigued by these intrepid travellers and for whom they willingly trekked for three weeks towards Lake Gashun. The detour involved fording the Etzingol river, where they nearly lost their mules in the quicksand bed of the stream. Worse was to come. Large tracts of the desert in this region were covered in tamarisk trees and, once having entered among these forests, it proved very difficult to keep any line of direction as no landmarks could be observed and the trees themselves (little more than thorny shrubs rising to some twelve or fifteen feet in height) were not strong enough to be climbed to obtain a lookout.

141

It was while wandering lost and in circles among the tamarisks that the ladies stumbled on a Mongol nomad encampment. They had not realized that telltale pieces of wool or cotton, hanging as though caught accidentally on the branch of a tamarisk, were in fact secret signs to a nearby camp. Armed men and fierce mastiffs were startled at their intrusion. 'We stood,' says Miss Cable, 'with hands open and arms thrown away from our sides, showing that we were unarmed and totally unable to defend ourselves.' The men were mystified at the sight of such bizarre visitors, and called for their womenfolk to cope. The women passed them on to the children. The children held their hands, patted them and took them into their yurts. Once more, the ladies had fallen on their feet metataphorically, at least; in practice they were crouched uncomfortably on the floor around a smouldering camel-dung fire watching the rich camel milk heat so slowly 'that the cream formed a thick crust which could be lifted from the pot dried and eaten as a biscuit'.

Here at last the missionaries were able to practise the etiquette of the nomad yurt which they had so painstakingly learnt. They admired the brass bowls that stood as offerings to a god (which did not rate a capital letter in their book); they remembered to leave their riding whips outside the quilted entrance curtain; they refrained from standing in the entrance or touching the cooking pots; they endeavoured to keep one knee flat on the ground while the other was raised (no easy task if they were as stiff after their ride as might have been expected); they helped to handfeed the newborn camels, and to play with the children and the newborn lambs. In fact, they were model guests.

'From one encampment to another we followed our quiet course,' records Miss Cable. They relished the feeling of being cut off from news of the outside world – even from the news of those revolts in the desert which had dogged their travels in other parts of the Gobi. They even rumbled the disguise of a sham nomad, who turned out to be a Chinese exile on the run (but they were too kind to embarrass him by their detective work or give him away). They do not say anything in their book about the success or failure of their missionary work; there are no self-congratulatory figures of baptisms and no grumbles about the pig-headedness of the heathen. They went on their quiet course. If at times they seem more intrigued by the excitement of finding and joining the nomadic people of the Gobi than they are by the prospect of converting the unenlightened, so be it. Their behaviour, in peril and in pleasure, remained unruffled, consistently Christian and very English.

BEATRIX BULSTRODE returned from her Mongolian travels to the plaudits of many who admired her adventurous spirit, and Miss Cable and Miss French were held in great respect by their missionary society and had a modest success with their book about the Gobi. But the greatest American explorer of the region was to have a very different reception in his own country: he was to be denounced as 'the top Soviet espionage agent in the US'.

Owen Lattimore was born in America in 1900 but brought up in China, where his father moved as a teacher of Western languages in 1901. It was a troubled time. There were such serious disturbances in 1911 that the Western community feared another Boxer Rebellion, and the Lattimore family was evacuated to Peking for safety. Even here the fear was not far away; the ten-year-old boy later recalled that 'when we went along the big streets we would see human heads nailed on telephone poles to intimidate the people'.

Young Lattimore was sent to school in England during the First World War and was disappointed at the end of this time not to win the scholarship to Oxford for which he had tried. His parents could not afford to send him to university without a scholarship, and he returned to China to work in an English import–export house. Soon he was moved to the insurance department, which involved travelling through the length and breadth of China. He started to learn Chinese and before long was undertaking more delicate jobs, such as negotiating with corrupt officials to lower their demands for bribes. But what distinguished Lattimore from other young expatriates was the manner in which he travelled aound the country. While other European businessmen in the 1920s took staff and provisions with them, Lattimore looked after himself, with no interpreter, no special food, no cook and no other servants. In fact, he went native, dossing down on the domestic sleeping shelves alongside the young Chinese. On one occasion he was sent to the railhead at Kweiha on the Inner Mongolian border and there saw the caravan trains coming in from Turkestan and transferring their loads on to the waiting steam trains: here indeed the medieval and modern worlds confronted each other. It made a deep impression on the young insurance clerk. As his biographer (Robert Newman) has recorded, he learnt much about politics, economics, banditry, landlordism and peasant unrest. It was a good initiation for one who was to become the greatest Anglo-American pundit on Central Asia.

In 1926 Lattimore married an American woman five years older than himself who was working at the Institute of Art History in Peking. They were to have one of the longest and most adventurous honeymoons on record. Lattimore was determined to follow the caravan route from Kweiha through Inner Mongolia to Sinkiang, the most westerly point of China which converges on Russian Central Asia, the Taklamakan Desert and northern India. But there could be no question of his bride travelling with a camel caravan across a vast tract of land at the mercy of marauding soldiery, so she was to travel by the Trans-Siberian railroad to its terminus in Sinkiang, where the couple would be reunited, cross the Heavenly (Tien Shan) Mountains, explore the fringes of the Taklamakan, cross the pass through the Karakoram Mountains and enter India at Hunza and Gilgit, those old staging posts in the Great Game. (It was similar to the route that Peter Fleming was to take ten years later and describe in *News from Tartary*.) Not everything went according to plan. Chinese warlords requisitioned Lattimore's camels at the outset, but with some subterfuge he managed to procure others and set out on the perilous trip he subsequently described in *Desert Road to Turkestan*. Meanwhile his wife succeeded in reaching by train Novosibirsk in Soviet Siberia and from there, in the depth of winter and speaking no Russian, she managed to negotiate a passage on a sledge carrying matches across the snowbound steppe into China to be reunited with her husband. After a month of recuperation, they set off together for six months of exploring Central Asia, mostly by horse-drawn cart. By the time they reached India, cold had given way to such intense heat that they needed to travel mostly at night. No wonder they then repaired to Rome to write their respective books and to London to lecture at the Royal Geographical Society.

Lattimore was now established as an Orientalist, and in the years that followed he obtained a number of academic posts in the United States and sponsorship for further journeys, particularly to Mongolia, the region closest to his heart. The pull of nomadic life, already established, was to dominate his travels and his writings. Some of the features of these travels and some of the conclusions he reached about nomadic life are described below. But while study, teaching and travel remained the mainspring of his activity, he also entered a more political world, and it was this that was so nearly to be his undoing.

Asian experts were a rare commodity in the United States as the Second World War got under way, and President Roosevelt encouraged the appointment of Lattimore as adviser to General Chiang Kaishek. As such, he was close to the decisions that preceded the Japanese attack on Pearl Harbor, and later the events that led to the Communist takeover in mainland China. By 1950 it was generally agreed that American policy towards China was on the rocks. The Cold War with Russia was also reaching its most alarming period. The American diplomat Alger Hiss had been indicted as a traitor. It was little wonder that American political and public opinion was jumpy and looking for scapegoats.

It was at this juncture that Senator Joe McCarthy launched his infamous witch-hunt in the ranks of the US establishment. Looking around for a plausible target, he named Owen Lattimore as not only the top Soviet espionage agent in the US but also 'the boss of Alger

Hiss'. Although the FBI had extensive files on Lattimore, there was no solid evidence to support these charges, and McCarthy eventually shifted his ground slightly to suggest that Lattimore had been more 'an agent of influence', working covertly to subvert American policy into channels that would undermine the national interest and play into the hands of the Communist Chinese.

Lattimore overnight found himself academically unemployable and labelled as a villain. For the next two years Senator Pat McCarran and the Senate Internal Security Committee carried on the witch-hunt McCarthy had initiated; Lattimore was cross-examined about papers he was not shown and accused of perjury when his memory faltered. It was not until 1955 that the US Attorney-General finally dismissed the case against him, and thereafter he found it more comfortable to transfer his academic career to Leeds University in England rather than to return to his former American campus, where his name had been dragged through the mud for so long. It was a relief to him to be able to go back to Mongolia in 1961 and undertake further travels, which were to result in his book *Nomads and Commissars*. He had paid a heavy price for his familiarity with both the ingredients of this title, but it was the nomads who still drew him like a magnet to their world.

Lattimore probably compounded the suspicion in which was held in the US and, at the same time, confused his Mongolian hosts by – as he put it – 'the anomaly of travelling like a Mongol but not being one, and being an American but not travelling like one'.

When, a few years after his memorable honeymoon, he set out in the 1930s on one of his longest treks across Mongolia, he decided to travel by camel rather than by horse, 'although it would have been more showy in Mongol eyes to travel with horses'. The 1926 crossing of Turkestan had been done as part of a Chinese caravan; he had covered an average of eighteen miles a day for thirty-two days. Now he was anxious to study the differences between travelling with a trading convoy of Chinese and a genuinely nomadic journey with Mongols.

He quickly observed the Mongol skills of tracking loose or breakaway camels, and of knowing whether the caravan had strayed from the intended route. A ten-year-old girl could sometimes pick up the trail of a stray camel even on a busy route (where there would be old tracks and new tracks and traces of camel caravans put out to pasture) by circling around until she found evidence of one camel having been grazing alone rather than with the herd and therefore proving itself a stranger to that part of the country; it could then be followed until it was retrieved. This was the simple part. An old man who was a real expert would be able to 'take up a handful of earth, sniff at it and say "No, this is not our road"'.

But even on a camel caravan the talk was endlessly of horses. Lattimore learnt how the Kazaks from the Altai Mountains in the west of the country would hunt with eagles in place of hawks; foxes would be their favourite prey, and often they would carry a greyhound across the pommel of their saddle and cast it to the ground in full stride when a fox had been set up, so that the hound could work with the eagle. If the quarry doubled back on its tracks, the greyhound would get it; if it carried straight on, the eagle would swoop on it. Such eagles had been known to attack much larger prey, including snow-leopard on occasion. It was said that if you see an Altai Kazak with eagle and hound, he is out hunting; but if he is armed and without an eagle or hound, then he is undoubtedly raiding. But even the raiding is carried out with a certain regard for the rules of fair play: night raiding, for instance, is considered bad form, and there is a taboo against raiding a camp when the men are away and only the women and children are left to guard the herds and flocks.

Lattimore heard in detail while he was on his travels about the code of practice for horse stealing. The Altai Kazaks and the Mongols themselves played the game by very similar rules. One was that you should boast of your intentions before a raid; the other was that, if caught, you should not confess. A Mongol horse thief does not steal from his neighbours; he rides into a distant part of the steppe to carry out his adventure. While on the journey, he will make no disguise of his intentions to those whom he meets along the way: he will – in effect – throw down a challenge that will go before him (like the hero of John Buchan's novel *John Macnab*, who announces in advance his intention of poaching a stag or a salmon from the forest of some Highland laird). As he gets nearer his quarry, the Mongol will take to travelling at night rather than by day, so making the precise timing and place of his appearance a surprise. The final approach will be by stealth: crawling into the camp or home grazing ground where he hopes to snatch his prize without disturbing the other horses or raising the alarm. The stakes are high. Mongol horse thieves, if caught, are not treated gently: beatings and breaking of limbs are to be expected. If the thief under such duress admits to his identity and to his 'banner' (or clan), then he will be prevented by his tribal chiefs from venturing on such exploits again. If he keeps his silence, despite the pain and torture, he will eventually be turned loose to make his way home in whatever sorry state he is in: crippled, perhaps, but unbowed and unrepentant.

While hearing all these tales of nomad life, Lattimore got into the rhythm of a Mongol camel caravan. Unlike the Chinese, who travel nose to tail in single file the Mongols ride alongside each other or even spread out over a wide front. This apparently dates from the time of the Mongol conquests, when it was necessary to be able to disperse or to concentrate rapidly in the face of attack; it also has the advantage that casual grazing can be carried out on the line of advance. The Mongols also observe the landscape closely as they cross it, as befits nomads who may wish to come this way again and may need to recognize natural features from different directions. The Chinese, on the other hand, keep their heads down and plod on unobservantly and unsociably. If Lattimore – exhausted from the day's march – fell in behind the leading camel and became silent, he would be chided with behaving like a Chinaman.

Lattimore obviously found that the Mongol style of conducting a camel caravan was much more relaxed than the Chinese in every way. For one thing, they did not stick slavishly to the track, but made a practice of camping a mile or two off the route, where the pasture was less eaten up, and where there was less chance of friction with other travellers. Equally, the Mongols would often wander off and leave a trade caravan for a day or two while they visited another camp and gossiped with friends. They knew the lie of the land around their route and were not, like the Chinese, apprehensive of deviating from it. Lattimore concluded that even while on a trading mission, a Mongol would deploy the skills and mental attitudes of a nomad.

One of the hazards of travelling with a Mongol or any other caravan on the steppes of Central Asia is the risk of being ambushed and robbed. Lattimore found that he encountered frequent pedlars or 'masterless boys' – usually Chinese who had run away from home and family. These got to know well the contours of the country and the pattern of caravan trade, and they were not above selling their knowledge to local bandits. Some of them even became bandits themselves.

He also got to know something of the prejudices of the Mongols. Although they did not think of pork as unclean, as Muslims do, they had a marked aversion to pigs and despised the Chinese for being pig-herders. This probably stems from the fact that pigs cannot be herded by nomadic peoples: unlike sheep and goats, horses and cattle, they cannot be taken on long treks. So it has come about that in Mongolia pigs have become a symbol of a settled and therefore unacceptable way of life.

More useful than noting prejudices was the opportunity to learn nomadic ways of coping with life on the steppes. Lattimore comments that even when there are shadows to give shape and contours to the land, it is very difficult for one accustomed to judging landscape in relation to trees, roads and houses to adjust his eye to the scale of magnitude of the open spaces. Misjudging distance can result in hours of weary trudging towards ever-retreating horizons. He started by thinking that the Mongols had wonderfully good eyesight, but came round to realizing that their vision was selective: they found it difficult to focus on handwriting or even things around the yurt, but their eyes were trained to put distant objects in focus. A white blob, which to Lattimore might either be a pale boulder a few hundred yards away or a felt yurt a mile away, would to the Mongol be recognizable by the detail surrounding it – tracks leading to the yurt or moving objects that might turn out to be men or dogs, for instance. Slowly Lattimore acquired these skills himself.

But above all on this trip he was preoccupied with the difference between the Mongol and Chinese attitude to everything, even tents. 'The tent of a Chinese always looks as if he had been glad to stop, the tent of a Mongol as if he were ready to go.' The whole question of tent and yurt positioning fascinated Lattimore: a lama's tent should be upstream or uphill from a layman's, so that his holy influence may flow down on the lesser mortal. More practically, although it seemed natural for Lattimore to relieve himself behind a yurt rather than in front of it, he came to appreciate that since all yurts are pitched on a slight slope and have their entrances facing downhill it is unhygienic to do so.

Like all travellers among the nomads of Mongolia, Lattimore ponders on the phenomenon of the great Mongol invasions of the thir-teeth century, the conquests that resulted in Genghis Khan ruling the largest contiguous land empire the world has ever known – from the Black Sea in the west to the Yellow Sea in the east. He points out that one of the features of nomadism is that it is equally suited to either attacking or to running away: all a nomad's property is as mobile as himself. He argues that when the centre of gravity lay in the steppe (as it did in the thirteenth century) and not in the surrounding cultivated areas, then nomad tribes adhered to each other and accumulated strength for conquests further afield. In reality the invasions were not a sudden occurence, however sudden they may have seemed to those who were on the receiving end of them. There had been a cycle of preliminary and gradually widening wars in which the Mongols tested their strength. Then their sheer mobility and single-mindedness swept all before it. They moved faster than their reputation for destruction.

The first rumours the Christian kingdoms of Europe heard about the oncoming menace were to the effect that a power had arisen in the East which was devastating the Muslim world; such a power seemed more likely to be an ally than a threat to rulers in Kiev or Kracow, in Vienna or Zagreb, who had for centuries viewed Islam as the prime enemy. Indeed, there was speculation in the capitals of Europe that perhaps the new star in the East was that of the dynasty of Prester John, the legendary Christian monarch descended from one of the Three Wise Men who had come to Bethlehem. The brutal reality – the Mongol or Tartar hordes surging like a plague virus across Asia and Eastern Europe – was a surprise as well as a calamity.

As a connoisseur of nomad peoples, Lattimore reckoned that the most genuinely nomadic of all the surviving steppe-nomad peoples whom he met were the Khalkha Mongols, who were fleeing from collectivization imposed by Communist influence in Outer Mongolia in the early 1930s. Many Khalkha had been shot down or captured before they reached the border to Inner Mongolia, where they had looked forward to coming under Chinese rather than Soviet Russian domination. But while others had lost their sheep, cattle and camels, they had managed to stampede with three thousand horses across the frontier. Lattimore encountered groups of these refugees on his travels. But they got little succour from their kinsmen on the Chinese side of the border, and were left to face near starvation for two winters until their herds began to grow again. Predictably, when they began to return to anything approaching prosperity, the local princes sent men to collect taxes from them. But the Khalkha had learnt a fierce independence by then. In answer to the princes' tax collectors, they tapped their guns and said: 'These are our princes: if you want taxes they will talk with you.'

In the course of his Mongolian travels, Lattimore observed that the nomadic prejudice against agriculture extends at times to a prejudice against hunting and fishing too. There have been periods in Mongol history when – even if falconry was always approved – there have been

151

taboos on shooting marmots and other animals sought for their furs. It is difficult to see why this should be so, but it seems that in periods when maximum mobility was required and expected (such as in the early years of Genghis Khan's conquests or during the 'times of troubles' in the seventeenth and eighteenth centuries) anything which tended to anchor people to a particular region was frowned on. A productive river, or even a good set of burrows for finding marmots, could come into this category. *Pure* nomadism demanded total reliance on herds and mobility: hence Lattimore's oft-quoted statement that the pure nomad is a poor nomad.

One of the truisms about pure nomads is that they leave no record of themselves: they do not leave archaeological monuments behind them because they are always moving on, and they do not write down their history usually because they cannot. As Bruce Chatwin wrote in the opening sentence of his unpublished book *The Nomadic Alternative*, 'the best travellers are illiterate and they do not bore us with reminiscences'. This was always assumed to be particularly true of the Mongols. But in 1866 a scholar-priest – happily named Archimandrite Palladius – attached to the Russian ecclesiastical mission in Peking made a remarkable discovery of a hitherto unknown work in the Chinese archives which described the achievements of Genghis Khan through the eyes of a Mongol. This document, known as *The Secret History of the Mongols*, purported to have been written very shortly after the death of Genghis, and not only to outline the origins of the Mongols but also to chronicle the birth, rise and conquests of their greatest leader. Once the initial discovery had been made, other fragments of the chronicle started turning up in archives and libraries all over China, where they had lain for several centuries attracting no attention from a people who tended to be almost exclusively interested in their own history. There are various theories as to why the history is called 'secret': possibly it was intended only for the edification of Genghis Khan's direct descendants. Even the language is obscure, being for the most part a Chinese transliteration of an original Mongol text. Lattimore was only one of many Mongol scholars who had found in *The Secret History* a mine of information about how a tribe of nomads had come to dominate the known world of their time.

When Mongolian nomads are gathered for any length of time in one place, there is a good likelihood of the 'three manly sports' (as defined in *The Secret History of the Mongols*) being exercised: horse racing, wrestling and archery. All three are part of the martial tradition that has been passed down from the era of Genghis Khan. And all three have very distinctive Mongolian features.

In horse racing for instance, the races are over longer distances than elsewhere, usually between fifteen- and thirty-mile courses. This is because, in all things to do with Mongol nomad life, stamina is at a premium. The jockeys are most often children under the age of nine; this is not only for reasons of weight but also because the owners wish to prove the spirit and determination of their horses and consider that older jockeys would impose too much of their own will-power on their mounts. (It is said that the children often surprise their sponsors by the way in which they impose their youthful enthusiasm on the horses none the less.)

Wrestling, too, has links with the nomadic life. The contestants approach each other for the fray dancing and leaping weirdly, and flapping their arms and loose sleeves in imitation of eagles or falcons about to descend on their prey. They keep their centre of gravity as low as possible, because whoever can toss or floor his opponent, so that any part of him – apart from the soles of his feet – touches the ground, is the winner.

Archery also is adapted, in this case to the equestrian lifestyle of the country. Mongols do not deploy longbows of the sort favoured by the English bowmen of Agincourt; they have shorter weapons, which are bent back to give added velocity to their arrows and to make them easier to manipulate in the saddle. The feather ribbing of the arrows is asymmetrically devised so as to make the arrow turn like a screw – or a rifle bullet – in flight and penetrate more deeply in consequence. The

153

targets, too, are different from conventional western targets: instead of being upright in the ground and shot at from in front, they are blocks of wood and are meant to be hit by a falling arrow at the end of its trajectory. It seems that oncoming horsemen traditionally were stemmed by a shower of arrows from on high, not by a volley of fire from in front. Thus all three manly sports have direct relevance to life as lived of old by the Mongol hordes. All this – sports as well as more serious occupations – Lattimore explains in his books.

So it is that anyone who wants to understand Mongolia and its inhabitants has to turn, preferably sooner rather than later, to the writings of Owen Lattimore, who not only travelled thoroughly and frequently in the country between the 1920s and the 1960s, but who spoke Mongolian as well as Russian and Chinese. While one could not claim that it was solely a fascination with nomad life that led him to Mongolia, because he appeared to be equally fascinated in every other aspect of its national activity, it is the case that he gave much thought to nomadic aspects and propounded with great authority theories that others – notably Bruce Chatwin – subsequently developed.

Chief among these theories was that concerning the relationship of nomads to settled pastoralists, of herdsmen to cultivators of the land. Lattimore has pointed out that the Chinese described the nomadic tribes on their periphery as 'following grass and water' as if this was a simple and unsophisticated process, whereas in reality it was a highly organized process requiring skills of timing, leadership and local knowledge. Flocks and herds that might appear too small adequately to graze their pastures in summer might prove too large for the more meagre winter pastures. Yaks and camels, horses and mules, sheep and goats . . . all required quite different grazing conditions and degrees of shelter from the winter blasts. Survival required a degree of mutual dependency: a single family would do well to own different varieties of stock as an insurance against disease or misadventure, but the family might need to farm out these varieties for grazing in different regions where the particular vegetation and cover provided the required fodder and protection. In reality, little was haphazard about the nomadism of the steppes of Central Asia.

Equally, there was nothing inferior in the nomad pattern of life compared with the settled pastoralist pattern. Lattimore is quick to point out that although farmers and city dwellers may – over the centuries – have looked down on nomadic peoples, the historical fact is that nomads are descended from ancestors who made a conscious choice of pursuing their way of life rather than the drudgery of agricultural labour. Farming, not hunting, was usually the immediate prelude to migratory pastoralism. The original nomadic tribesmen – whether they were Arabs, Turks, Lurs or Mongols – did not stumble into nomadism; they chose it as a preferred alternative.

Of course there were other advantages to a life of movement: authority was further away and therefore less oppressive; it was a bold tax gatherer who took to the open steppe. The Mongol hordes were for ever outsiders – not just metaphorically, but literally outside the Great Wall of China.

In Mongolia dependence on animals does not imply sentimentality towards them. An Arabian may have a special relationship with his steed, and a Tuareg may have an affection for a favourite racing camel, but Mongolian horsemen tend to treat their horses (which are more like ponies to Western eyes) as interchangeable units of transport. They will be pressed to the full limits of their stamina one day and left to rest or travel burdenless the next while another pony is ridden. Abundant remounts were one of the keys to the success of Genghis Khan's army, and they are still one of the keys to the smooth migration of Mongol nomads.

If the horse is the essential element of transport, the sheep is the essential element of almost everything else: mutton is for eating, ewes' milk is for drinking and churning into pungent butter, sheepskins are for winter coats, wool is for making felt for the roof of yurts and for making rugs for sale, and finally sheep-droppings are for compacting into bricks of fuel for the cooking and camp-fire.

155

Owen Lattimore was not only the most controversial and the most sophisticated traveller among the nomads of Mongolia, but he was also the most philosophical. As well as observing and recording what he saw and experienced, he interpreted it too. Curiosity drove him on: his mother once said of him: 'Owen just learns languages because he can't bear not to know what other people are saying.' He did a lot of listening and a lot of talking. The American authorities would have done better to have listened to him than to have castigated him.

Serious-minded and highly focused as he may have been, Lattimore also lived up to the reputation for eccentricity which was a characteristic of so many Englishmen and Americans who set off on the nomad trail. As a young man he wore a monocle, even when in the desert; in fact, he was said to carry a box of two hundred spares as they were always being blown away in the wind. Impractical as this may seem, it had its compensating factors: the glint of his monocle in the sunlight made it possible for people to spot him and his caravan from a great distance. And having once spotted him, few could resist riding over to meet him.

# 5

# Afghanistan

———⟫◆⟪———

Here at last is Asia without an inferiority complex.
Robert Byron on entering Afghanistan,
from *The Road to Oxiana* (1937)

AFGHANISTAN has always been a catchment area for those on
the move across Asia. Mongols and Tartars have loitered there;
Huns and Turkomen, Tajiks and Uzbeks, Kafirs and Hazaras have
passed through, leaving communities behind. Even Alexander the
Great's Greek army left its mark here. And everywhere there are
Pathans – the nearest thing to a native and dominant race. It is a
land of movement where tribal peoples pass from valley to valley, with
their families, their flocks and their scant possessions – traditionally
paying little regard for authorities. It is difficult here to lay down
patterns of migration (as one can do in Iran) or clear ethnic
distinctions (as one can do in the Sahara): this is a motley land of
warriors, more nomadic than settled – in spirit if not in census statistics. Most activities involved raiding: even an Afghan wedding
frequently required the bridegroom to make a ritual kidnapping of
his bride before carrying her off to his own family's tents. All males
tended to carry firearms, and the Lee-Enfield rifle (looted from the

British) eventually gave way to the Kalashnikov (captured from the Russians).

Most of those who came here from the English-speaking world in the nineteenth century came as soldiers or spies, agents in the Great Game struggle – between imperial Russia and the British Raj in India – for the heart of Central Asia. One of the first of them was William Moorcroft, who had his own very special reasons – concerned with Mongol horses, as explained below – for mingling with the nomadic tribes. Other names ring out like battle honours of some ghostly regiment: Bokhara Burnes, Elphinstone, Macnaughten, Cavagnari, Roberts of Kandahar . . . few of them survived their Afghan experience. As if the reality of adventure were not enough, Afghanistan featured in fiction too: John Buchan's hero in *Greenmantle* is told of 'Afghan horse-dealers, Turcoman merchants and sheep-skinned Mongols' who know the secrets of deep-laid plots against British India.

As the twentieth century got under way, some less military Englishmen were venturing through the Khyber or other passes into Afghanistan. Robert Byron came in 1936 in search of Islamic architecture; Eric Newby came in 1957 to climb in Nuristan (as Kipling's Kafiristan had come to be called); Wilfred Thesiger came also in the 1950s to explore a country that had all the ingredients that most attracted him – mountains, deserts, brigands and other assorted dangers. And some came seeking to find and study the nomadic peoples of this troubled land: among such latter-day travellers were Freya Stark, Bruce Chatwin and Peter Levi (who had his own separate classical interests). It is among these last that I was to find further examples of the Anglo-Saxon preoccupation with the search for nomads.

But first, as in Iran with the Qashqai and in the Sahara with the Tuareg, I had had my own encounters to lend colour to my theme. In the late 1950s, when the Afghan royal house was still apparently firmly on the throne, I made a largely overland trip to Afghanistan from Soviet Russia, where I was serving at the British embassy in Moscow as a junior diplomat. Arriving at the embassy in Kabul, with no very definite plans for the following few days, I was gathered up in an invitation to a dinner at a royal palace and found myself sitting next to an elderly Afghan tribal chief with a back like a ramrod and a profile like a well-bred peregrine falcon. We talked about deerstalking in Scotland, about which he had heard and of which I had some limited experience. He enquired politely about my plans for my stay in his country and, on hearing I was on my first visit and had no specific plans, he invited me to join a small shooting party he was taking into the hills the following morning for a few days hunting ibex, Marco Polo rams, possibly a local version of mouflon, and other exotic mountain prey – including wolves. It was far too exciting an offer to decline: this was surely a better way of seeing something of Afghanistan than trundling around Kabul in an embassy limousine.

On my way back to the embassy after dinner, I told the ambassador of my invitation. He was somewhat taken aback, and explained that my proposed host on the hunting expedition was the most intimidating man in the kingdom – a kinsman of the King, he had himself swept down from the hills in 1929 to play a major part in the overthrow of the regime following the fall of King Amanullah, whose modernizing measures had provoked the disapproval of the tribes. For his efforts, the tribal chief had been granted the title of 'His Royal Highness the Conqueror of Kabul', and he was to be addressed (the ambassador seriously assured me) in this manner 'on all occasions however informal'. Nothing daunted, I set off at dawn the following day to our agreed rendezvous.

My formidable host was waiting for me. His party was a small one: two or three friends and two or three retainers, all with their own mountain horses. A mount and a rifle had been brought for me, and I was invited – at some dusty spot on the outskirts of the town – to shoot at a stone from a hundred paces to prove that I could handle the rifle adequately. I passed the test, silently thanking my military service of a few years earlier. Then we headed north, and into what must have been the lower foothills of the Hindu Kush. The hillsides were so bare that it seemed no life could be sustained. But I was wrong in this.

My memory of the next few days is conditioned by the passing of nearly fifty years, but I recall seeing most of the anticipated game. Wolves were much in evidence, and invariably shot at. My host proved a predictably hawk-eyed marksman: on one occasion, I heard a report from his Winchester .30-06 at my side before I had seen anything, and on going forward found he had shot a wild cat through the head at a distance of nearly two hundred paces. He was a tolerant and generous companion, full of congratulations on the rare occasions one merited it, and full of commiseration on the more frequent occasions that one did not. It was said of him that on one occasion, when a foreign ambassador had been his guest on a hunting expedition and returned after a considerable expenditure of cartridges with nothing to show for it, he had politely told his guest that it was in no way his fault as it was one of those days 'when Allah is merciful and protects the birds and the beasts'. On difficult passages through the mountain trails – some were distinctly vertiginous – he would lead and look around regularly to see that his companions and I were all right. If he got far ahead of us, he would wait just below the crest of the hill, but never silhouetted against the skyline – old military campaigning habits did not desert him even in peace.

When we camped in valleys, my host's retainers would go ahead to pitch tents and would often be joined and assisted by tribesmen who appeared as it were from nowhere – rather like small children will appear miraculously in the apparently empty landscape of Morocco. They would be deferential towards my host, whose figure was instantly recognized and whose reputation was known to every compatriot. He would explain that many of those who so mysteriously appeared were travelling with their small herds or flocks – often only a handful of animals – and were part of a pattern of almost continual movement in search of pasture. When I asked if particular groups were nomads, he would reply: 'We are all nomads here . . . it is better thus . . . this is no country for what Americans call real estate . . . we are ships that put down anchor where we will and sail on when we are ready.'

I remember best our last night in the mountains. We were not in tents, but all in one big cave (which looked to me uncomfortably like the normal abode of a bear or a wolf pack). Islamic conventions were disregarded and a bottle of scotch whisky was produced from the depths of a saddlebag. Small metal cups were distributed and the bottle passed around several times. Even when everyone was totally relaxed, I had continued to address my host in the formal manner prescribed by the British ambassador, as 'Your Royal Highness the Conqueror of Kabul' and he had never seemed to find this odd or out of place. But on that final night I knew I had arrived, had been accepted as one of his circle, when he turned to me with a serious but gentle smile and said quietly: 'Up here in the hills, my boy, we are very informal people: just call me Conqueror.'

WILLIAM MOORCROFT was not primarily a man in search of nomads. This East India Company veterinary surgeon had many other things on his mind when he came to India in the first decade of the nineteenth century. He had been appointed as director of the Company's stud farm at Pusa near the Nepalese frontier and was much concerned with horse breeding, and early in his career he became obsessed with the imperial Russian threat to the British Raj in India. Neither of these preoccupations – on the face of it – was very directly related to nomads.

But in the event Moorcroft became the first really significant modern explorer of the Central Asian steppes, the homeland of nomadic peoples, and he also developed a passion for two of the subjects that absorbed the attention of these nomadic peoples: horses of all shapes and sizes, and the fine Kashmir goat wool found in the foothills of the Himalayas.

His interest in horses was initially focused on superior horseflesh – on the stallions that might improve the strain of the military horses that were bred and reared at his stud farm. But such steeds were rare even in the legendary horse markets of Central Asia. As he sought them in vain – in Tibet, in Nepal, in Afghanistan and in the desert plains around Bokhara – he became enamoured of the sturdy small horses that were the usual currency of these regions and which on more than one occasion saved his own life.

His interest in 'shawl-wool of the finest texture' was closely linked to the nomadic peoples who tended the herds of goats from which this wool was derived. Moorcroft was intent on opening up a trade route to bring this fine wool south into India, from where it might be transported to the looms of Calcutta or Lancashire, rather than allowing it to filter out of Central Asia northwards towards the factories of Moscow or westwards by overland caravan routes to the cities of the Muslim world. He was – among other things – a strategic marketeer ahead of his time, and his remarkable story bears retelling in this context.

William Moorcroft was born in Lancashire in 1767, an illegitimate child from an agricultural and well-educated background. He qualified as a veterinary surgeon in England and in France, and set up a practice in London, specializing in horses. The horse was still the pivot on which not only transport but many aspects of social life turned: it was the age of the stagecoach, the private carriage, the phaeton, the curricle and the gig as well as the hack and the hunter. When the risk of invasion by Napoleon's armies from across the Channel became a matter of national concern in 1803, Moorcroft joined the Westminster Volunteer Cavalry. Meanwhile, his veterinary business flourished and, as head of the best-qualified horse practice in England, his clients included King George III and the Prince Regent. He also became acquainted with the former Governor-General of India, the celebrated Warren Hastings. When it became apparent that the East India Company were delighted with the work Moorcroft had done for them in London, but were concerned about the inadequacy of their stud in Bengal, it was not surprising that they invited him to run their Indian operation. In some ways it was a natural progression from his equine, military and social connections that he should consider the wider horizons of empire. In other ways a move away from England, when he was already nearly forty and had a well-established professional practice behind him, must have involved personal sacrifices. Moorcroft agreed to go, but negotiated a salary (at 30,000 rupees) that was almost in the same bracket as the commander-in-chief. It was little wonder that later this was to arouse jealousies.

To improve the quality of the Company's stud at Pusa, it was necessary to introduce new bloodstock. India was full of rumours of magnificent thoroughbred horses raised on the open spaces of the steppes beyond the great natural barrier of the Himalayas; and history was full of stories about the fortitude and endurance of the compact and squat Mongol horses that had been the driving force of the invading Mongol hordes of the past. If the elegance and spirit of the former could be blended with the toughness and mettle of the latter, the cavalry of the Raj would reap the benefits indeed.

Moorcroft's first major journey in 1811, ostensibly on behalf of the stud, was through the northern plains of India to the foothills of the Himalayas. It gave him a taste for adventurous travel, and the following year he succeeded in entering Tibet, but on his return he was captured and briefly held prisoner by the Gurkhas (who were not yet incorporated into the Indian army). Nothing daunted, after a further spell at the stud, he set out on his great journey of 1820 to 1825 with the firm intention of reaching the fabled city of Bokhara, which no Englishman had visited since Tudor times and which was reputed to be the greatest staging post on the caravan routes that carried merchandise from east to west. Already aged fifty-two, Moorcroft well knew the dangers and discomforts that lay ahead of him, but his motivation was strong even if mixed: apart from seeking horses, he also sought fine wool or the fine-wool goats themselves, and in addition he had the wider motives of opening up a network of trading routes orientated towards India. His final and least-declared motive was spying out evidence of Russian infiltration into the heart of Central Asia.

This last motive had been given added impetus by an event on his previous journey in Tibet. He had encountered two small dogs – a terrier and a pug, breeds unknown in that part of Asia – which were

163

clearly of European origin. Not only was this strange, but the dogs appeared to recognize Moorcroft as a European and performed trained antics for him which, he was persuaded, had a military significance. Moorcroft concluded that without a doubt the dogs had been left behind by a Russian military reconnaissance party. This was what had given his fears fresh force.

Moorcroft set off for Bokhara with several stalwart companions and a sizeable caravan of trade goods, as he reckoned that barter might be more effective than purchase if he found the horses or goats he sought. He also packed numerous presents, ranging from valuable watches and firearms for rulers whom he wished to placate, to strings of pierced and threaded beads for lesser mortals who helped him along his way. He himself constituted the sort of trading mission for which he hoped to open up the mountains and steppes of Central Asia.

To reach Bokhara Moorcroft first tried to approach from Chinese Turkestan. He was delayed indefinitely on the western side of the Karakoram range and finally decided to change his approach route and go through Afghanistan, despite the dangers inherent in that disturbed and frequently hostile country. It took him nearly eight months from crossing into Afghanistan at the Khyber Pass to reach the Oxus river in the north. He was probably the first European ever to set foot on the banks of that mysterious and romantic river, and to see how Matthew Arnold's

> . . . majestic river floated on,
> Out of the mist and hum of that low land.

It was February 1825 before Moorcroft saw the evocative skyline of Bokhara's minarets and knew he had at long last reached his goal.

But further disappointments lay ahead. Although he was amiably received by the Emir (in marked contrast to the reception accorded to his compatriots Stoddart and Conolly, who fifteen years later were to be incarcerated in a vermin pit and then beheaded, after a failed diplomatic mission to Bokhara) he found the horses still elusive. Just when he thought he had arranged to buy some fine specimens, they were whisked away by the Emir to take part in a military campaign against the insubordinate Kitay-Kipchaks, a nomadic tribe who frequented the steppe between Bokhara and Samarkand. The stallions of the nomads were no more available than the Emir's own mounts, although he did manage to obtain, in exchange for some of the goods he had brought from India, about forty 'moderately good horses'. One of the finest animals he was shown – 'a breathtakingly magnificent Turcoman horse' (according to Moorcroft's biographer, Dr Alder) – was denied to him after he declined to help the Emir fight his nomadic rebels. Even Moorcroft, with his propensity to get involved in exploration and geographical espionage, baulked at the prospect of intervening in Central Asian warfare. Had the risk of such involvement been less, he would doubtless have liked to spend more time with the Turkoman nomadic tribes rather than in the hothouse atmosphere of the Emir's court and camp.

Indeed, the more time Moorcroft spent at Bokhara the less he relished it. For one thing, much as he mistrusted the Russians, he was distressed to find some of their citizens in slavery there. He even bought the liberty of three such Russians and set them to work as grooms, but the Emir insisted that he sold them back into slavery – much to the distress of both Moorcroft and the Russians. He also fretted under the corruption and licentiousness that were now part of life in a city that traditionally had been so holy that it was said that 'while elsewhere on earth the daylight shone downwards from the skies, from Bokhara it radiated upwards to illuminate the heavens'.

Eventually Moorcroft resolved to return to Bengal before winter closed in and blocked the passes with snow. He was under heavy criticism for his long neglect of the stud, and may have realized that his position was in jeopardy. Having sent a guide ahead to explore the possibility of going back by a more direct route through Chitral, he opted for returning the way he had come. It was not without fresh problems. At Karshi, four days' march out of Bokhara, the local prince extorted a high price for his safe passage: some of the best of the fine-wool shawls were taken off him together with one of the better horses. At Balkh in Afghanistan he had further disappointments with the quality of the horses he was offered, and he went off in search of superior animals among the semi-nomadic peoples of the surrounding desert. He took only two or three personal servants with him and left the rest of the party at Balkh, telling them he would rejoin them after a circuit of about three weeks' duration. The desert terrain around was known to be dangerous: itinerant robbers preyed on passing caravans. But it was not an attack that was to be the cause of Moorcroft's death; he had been unwell for some time and while parted from his companions succumbed to 'the scorching sand, venomous flies' and consequent fever. He died on 27 August 1825.

But the mystery that hung around his motives and travels were even then not put to rest; some years later a report that his papers had surfaced in Tibet (2,000 miles east across the Himalayas) started speculation that he had himself been living there in disguise, having presumably chosen to disappear into the fastnesses of Central Asia rather than return to his neglected stud farm in India. Dr Alder argues convincingly against any such theory. It must be assumed that he did indeed die a lonely and fevered death among the wild tribesmen of northern Afghanistan.

Moorcroft's interest was in horses and goats, in exploration and in the military threat to India, rather than in nomads or the nomadic way of life for its own sake. But he blazed a trail, physically and emotionally, and in doing so had a profound effect on his countrymen's enthusiasm for the steppes of Central Asia and the Mongol-descended horsemen who had stamped their identity and lifestyle on so much of this region. He was perhaps the chief among those who were to initiate an obsession among many of his compatriots, and as such he deserves a place in their chronicles.

F REYA STARK is best remembered as a traveller and writer who made the Middle East her stamping ground and made her canvas

Iran and Iraq, Syria and Lebanon, the Hadhramaut and the shores of Asia Minor. These are the regions with which her name is most often associated. She had always been attracted by the ways of the desert and by the patterns of itinerant existence but, when she came to analyse the essence of nomadic life, it was to the migratory peoples of Afghanistan – rather than to the Arabs – that she turned.

Freya herself was not a simple character. After an unhappily broken-off engagement to an Italian doctor during the First World War, she established herself as an intrepid and percipient traveller in little-known parts of the Levant, although there were always those – such as Wilfred Thesiger and Ivy Compton-Burnett – who were dismissive about her achievements as a genuine explorer. Her reputation as a writer stemmed largely from her journeys through the Elburz Mountains in northern Iran and into the Valleys of the Assassins (the title of her first significant book in 1934). Her particular quality was an empathy with the ordinary peoples she encountered on her journeys. She seemed able to respond to Arab women in their veiled seclusion, or to nomadic men crouched around a camp-fire, in a way that established a distinction between herself as a sensitive traveller and others who remained tourists in an alien world. Her writing could rise to heights of poetic description that made her readers feel that she inhabited (in the words of her biographer, Molly Izzard) 'a private world into which the mundane and the commonplace did not intrude'. Coupled with this ability, she possessed a well-honed capacity to project her own image and enhance her own reputation. Her work in the Second World War as an information officer promoting British government policies in the Middle East did much to consolidate her self-confidence and convince official circles that she could recruit support from quarters that others could not reach. Her most ambitious project – 'the Brotherhood' – was a self-consciously secret society based in Cairo and of mixed nationalities which helped to spread British propaganda by an orchestrated whispering campaign; the orchestration was done by Freya. She was ambitious to achieve acceptance by the Establishment –

an acceptance eventually recognized by her creation as a Dame of the Order of the British Empire. There was a purposefulness about Freya that makes her contemplative approach to the 'alternative world' of nomads all the more remarkable and memorable. And nowhere is this better expressed than in her book about Afghanistan.

Comparatively late in life – in 1968, when she was already seventy-five – Freya Stark accepted an invitation to make a trip deep into Afghanistan to find and view the minaret of Djam, a remarkable edifice built in the thirteenth century but rediscovered only in the 1950s. A pilot straying off course had first spotted this tall, strawberry-coloured brick finger pointing to the sky and set at the conjunction of four steep gorges, far from any roads or tracks. However, it was deemed to be reachable – according to Freya's friends – by Land Rover. In the course of an exciting journey, she encountered the caravans of camel-borne Afghans moving with their families and belongings to the pastures beyond Herat, where they would spend the four months of autumn, before moving on with the onset of winter to fresh pastures near Kalat in Baluchistan.

As Freya watched them crossing the rivers in spate, she meditated on the life they led and the philosophy that underpinned it – a philosophy that appealed to the rolling stone in herself. She recognized that the nomads were free of all laws except their own, and appeared aloof to the conventions of those whom they passed by in settlements along their route. She noted with approval that the severity of nature pressed them into a certain conformity: above all, their arts and artefacts had to be simple and portable. Silver amulets and bangles were sported by young brides; bright coins and charms were sewn on to the quilted doublets of the children; everything was easy to transport and 'no one is much harrowed by choice'. Even the bright patterns of their art – incorporating significant meaning unrecognized by outsiders – were repeated without the agony of creative decisions: repeated on rugs and saddlebags and saddlecloths, and repeated from one century to another.

Ruminating on this, Freya Stark argues that although such constraints may make nomadic life circumscribed in some respects, it is less constrained than the 'comfortably padded' walls of the cells that constitute so-called civilized Western life. She found that her sedentary compatriots stumbled on their journey through life, beset by 'divergencies of accent or behaviour that show the fences and partitions of our world', while the nomad 'does not feel himself particularly either sheltered or exposed, but is at home in the world like an animal'.

Freya goes on to philosophize about the cardinal virtues: only two – love and delight – she feels transcend the world that encompasses us and have a place in eternity. And the second of these – delight – is brighter in the nomadic world than in the settled one because 'they accept their scanty blessings as gifts and not as dividends', and welcome the unpredictability of life's blessings and cruelties as being subject to elements beyond their control: the tempered wind that saves the newborn camel, or the melting mountain snows that fill (or fail to fill) the streams on which they depend for water and life. In the remotest corners of Afghanistan, Freya is reminded of the delight that she herself experiences when at one with nature; among the black woollen tents (which have here replaced the yurts of the Mongol steppe) and the browsing herds of camels, she feels a release from the stresses and complexities of her domestic existence.

Even the raids and small wars which have from time immemorial been a feature of life among the nomads are, she feels, less activated by greed and lust for possessions than by an unconscious desire to mitigate boredom; and – as a latent feminist – she concludes that, since women are less easily bored than men, the mountains and valleys of Afghanistan would be a safer place if women managed the affairs of the tribes. (The events of the closing years of the twentieth century perhaps confirm that view?) Not that she feels any sense of being in danger there herself. Indeed, when asked what she does about security, Freya replies: 'We give sweets to the children.'

A visit to the minaret of Djam was also the high point on an Afghan journey by that indefatigable seeker after nomads – Bruce Chatwin. His trip was in fact his third visit to that country, and took place in 1969, only one year after Freya Stark's.

Chatwin's earlier Afghan ventures had ostensibly had other objectives. His first, in 1963, had been a pilgrimage in the steps of Robert Byron, whose *Road to Oxiana* was the inspiration for the journey. Chatwin was not yet committed to his book on nomads and still saw himself as a potential archaeologist rather than as a writer. (He had already behind him his short career as a Sotheby's art expert and negotiator.) But the country exerted an irresistible pull on his imagination: 'the bazaar is really Arabian Nights!' He went back the following year, this time as a botanist: his equipment included a large flower press. Always something of a hypochondriac, Chatwin found himself dispensing medicines to Afghans whose ailments were considerably more serious and dramatic than his own.

It was only on his third Afghan journey that Chatwin made the pursuit of nomads his main objective. By then he was already committed to the publisher Jonathan Cape to write *The Nomadic Alternative*, and the collection of material for that book was his motivation. His travelling companion was Peter Levi – the poet, classical scholar and Jesuit priest – who was something of a role-model for Chatwin, and whose own motivation for visiting Afghanistan was to collect material for a book on the Greek influence in a region that had been a staging post on Alexander's march to India. Together, Chatwin and Levi would explore the Silk Route.

They were a strangely assorted pair of travellers. Although married (and indeed joined by his wife Elizabeth for the final stages of the journey), Chatwin was highly susceptible to the charms of his own sex, and they were equally frequently susceptible to his charms. His notes refer to 'syrupy looks' and 'deep, deep glances' from boys encountered en route. But Levi states emphatically that while on his Afghan trip Chatwin 'didn't go to bed with any monkeys or goat-boys . . . he led the life of a Cistercian monk'. Levi, for his part, had as richly varied a professional life as Chatwin's: though not a Cistercian monk, he was still a Jesuit priest (though he later resigned from the priesthood), and as well as lecturing on classics at Oxford he was to be the architectural correspondent of *The Times* and go on to be Professor of Poetry at Oxford. At the same time as these varied activities, he was a prolific writer, not only of poetry but also of serious – some of it very serious – prose, and – for good measure – of thrillers. They must have appeared an attractive and formidable couple to the random strangers they met in the wilds of Afghanistan.

Chatwin did indeed find material for his book, which was never to appear. Early in their travels they stumbled on nomad burial mounds in a valley behind Shar-i-Golgola. 'It was too good to be true' from Chatwin's point of view, wrote Levi. Later they reached the barren ground of Chagcheran, where Chatwin had heard there was an annual nomad fair of vast proportions. Such a gathering would have provided him with an opportunity to study the elements of nomadic culture that had survived from remote antiquity. But this time they were less lucky, and they mistimed their arrival: where there had been a thousand nomad tents the previous week, they found only some forty, largely deserted and flapping about in a dust storm. Even then, they noted that the last remnant of the nomad assembly was encamped like a medieval army, with lines of horses and camels behind the tents. However, not everything was as disciplined: as a local police chief said to them, 'Desert is toilet, all Chagcheran is desert, all Chagcheran is toilet'. Those still at the fair were from the Firuzkuhi tribe, who had first come into Afghanistan with an army of Turkish mercenary cavalry.

It was the Firuzkuhi who had built the minaret at Djam which was to be Chatwin's next objective. He and Levi hired horses and rode for fourteen hours to get there. The minaret did not disappoint Chatwin, who described it as 'rearing to the sky like some triple-tiered Moon Rocket' and having the same aspiration of reaching to the heavens. With his ready sense of the macabre, Chatwin also observed that the minaret owed its longevity to the strength of the mortar with which it was built, which in turn was alleged to owe its strength to the fact that, when the prisoners who carried sacks of earth to the building site had outlived their usefulness, they were beheaded and their bodies mixed in with the mortar to 'form a paste'.

Unlike Chatwin, who never published a proper account of this trip, Levi produced a book called *The Light Garden of the Angel King* three years later, much to the annoyance of Chatwin, who claimed that many of his own wittiest comments had been absorbed into the text. (In fact, Levi is extremely generous in his remarks about Chatwin and gives him credit for 'most of the best observations and all the best jokes'.) So although it was not Levi whose main interest was the nomadic life, it is in his writings that much of the best material on the subject is to be found.

Most of the Afghan nomads had originally come – like the Kazaks – from further east: the descendants of the Mongol horsemen who first penetrated this region in the wake of Genghis Khan. This was not surprising: the higher pastures through which Chatwin and Levi passed on some sections of their trip were lush compared with the barren stony wastes of the Central Asian steppe. There had also been nomadic pastoral tribes pressing downwards into Central Asia from Siberia. Everywhere the visitors found current evidence of such nomads, their tents and flocks being visible even from the air on the approach to Kabul.

Often the finest horsemen and the most magnificently dressed and bejewelled were Turkoman nomads from the eastern frontiers; equally often the tattered tents of other nomads were evidence of poorer migrants from Siberia. From whatever quarter they came, and however rich or poor they might be, they were uniformly impervious to the attempts of Buddhists or Christians to convert them from their own severe tribal beliefs. The influx of nomads had over the centuries terrified the indigenous inhabitants, but the culture that the invaders brought with them was not always inferior to that of the settled inhabitants. Levi comments that 'if we think about the past in Central

Asia, we ought to think of most of the time and most of the territory as the grazing ground of nomadic herdsmen'.

Chatwin and Levi were particularly intrigued with the Kuchi, a frontier people who used to move indifferently between Afghanistan and the North-West Frontier province of British India. In the 1960s they came up once a year from their own lands south of Gardez (which in turn is south of Kabul and within Afghanistan), although if they strayed they had problems with the Pakistani authorities, who tried to control their movements and to insist on passports – an alien concept to the Kuchi. They took about four months each way on the journey, only spending the remaining four months of the year in the north-west grazing grounds they had taken so long to reach; it was a way of of life that constituted a total commitment to nomadism. Along their route, Chatwin and Levi found sheep-dips and places where the Kuchi had forded the rivers, all evidence of the well-worn trail to the summer pastures.

Although no longer in evidence when Chatwin and Levi got there, it was the Kuchi who had formed the largest element in the big nomad fair at Chagcheran. They preferred this gathering to the smaller fairs because, as Levi reports, 'there was a lot of thieving and murder at the old scattered sites'. They came to the fair without their families, and they brought clothes and guns to sell, while they bought sheep for resale at a profit in Kabul on the return journey. In earlier times, fragments of lapis lazuli – long found in this area – would be used as currency for such purchases. Carpets, too, had long been a trading item, and in the back quarters of one carpet shop Chatwin found the complete trappings of a Kazak nomad tent. His immediate recognition of its provenance delighted the Kazak shopkeeper, who had brought these handsomely crafted accoutrements with him as a refugee from Soviet Kazakhtan some twenty years before. Chatwin's unfaltering eye, which had stood him in such good stead at Sotheby's, had once again made him a friend.

Levi also noted that the Kuchi had big military-looking tents, some of which he suspected were looted from or left behind by the British army. Indeed, it was clear to him and Chatwin that folk memories in this part of the world stretched back as far as the Afghan wars of the nineteenth century. The nomad camps they passed through had other features: recent rock carvings and drawings of goats tempted them to loiter, while packs of predatory dogs tempted them to spur their horses on. Sometimes they would see a long procession of camels and horses, together with young animals born in the summer pastures, leaving the nomad camps as their camp-fires smoked in the evening light, and trickling down towards Faizabad. This was what Chatwin had come for. He felt his book taking shape in his head. He had seen for himself something of 'the princes of felt and furs'.

# BOOK IV

# THE TUAREG AND
# THE MOORS OF THE SAHARA

'The desert people are closer to being good than settled people because they are closer to the First State and are more removed from all the evil habits that have infected the hearts of settlers.'

Ib'n Khaldun (fifteenth-century philosopher and historian who recruited mercenaries from the Sahara)

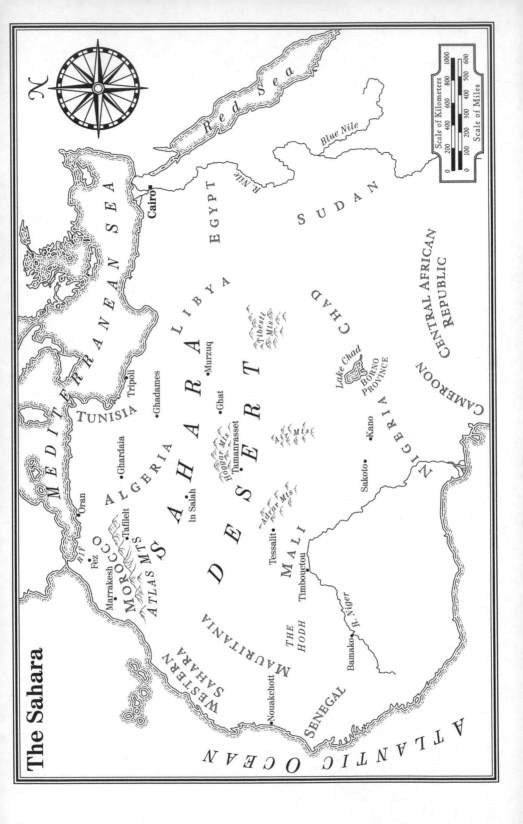

# The Sahara

MEDITERRANEAN SEA

Red Sea

Blue Nile

R. Nile

Cairo

EGYPT

LIBYA

SUDAN

CHAD

CENTRAL AFRICAN REPUBLIC

CAMEROON

NIGERIA

Tibesti Mts

Murzuq

SAHARA DESERT

Lake Chad

BORNO PROVINCE

Kano

Aïr Mts

Ghat

Ghadames

Tripoli

TUNISIA

Ghardaia

ALGERIA

Hoggar Mts

Tamanrasset

In Salah

Sakoto

Oran

MOROCCO

Tafilelt

Fez

RIF

Marrakesh

ATLAS MTS

Adrar Mts

Tessalit

MALI

Timbouctou

R. Niger

Bamako

THE HODH

MAURITANIA

WESTERN SAHARA

Nouakchott

SENEGAL

ATLANTIC OCEAN

Scale of Kilometers
0  200  400  600  800  1000

Scale of Miles
0  100  200  300  400  500  600

N

# 6

# The Tuarag and the Mauritanian Moors
# of the Sahara

———⟫⋅◆⋅⟪———

THE Tuareg – the 'veiled people of the Sahara' – have exercised a dangerous attraction to outsiders for many centuries. Herodotus provided the first introduction to their lands in the fourth century BC, and Ib'n Batutah in the fourteenth century AD and Leo Africanus in the sixteenth century somewhat increased the slender sum of knowledge about them available to Western travellers. But they have remained enigmatic.

The Tuareg are not a tribe but a people, and their name was originally a term of opprobrium applied to them by their enemies. They are thought to be separate in origin from the Berbers, with whom they are frequently confused, and are a Libyan race (indeed, Herodotus described them as 'Libyans') who were in Africa long before the arrival of the Arabs. Their own language is Tamachek, which varies in dialect from group to group. They have always been nomadic by instinct, and have tended to remain distinct from their neighbours both in ethnic terms and in characteristics. Their heartlands have traditionally been deep in the Sahara, and they have ranged widely over the Hoggar mountains in southern Algeria, the Aïr Mountains in Niger and (together with the Toubou) the Tibesti Mountains in Chad.

The most memorable trait of the Tuareg has usually been their fierce resistance to penetration of their homelands from outside. Dominating the caravan routes themselves, they have resented the intrusion of outsiders, and almost all the early travellers in the region have brushed with them – notably the French, whose Foreign Legion was at times badly worsted by Tuareg attacks. The most romantic of Saharan peoples, the Tuareg have been both a magnet for European adventurers and, in many cases, the most formidable of the obstacles to a safe crossing of the desert which they have encountered.

Further to the west and based on Mauritania, a state with an extensive Atlantic seaboard and twice the size of France, is to be found the other great confederation of Saharan nomadic peoples – the Moors. Like the Tuareg, the Moors are made up of a collection of different tribes, perhaps as many as a hundred. They, too, reacted ferociously to European intruders, and it was not until 1934 that the French managed to bring Mauritania under their control. They also are 'blue men', wearing indigo robes that rub off some of their colouring on the skin of the wearers (although the Moors do not veil themselves from view as do the Tuareg).

One thing that distinguishes Mauritania from other Saharan countries that have a large nomadic population is that here the leaders of the state themselves have tended to come from nomadic backgrounds. For this reason there is none of the suspicion of the nomadic lifestyle which dominates so many countries, where central government is mistrustful of a part of the population which has difficulty in complying with the norms of modern life: taxation, military service, settled education and health care. At the time of independence in

178

1960, eighty-five per cent of Mauritania's Moors were nomadic; but since then there has been a large-scale settlement of the population, resulting largely from the appalling droughts of the decade after independence. Some have moved to the small towns; others have taken up settled agriculture; but many still pursue their pastoral way of life, particularly in the eastern part of the country – the Hodh – which is nearly a thousand miles from the coastal capital of Nouakchott.

The Moorish nomads of Mauritania tend to move in small groups – extended families – rather than in large tribes (as, for instance, in southern Iran). If the pasture is good, some score of tents may be found in one place; but if it is sparce, as is more often the case, then only a cluster of two or three tents will usually be found together. Almost all the travellers whose experiences are related in the following pages have found that they seldom encountered more than a handful of Moors on any single occasion. Fewer and fewer of their tents are now woven from the traditional goatskins, and heavy cotton is imported from neighbouring Mali as a substitute. Frequently such cotton tents are embroidered by the Moorish women with highly coloured panels, which make them easy to distinguish from Tuareg encampments.

The women do not only embellish the tents: they are normally the ones who set them up and take them down. If travellers have temporarily lost their bearings, at night or in a storm, they can check the compass points by the fact that Moorish tents (especially those of the Hammunat, the largest tribe in the Hodh) always have their opening facing west. The Hammunat Moors probably move on average about once every ten days, and the striking and pitching of camps will take several hours on every occasion. The loading of the camels (which will be done by the men) will also be a long process, as traditionally the Moors keep their possessions in tin trunks – like English children setting off for boarding school – which are awkward loads on camels.

Camels are of course the key to life. Wealth is measured in heads of camels and herds, but the Moors appear to visitors to be very relaxed in the way they allow these prized possessions to roam freely over large areas. They calculate that where grazing is so hard to come by, the animals need the freedom to range widely, and they are confident they will eventually gravitate towards the few existing wells; but because of this relaxed philosophy, much time and effort is expended in tracking down and rounding up animals almost every day, and certainly every time a move is contemplated. European travellers have had the same experience, and most of them record hours spent every morning finding the camels before they can be loaded. Even when hobbled, it seems that camels will cover considerable distances in search of anything to nibble.

Those intrepid travellers who have crossed the Hodh, usually en route for Timbuctoo, have often been surprised by the location of these small nomad encampments. But on investigation there are usually sound reasons for the site. The Moors do not like camping on top of another family and usually will prefer to distance themselves by at least a mile, largely so that they are not encroaching on each other's grazing. The presence of firewood is another factor dictating the site. But too much vegetation, particularly in the form of scrubland, can have its own hazards: wolves, hyenas and jackals all frequent this part of the Sahara, as some of the travellers recorded below have found out to their discomfort. Further east, in the Tuareg regions, there was evidence of activity by lions until relatively recent times; camels were occasionally attacked and dragged away to lairs among distant rocks – a feat no lesser animal could have achieved – and a lioness was found drowned in a well on a different occasion (her cubs ending up in a Paris zoo). Scrub also makes it harder for those camping to spot snakes – the horned viper is the most frequent – scorpions and some of the carnivorous beetles which frequent the desert. For such a barren landscape, there are surprisingly many horrors.

For this reason alone, it has taken an unusual type of person to seek out those nomads who have chosen to lead their lives beyond the baking gravel and the shifting sand-dunes of the Sahara.

LARGELY inspired by James Bruce's discovery of the source of the Blue Nile in the 1770s, an Association for Promoting the Discovery of the Interior Parts of Africa was set up in Britain in 1788. Its aim was to send expeditions to penetrate the 'Dark Continent', as it was known, and to chart and possibly colonize the regions they discovered. Also much in their minds was the desirability of ending, or at least containing, the active slave trade that was known to be carried on by the Arabs and others at the expense of the Negro peoples from south of the Sahara, although in practice most anti-slavery activity at that period was concentrated on the European-dominated transatlantic trade from West Africa to the West Indies and the United States.

The southern cone of Africa was considered by the Association to be reasonably accessible already, and the preferred method of entering on exploration of the centre and north of the continent was either from the east coast (later explorers were to use Zanzibar as a jumping-off point) or from the rivers of the western (Atlantic) coast. The Association's earliest major achievements were the expeditions of Mungo Park, first overland from the Gambia and then down the Niger river – which many geographers in London believed at the time to be linked to the Nile. Although Park skirted the southern Sahara and was aware of the fierce Tuareg and other desert tribes, he was not involved with these nomadic peoples: 'black' Africa was his fief.

Soon after Mungo Park's death on the Niger river in 1806, the Association turned its attention to the possibility of penetrating the heart of Africa from the north. Simon Lucas had already made one attempt to cross the Sahara starting from Tripoli, but it was not until after the appointment of Colonel Hanmer Warrington as British consul-general in Tripoli in 1814 that the northern route was seriously considered by him and others as 'Britain's exclusive highway into Africa'. With the final defeat of Napoleon in 1815, Britain achieved recognition as the leader of European overseas expansion. Warrington was to hold his post for thirty years and to establish a dominant relationship with the Pasha of Tripoli which facilitated the dispatch of further expeditions. He even arranged for the appointment of a British vice-consul at Murzuq, some six hundred miles due south of Tripoli and deep in the Sahara; but unfortunately the gentleman selected to fill this post – Dr Joseph Ritchie – proved to be more interested in entomology than in geography (his baggage included a camel-load of corks for securing dead insects) and in any event he died shortly afterwards on an abortive expedition.

The most serious explorer of the northern Sahara to be commissioned by the Africa Association was a much more committed character: Lieutenant Hugh Clapperton of the Royal Navy. Like many adventurers who were to fall under the spell of nomadic tribes in the course of their explorations, he was something of a nomad himself. He was born in 1788 in Dunfriesshire in the lowlands of Scotland, the son of a hard-drinking provincial surgeon who remarried shortly after the death of Clapperton's mother and who left the boy largely to his own devices. After a sound basic education at the village school, not altogether surprisingly at the age of thirteen Clapperton ran away to sea. He signed on as a ship's boy on a schooner trading with the Baltic states and North America. As frequently happened at that period, Clapperton was then press-ganged into the Royal Navy at the age of seventeen and forced to work as a cook's mate on a ship-of-the-line. Once again, he ran away, this time to join the crew of a privateer, where the rewards were greater and the dangers not much more than those of service with the fleet. But life as a privateer – often little more than a licensed pirate – did not suit him, and after a few months he managed to rejoin the Royal Navy without apparently undergoing any disciplinary action. Sailors were always in demand.

Although he was still before the mast, Clapperton now managed to invoke the help of an uncle who was a commissioned officer in the Royal Marines. A little nepotism, added to his already considerable maritime experience, eventually secured a midshipman's post for Clapperton, and more far-flung experience quickly followed – in the East Indies, South America, southern Africa and the China Seas. He participated in the brief and unhappy war between Britain and the United States in 1812 and, having seen active service in a number of corners of the world, was finally given command of his own ship. His duties included charting and exploring wild regions around the Great Lakes of North America, and he found that the life of a back-woodsman appealed to his sense of self-reliance and rough and tumble. It was no coincidence that he had earlier been selected as an instructor in cutlass-fighting. This was a man who could look after himself in almost any circumstances and was footloose for further adventures.

When he was prematurely retired on half-pay in 1817 (a frequent experience of officers after the conclusion of the Napoleonic Wars), it was not surprising that this obviously rough diamond was to find himself recruited to join an expedition to open up the interior of the Dark Continent and to learn to live alongside the itinerant peoples of the desert. Settled life was no part of his make-up.

The motivation for undertaking journeys deep into the Sahara was mixed. Partly the appeal was simply that of the unknown: it was there, so it ought to be explored. But a more important consideration was the network of trade routes which traversed the great desert. Traditionally, gold and salt had been exchanged; more recently, manufactured goods had begun to go south, while slaves, hides and other native com-modities had begun to become a feature of the northward-bound caravans. In the case of the slaves, they would usually be marshalled in herds, often manacled, and more frequently than not failing to survive the appalling conditions of the route-march through the cauldron of heat and sand which divided the lush green forests of central Africa from the Mediterranean coastline. It was felt that if a European power – preferably Britain – could once dominate the caravan routes, new (and more wholesome) trade would begin to flow into Europe.

The problem was not only the physical conditions of the Sahara: the vast distances, the heat, the sparseness of the wells and so on. The biggest difficulty of all was that the caravan routes were under the sway of fierce nomadic tribes who resented intrusion into their domain and threats to their livelihood. The nomads of the Sahara had three immediate ways of making a living out of the routes that crossed their traditional territories: they could act as guides themselves, and hire out their camels as transport; they could plunder those caravans that had not hired them as guides; and they could indulge in a little trafficking on their own behalf.

Each tribe had its own stamping ground. The Tuareg peoples were spread widely: their four major 'confederacies' were each based on one of the mountainous or upland regions of the desert – the Ajjer and Hoggar Mountains, the highlands of Aïr, and the Adrar. The Garamantian road (one of the most celebrated of Saharan caravan routes) roughly formed a frontier between the Tuareg and the Toubou, who were based in the Tibesti Mountains. The Toubou were, if anything, even wilder and more unpredictable than the Tuareg, and were described (by L. C. Briggs in his *Tribes of the Sahara*) as having raised the principle of freedom 'almost to the level of anarchy'. These were the peoples who bestrode the caravan routes. It was essential they should be contacted and placated or vanquished.

Clapperton seemed to have the right credentials for the job. An expedition to Borno, near Lake Chad and a thousand miles further south than Murzuq, was mounted with the intention of carrying out the task that the unfortunate Ritchie had failed to achieve. But the expedition was not solely entrusted to him; in fact, shortly before its departure he was informed that he was not to be its leader but that another officer – Lieutenant (later Major) Dixon Denham from the British army, who had more influential patronage than Clapperton – was to be in charge. The third member of the party was a thirty-one-year-old Scottish doctor called Walter Oudney. Denham and Clapperton did not get on together, the former finding the latter 'vulgar', and the latter resenting the fact that Denham had been super-imposed to take command. Matters were aggravated by Denham delaying their departure by attempting to return to London for fresh instructions. At last, in 1822 they set out southwards with a sizeable entourage: the three principals were accompanied by five servants (all freed slaves), their three horses, four camel drivers, thirty-three camels and a mule. Together with their escort and various hangers-on (mostly merchants wanting protection and freed slaves returning home), they numbered some three hundred in all. Some of the camels were carrying trade goods, some of them medicines, some of them weapons for hunting and protection, and some of them rich gifts for local chiefs who might need buttering up along the way.

Despite the fact that Oudney, like Park and Ritchie before him, died on the journey, the expedition was – by any standards except that of harmony between the participants – a great success. Not only was the Borno region extensively explored and mapped, but they went further into the heart of the continent than had been expected of them. Clapperton reached Kano, already a great trading centre in what was to become Nigeria; and the Sultan of Sokoto, who presided over another formidably properous Central African state, had been contacted. The way for future expansion, be it commercial or colonial, lay open. But surprisingly and inexplicably, Britain, whose government had other things on its mind, did nothing to follow up this promising lead for another quarter of a century, and by the time of the real 'scramble for Africa' towards the end of the nineteenth century, the French had consolidated their position in most of Saharan Africa.

But for Clapperton (as his recently published journals reveal) the real interest of the expedition had been largely in the encounters with the people who had straddled the route to Central Africa – the Tuareg who, despite their nomadic lifestyle, felt fiercely possessive about the Saharan territories across which they roamed. His diaries are full of observations and comments about the Tuareg. He sympathizes with their attitude of superiority towards settled peoples. 'The Tuareg hold as mean to cultivate the ground,' he remarks, and goes on to point out that they live principally on the milk and flesh of goats, sheep and camels, which they raise, and on mouflon, which they hunt. He compares their capacity to stock up with food before desert journeys with the well-known capacity of camels to do the same with water: 'Like all wandering people, the Tuareg are able to eat a great deal of meat without injury and to fast for a long time.' He also noted that they were not adversely affected by anything they ate or drank, however rank the meat or fetid the water might be. He was one of the first to observe and record how the Tuareg live in black goatskin tents – a feature that enabled subsequent travellers to recognize them from far off – and how they wore indigo robes and went veiled against the burning sun and swirling sand.

With his background of naval warfare and cutlass-fighting, Clapperton was particularly intrigued by the Tuareg's weapons. He noted that they had swords and daggers of European make, and he even found one that had a blade inscribed with the date 1577 and a ducal coronet – surely the relic of some extraordinary past adventure. He also observed that the Tuareg never shed their daggers except to say their prayers, and even then they kept them always in view and readily to hand.

Clapperton and his party were fortunate in not provoking attack from the Tuareg they encountered. Perhaps their numbers and arms deterred aggression, but that was not to prove a sufficient deterrent in the case of later French incursions – many of them much more heavily armed – into the Sahara. Their capacity to intimidate was not lost on Clapperton; he noted that young women and other vulnerable citizens tended to flee from settlements when the Tuareg appeared on the horizon. But he found that they were friendly among themselves, although, he commented wrily, 'murders happen at times'.

As guides, Clapperton found the Tuareg less than reliable. On more than one occasion they failed to show up with their camels after arrangements had been made for them to act as escorts. He was inclined to give them the benefit of the doubt when one of them claimed to be sick 'with worm in his knee'. Their usefulness as guides and allies was further qualified in Clapperton's opinion by the fact that they were gullible and superstitious.

Dr Oudney, who before he succumbed to fatal illness himself was often allowed to visit the women's quarters in his medical capacity, told Clapperton that he found Tuareg women free and easy in their manner and not as coy as their permanently veiled condition outside their tents might have implied. But there is no suggestion they were flirtatious (and Oudney would certainly have been living dangerously indeed if he had found himself even on the receiving end of any such advances).

Clapperton contributed to the official account of the expedition he made with Denham entitled *Narrative of Travels and Discoveries in Northern and Central Africa in the Years 1822, 1823 and 1824*, but his role was played down as much as possible by Denham, who was jealous of his own nominal leadership. In particular, no proper account was given of the travels which Clapperton and Oudney made without Denham to Ghat, on the edge of the Hoggar Mountains. It was only later with his own *Journal of a Second Expedition into the Interior of Africa* (published in London in 1829) and the appearance of his diaries (edited under the justified title of *Difficult and Dangerous Roads* in London in 2000) that Clapperton really comes into his own.

Clapperton's incursions into Africa 'from the wrong direction' (that is, from the north rather than from the more favoured western or eastern approaches) demonstrated to later travellers like James Richardson of the Anti-Slavery Society and Dr Heinrich Barth (who despite his German name and origin went as a geographer on Richardson's British-sponsored expedition in 1849) that it was possible to survive both the desert and the Tuareg. His obvious fascination with them both was to prove a spur to future explorers.

ALTHOUGH CLAPPERTON reached Kano and Sokoto (on the southern fringes of the Sahara in what is now Nigeria), he abandoned any attempt to reach the fabled Saharan city of Timbuctoo. This achievement was left to another contemporary Scotsman – Alexander Gordon Laing – in 1826. Laing was not so much obsessed by the Tuareg nomads as overinclined to trust them: they were first grievously to wound him, and later brutally to murder him.

Laing was born in Edinburgh in 1794 and accepted as an under-graduate at Edinburgh University at the age of thirteen; he was expected to follow his grandfather and father into an academic career. But, like Clapperton, he was footloose; instead of joining the navy, he joined the army at the age of seventeen, being commissioned into the West Indies Infantry (a colonial regiment for which no private income was required). But regimental soldiering bored him, and when posted to West Africa he applied to the Secretary of State for War, Lord Bathurst (who was to give his name to the capital of the Gambia), to be allowed to lead an expedition to Timbuctoo, which had not previously been reached by any European and which was thought to be an Arab city of glistening golden mosques and rich potential markets – an African Baghdad.

Bathurst was convinced that the right line of approach was across 1,500 miles of Sahara from the north, rather than from the much closer West African coast. Colonel Warrington, the redoubtable consul-general in Tripoli, was the man to launch Laing on his way. What no one had anticipated was that Laing would fall hopelessly in love with Warrington's daughter and refuse to leave on his expedition until he had been allowed to marry her; Warrington reluctantly agreed to use his consular powers to marry them, but made it a condition that the union should not be consummated until Laing returned safe and sound from Timbuctoo. Rather surprisingly, all parties consented to this arrangement.

When not escorting Emma Warrington, Laing spent his time in Tripoli trying to extract funds from Lord Bathurst in London for the expedition (on the grounds that it would be a national disaster if the French got to Timbuctoo first) and trying to fend off the exhorbitant demands of the local Pasha for bribes to facilitate the venture. Eventually he set off with a train of camels and local servants, but no other European companion – having (probably fatally, as it turned out) rejected the offer of taking a doctor with him, as he thought this might diminish the glory and uniqueness of his achievement.

Laing wrote copious letters from the desert, only some of which got back – by courier – to Tripoli; as well as recounting his adventures, the letters had two recurring themes – his passion for Emma, and his dissatisfaction about his own promotion prospects. For a man whose life was continually at risk from hunger, thirst, disease and attack, he showed a remarkable preoccupation on whether Lord Bathurst would agree to convert his temporary rank of major into a substantive promotion. He was also much concerned about whether Clapperton, his rival explorer, might not be making a sly advance on Timbuctoo from another direction and thus outflanking him in the race for glory.

Possibly because of these personal considerations, possibly because he – like so many of his compatriots before and after – was attracted to the brave and dashing lifestyle of the Tuareg, or possibly because he was in no position to choose who his protectors might be, he put his trust to an unwarranted degree in the nomadic tribes who frequented the Saharan caravan routes.

Laing's first major halt in the desert was at the oasis town of Ghadames (still in Libya), where he spent five weeks gathering provisions and guides for the next stage of the journey. He decided not to conceal that he was Christian, and this, together with the fact that he could not hide that he was carrying a relatively large amount of money and precious gifts, made him particularly vulnerable to robbery. The rapacity of the inhabitants of the oases further prejudiced Laing in favour of the freer and more generous spirit he detected among the nomadic tribes.

From Ghadames a further month's travel took him to the walled mid-Saharan town of In Salah, never previously visited by any European. Here he was such a curiosity to the local women that he had to nail up the door of his house to avoid their intrusions and attentions. Along the route he had had to make lengthy diversions to avoid desert conflicts between the Tuareg and their darker-skinned neighbours from further south. Again, his sympathies tended to be more with the Arabs than the Africans.

It was Laing's impatience to move off from In Salah that exposed the caravan to the danger of attack from a particularly fierce tribe of Mauritanian Moors who were ranging the area; when a scout returned on a racing camel to report that the Moors were alarmingly close, it was all Laing could do to persuade his companions not to return immediately to In Salah and further indefinite delays. Nerves were getting very frayed. It was against this background that Laing made a near-fatal mistake.

Just when Laing thought he was losing the argument about not returning to In Salah, a party of some twenty apparently friendly nomads appeared over the horizon and offered to take the caravan under their protection. Laing jumped at the offer: now his companions (merchants with whom they had joined up for this stage of the journey) could stop their whining requests to go back on their tracks. After five days of travelling in convoy, so reassuring did the newcomers seem that his leading guide persuaded Laing that he should give them some powder for their muskets, and that he could relax his grip on his own firearms. The new escorts were Tuareg, and Laing had already developed a better rapport with them than with the Moors or the 'blackamoors' from further south.

At five in the morning on the sixth day, the Tuareg struck. They concentrated their attack on Laing's tents and fired into them before rushing in with sabres to cut down survivors. Several of his party were killed outright. Laing himself received a bullet in his side, and sabre slashes on his head and thigh, neck and face, arms and hands. Having wrought their vengeance on the Christian and robbed him of most of his money and gifts, the Tuareg melted away into the sand-dunes. The accompanying merchants were left unharmed but more nervous than ever; as they left the scene of the attack as rapidly as they could in the direction of Timbuctoo, Laing was left crippled on his own camel – tied on to prevent his falling off – lagging behind his companions and catching up with only after they halted at night. Eventually, after some further four hundred miles of travelling in this condition, he was given shelter, food and medical care by a friendly local chief (who unhappily died himself of fever before he finished tending to Laing). Some measure of Laing's will to live may be gathered from the text of a letter he sent back to Warrington after the attack:

> To begin at the top, I have five sabre cuts on the crown of the head and three on the left temple, all fractures from which much bone has come away; one on my left cheek which fractured the jaw bone and has divided the ear, forming a very unsightly wound; one over the right temple and a dreadful gash on the back of the neck, which slightly scratched the windpipe . . .

There are then several lines of further detail enumerating the twenty-four wounds in all, and ending with the verdict: 'I am nevertheless doing well.' His main concern was that his disfigurements might distress his bride Emma.

After a period of rest, and against all advice, Laing pressed on for the final lap to Timbuctoo. The journey from Tripoli had taken him thirteen months, and he had had to cover nearly 2,500 miles (rather than the estimated 1,500) by the time all the necessary detours had been taken into account. His was the first north–south crossing of the Sahara at its widest point. But August 1826 was not a good time to arrive in Timbuctoo; the city was in confusion and under a new regime. And, worse, Timbuctoo itself was an anticlimax: it was not the gilded city of *Arabian Nights* which Europe had been expecting. It was a drab place of mud houses with a squalid slave market.

Laing spent five uncomfortable weeks in Timbuctoo. He wore European clothes, did not dissemble his Christian origins  and announced that he was the representative of the King of England. There was a brittle tolerance of him in the city itself, but when he wanted to explore the outskirts he found it more prudent to do so alone, at night and on horseback.

Eventually he set out for home, with a small caravan on a northerly course. It is unclear whether it was his intention later to go west towards the parts of West Africa which he already knew, or more likely to take the most direct route back to Tripoli and his bride. Whatever the intention, he did not get far. The caravan was under the direction of a certain Sheik Labeida, who had a reputation for being a fanatical Muslim and a part of the Tuareg hierarchy which dominated Timbuctoo. The sheik was loud in his protestations of friendship and goodwill towards the travellers under his protection, but doubtless he persuaded himself that such assurances were not binding when given to infidels. As on previous occasions, Laing was naively trusting. He still believed in the nomadic lore of the desert.

On the third night out of Timbuctoo, Labeida and some of his men fell on the companions entrusted to their care. Laing had let his defences down once too often. Most reports said that he was again attacked with sabres and this time beheaded; other reports said that he was strangled with a Tuareg scarf. At all events, he was killed, robbed of his few remaining possessions (including a brooch given him by Emma) and left unburied by the wayside. Even his papers, some of which had been given to separate couriers for safety, went astray and were thought to have been improperly acquired by the French author-ities in their search for information about Timbuctoo. It was years before Emma knew the truth about his fate, and when she did she remarried and died of fever shortly afterwards. The glory for which Laing craved was largely captured by his French rival, René Caillié, who reached Timbuctoo two years later and – more important – survived to tell the tale.

Gordon Laing set off on his quest out of ambition as an explorer not out of curiosity about the nomads of the Sahara, but his tendency to fall under the spell of the Tuareg was largely responsible for his terrible wounds and subsequent death.

IT has been related how Colonel Warrington, as British consul-general in Tripoli, managed to exert a powerful influence over the Pasha there early in the nineteenth century. Further west, along the North African coast, and some half-century later, a small group of less official Englishmen (and Scotsmen) were to exert an equally effective influence over the Sultan of Morocco. One such was Walter Harris, the correspondent of *The Times* and a frequent volunteer for hazardous diplomatic missions; another was Lord Loch, whose Guards-officer's bearskin (or 'busby') topping his six-foot-five height so impressed the young Sultan Mulai Abdul Aziz that he invited Loch to become a semi-permanent fixture at the Moorish court; and a third was the most remarkable of all – Sir Harry Aubrey de Vere Maclean, to become universally known in Morocco as 'Caid Maclean'.

It could be argued that the motivation of this distinctive little group of expatriates was entirely governmental and had little or nothing to do with the nomadic peoples of southern Morocco, that they were political manipulators rather than students of the tribes, functionaries rather than explorers. But whatever may be true of the journalist Harris and the military attaché Loch, Caid Maclean seems always to have been fascinated by the prospect of contacting and harnessing the wilder nomadic peoples who inhabited the fringes of the Sahara. As a military trainer and adviser to successive sultans, he appears to have harboured ambitions not dissimilar to those of Glubb Pasha (another Briton who assumed a local title) in Jordan: he believed that the key to the defence of the realm lay in the hands of those who were its traditional tormentors – unruly tribesmen with roving inclinations.

In 1877 Maclean was pitchforked into a turbulent Morocco in a way that he could never have forecast. He had been born in 1848, the son of the inspector-general of Queen Victoria's Army Medical Service, an institution then (pre-Crimean War) still in its infancy. He joined the army in 1869 and served for seven years in a range of frontier-like assignments in Canada, Bermuda and finally Gibraltar. It was to that British enclave that the then Sultan of Morocco – Mulai Hassan – sent a small contingent from his Berber army to receive training at the hands of the British. It fell to Maclean to do the training. So successful was he that the Sultan invited him to return to Morocco with the soldiers and to carry on training his army on a larger scale. He was quickly granted the title of Caid and made responsible not only for the infantry but for the household troops attached to the court. He was encouraged to learn fluent Arabic with inducements of enhanced pay and soon achieved this, becoming one of the few Britons at the court with such a qualification. He was provided with a cavalry mount and a residence – frequently no more than a tent – wherever the Sultan might happen to be. The trickiest part of his assignment was that it had a built-in paradox: the Sultan wanted his praetorian guard to be efficient bodyguards, but he did not want them to be too proficient at their musketry lest they should get ideas above their station and become a threat to the Sultan rather than a protection. The right balance was left to Caid Maclean to decide.

The most challenging aspect of Sultan Mulai Hassan's reign was the periodic subjugation of the warmongering and highly mobile tribes, particularly in the south of the country beyond the Atlas Mountains. Maclean accompanied the Sultan on these *harkas*. The court would descend on a frontier region and live off the local resources until they had effectively impoverished the tribes and their leaders, rather as Henry VII or Elizabeth I had impoverished over-mighty subjects in Tudor England by laying unreasonable demands on their hospitality. So frequent were the Sultan's forays that it was said that – 'the imperial tents are never folded away'. In the course of these royal progresses through the remotest parts of the kingdom, Maclean developed an interest in and fascination with those who lived outside the normal discipline of the state. Such peoples were – then as now – mostly to be found south of the Atlas Mountains, or sometimes in the Rif Mountains.

In 1893 Sultan Mulai Hassan decided to embark on one of the most arduous of his *harkas*: he was to take his army on a tax-gathering expedition to the desert oases beyond the High Atlas. In particular, he aimed to reimpose his rule in the disturbed region around the great palm oasis of Tafilelt, where the Saharan tribes tended to be a law unto themselves. Maclean, as usual, accompanied the expedition, but things did not go well. The royal cavalcade made itself extremely unpopular as it progressed through the tribal areas: viziers expected to be bribed, soldiers looted and pilfered, vast numbers of men and animals had to be fed, audiences were sought and petitions put forward – all too frequently to be rejected. Each day the Sultan and his entourage moved on, pitching the royal tent – surmounted by its golden globe – with its adjoining harem tents, and its surrounding white canvas township of lesser tents. The viziers and commanders would not have direct access to the royal enclosure but would be stationed nearby in order of importance. On the periphery of the camp would be the encircling tents of the Berber infantry, providing a wall of defence against assault or intrusion.

The cavalcade had set out from Fez towards Tafilelt in the summer, and the heat of the desert beyond the mountains had been abnormal, even for Morocco. Food had run out and local provisions were difficult to requisition. The wells were brackish, the tribesmen recalcitrant, and fever endemic among the troops. It was winter before they reached Tafilelt, so the return march had to be made across snow-blocked passes. Any thought of reaching Fez was abandoned and the less-distant imperial city of Marrakesh became the destination.

Caid Maclean had been impressed by the wild Saharan horsemen he had seen, harassing the royal cavalcade or withdrawing before them into their desert fastnesses. But far from being able to recruit them or even indulge his admiration, he was fully occupied with the task of trying to steady morale in the more-pedestrian ranks of the imperial troops whom the tribes had been molesting. Being of a powerful physique, Maclean was able to deal summarily with insubordinate individuals; but more effective still was the fact that his men liked and trusted him. Although (as we shall see) he was not above making a quick profit when an opportunity came his way, he was less venal and demanding than most of the Sultan's viziers and officials. He had already – the previous year – distinguished himself by suppressing an insurrection of the Anjera tribe. But it took Maclean all his forcefulness and all his powers of leadership to persuade the raggle-taggle army to brave the snowbound passes and head on towards Marrakesh. His influence on his men may have been enhanced by his commanding, if bizarre, appearance: he was accustomed to wearing a white turban, highly polished English hunting boots and a Berber cloak woven in the pattern of his own – Maclean – clan tartan. And he played the bagpipes.

On the way to Marrakesh a significant event occurred. The Sultan decided to seek shelter at the Glaoui fortress kasbah of Telouet, which commanded the Tiz-n-Tishka pass through the High Atlas. El Glaoui – the head of the clan – received him and his weary troops with generous hospitality (something that could not have been taken for granted in these wild parts), and in return the Sultan gave El Glaoui his Krupp cannon, the most formidable piece of artillery in all Morocco. It was to be the making of the prestige and power of the Glaoui; this mountain dynasty, far more than the wild desert nomadic tribes which had so attracted Maclean as possible sources of support, was to prove a formidable factor in the making and breaking of future sultans.

Sultan Mulai Hassan's health never really recovered from his abortive expedition to Tafilelt, but this did not deter him from undertaking another *harka* the following spring – this time to the north-east of Marrakesh. Once again, Maclean accompanied him, but on this occasion the service he was to perform to the sultanate was of a macabre nature. As Maclean had discovered on previous expeditions, the main factor in holding the army loyal was the presence of the Sultan himself. Any power vacuum invited the tribes to sweep in from the desert or down from the mountains and usurp the royal control.

Mulai Hassan left just such a power vacuum: he died on his campaign. His chamberlain was quick to realize the danger, and confided in Maclean (who as a foreigner was unique in presenting no personal rivalry). Between them, the royal chamberlain and the 'English' Caid decided on a bold subterfuge. Not only was the Sultan's death not announced, but life went on as if he were still alive. 'The Sultan died in the recesses of his tents, themselves enclosed in a great canvas wall, inside which . . . no one was permitted to penetrate,' wrote

196

Walter Harris. The knowledge of his death was therefore limited to his personal slaves and his chamberlain.

If the power vacuum was to be concealed, two things were necessary: life had to continue with the military advance as if nothing had happened, and messengers had to be sent post-haste to the Sultan's chosen son (not necessarily the eldest) who was to succeed. In both tasks, Maclean assisted the chamberlain.

The morning after the Sultan's death, it was announced in the camp that the next stage of the journey would start at dawn, and before daylight the state palanquin was carried into the tented imperial enclosure, the corpse was propped up inside it and its curtains drawn. To the usual fanfare of trumpets, and with banners flying, the cavalcade moved off with cries of 'May Allah protect the life of the Sultan!' When the cavalcade halted for rests, tea was elaborately brewed up and refreshments were carried into a specially erected tent by the slaves who were party to the secret. The day's march was a long one, since it was clearly important to reach Rabat as soon as possible, and when darkness came the chamberlain announced that his majesty was too tired to give any audiences that night. Urgent business was confined to documents that were taken in to the royal tent and emerged in the chamberlain's hand bearing the seal of state.

By the time they reached Rabat after another long day's march, the summer heat was taking its toll and it was increasingly impossible to disguise the nature of the palanquin's contents. But the objective had been achieved: the new Sultan – Mulai Abdul Aziz – had been proclaimed in Rabat, despite the fact that he was only a twelve-year-old boy. An attack on the dead Sultan's entourage had been averted. When the fatal cavalcade eventually arrived at the gates of Rabat, a hole was made in the city walls to allow for the entry of the reeking palanquin (no dead body could pass through the gates – least of all one that had been five days decomposing), and the overdue burial rapidly took place. The tartan-clad Caid had completed his part in steadying the troops and ensuring a peaceful handover.

Other Caids throughout Morocco were frequently less loyal. The greatest threat was thought to come from the faction of the Grand Vizier, who had remained at Fez – the spiritual and social capital of the country – during the late Sultan's final campaign. When Mulai Abdul Aziz reached Fez still accompanied by his powerful chamberlain, the latter managed to get the boy Sultan to authorize the arrest of his father's Grand Vizier, who was to spend the rest of his life chained in fetters in a dungeon (such being the fate of those who fell from office). Uprisings among the tribes were brutally suppressed: one tribal leader was brought on camel-back to Marrakesh in a cage made out of the rifle barrels of his supporters, before being starved to death. The most effective instrument in the hands of the chamberlain during these campaigns of repression was the support of the Glaoui chieftain and his Krupp cannon.

While the chamberlain assumed direction of the affairs of state, he attempted to ensure that the child king was kept amused with ever more extravagant foreign toys – fireworks, model railways, gold cameras, musical stuffed birds and even a miniature rifle range. The agent for obtaining all this imported paraphernalia was none other than Caid Maclean. While his heart no doubt lay with the untamed tribes on the fringes of the Sahara which he had hoped to bring within the Sultan's orbit, his pocket dictated that he should busy himself with taking a commission on all the orders for these childish luxuries from London and Paris. He was not only a passive agent: the hunting-booted Caid was also instrumental in dreaming up fresh orders for ever more improbable diversions for the young monarch: a scarlet state coach reached Fez from London, although there was scarcely a single stretch of road level enough for it to trundle with its giggling royal incumbent. Among those whom Maclean brought out from England was a fireworks operative who became a permanent member of the royal household. The Caid himself was now a wealthy man.

From time to time Maclean managed to escape long enough from the young Sultan's court to visit the tribal areas beyond the Atlas, where he still hankered after established recruiting contacts with the nomadic tribes. In 1901 he took Lady Grove, a spirited English lady traveller, to stay at Telouet – the Glaoui fortress in the Atlas – on his way further south. (She complained so vociferously about the inadequacy of the accommodation she was offered at Telouet that she had to be placed in the royal suite.) But dangerous as these trips were, it was not here but in the Rif Mountains further north that Maclean nearly met his end.

During the sultancy of Mulai Abdul Aziz, a notorious bandit by the name of Raisul terrorized whole regions of the kingdom. Raisul was an aristocrat, descended – so he claimed – from the Prophet Mohammed himself; with a soft voice, a handsome profile and a tendency to smile in a sad manner, he was no common brigand. But his misdeeds led to his arrest and incarceration in a dungeon; after four years he escaped following many months of nocturnal filing at his fetters, only to be recaptured almost immediately (he had found himself unable to run away after so long in leg-irons). When eventually he was released, he soon reverted to his old ways, kidnapping – among others – Walter Harris in 1903. Harris's release was negotiated fairly rapidly, but not before his captors had shown him a less fortunate prisoner, 'his corpse swollen, an apple stuck in his mouth, his eyes gouged out, and his naked body horribly mutilated... his hands pegged to the ground by stakes driven through his palms'. Capture by Raisul was not a risk to be lightly undertaken.

Yet this was exactly what Caid Maclean did. He volunteered to hold negotiations with Raisul on the Sultan's behalf in April 1907. The meeting appeared to go well, and a second one was proposed. A month or so later, a further rendezvous was arranged on the borders of the Ahlserif tribal lands in Raisul's territory. Raisul said he would accept a safe-conduct to meet the Sultan, if Maclean would accompany him to his camp before setting out for Rabat the following day. Maclean agreed and entered the mountains with his host. But there was no setting out the next day; Maclean found himself a prisoner and was to remain so for a harrowing seven months.

The negotiations for his release were handled less well than in the case of Harris. In the end, a ransom of £20,000 was paid, and Raisul was made a 'protected British subject' – in effect, granted a degree of immunity against the Sultan's further wrath. Although Maclean had endured his ordeal with 'courage and coolness' (according to a contemporary), the experience seriously undermined his health. When the following year Mulai Abdul Aziz was deposed as Sultan, it was hardly surprising that Sir Harry Maclean declined to accept an invitation to stay on as a Caid at the court of his successor. Instead he retired to Richmond in England, remarried (to the daughter of Sir Harry Prendergast VC) and continued to spend part of every year in Morocco, but now in the relative safety of Tangier and far away from both his beloved trans-Atlas tribes and the dangers of kidnap.

The tartan Berber cloak, the highly polished English hunting boots and the sound of the bagpipes were to become a memory only in the distant oases.

THE Hon. Francis James Rennell Rodd was a quintessentially Establishment figure throughout the first three-quarters of the twentieth century: at first appearances, no one could have been less of a nomad. His father – the first Lord Rennell of Rodd – was an immensely distinguished diplomat, serving as ambassador in Rome from 1908 until 1919 and playing a large part in bringing the Italians into the First World War on the British side. As well as a peerage, Lord Rennell amassed other honours – being a knight grand cross of no fewer than three British orders of knighthood, including the Bath.

The young Francis Rodd was educated at Eton and Balliol College, Oxford, and spent much of his childhood following his father around the world and acquiring fluency in French, German and Italian. After serving in the army throughout the First World War, he followed his father into the diplomatic service and seemed set for a conventional career in diplomacy. But it was not to be. In 1922, taking extended leave from the Foreign Office for nearly a year (these were more leisured days), he set off with two friends to explore the Sahara, having concluded that 'neither the Tuareg people nor this vast area of the world's surface had been adequately examined'. In the book he subsequently wrote about his travels – *The People of the Veil* – he disclaims any pretension to be an anthropologist; but the book is an in-depth study of the Tuareg, their terrain and way of life, and would not have disgraced a professional anthropologist.

Perhaps his long absence from his post, or the wider horizons he had experienced in the desert, unsettled his career; at all events, he resigned soon after his return in 1924 and returned to the Sahara for another long trip in 1927, thereafter being awarded the Founder's Medal by the Royal Geographical Society for his travels and writing. But he did not abandon his conventional lifestyle: he became a stockbroker, then he joined the Bank of England and went on to become one of the leading merchant bankers of his time. When the Second World War broke out, Rodd rejoined the army as an administrator in the Middle East and East Africa, quickly rising to the rank of major-general and being awarded numerous honours, like his father. He was a natural choice as president of the Royal Geographical Society after the war, and was remembered among other qualities for his panache in waving a gaily coloured silk handerchief as he sniffed snuff like an eighteenth-century grandee.

What had drawn Rodd – this figure of clubland and the City – to the Tuareg? Many things no doubt, including the romance of the desert and the fascination of a fast-disappearing way of life. But on reading his book, it is clear that there was something else and something special that attracted him to them – a panache which matched his own. Rodd was a man who did things in style. When he was on his trip deep in the Aïr Mountains of the Sahara, news was received of an impending raid by other tribesmen; the French officer commanding the nearest Foreign Legion outpost at Fort Agades had heard of Rodd as a man of spirit, and he immediately sent a message to him asking him to take command of a reconnaissance by an armed band of

Tuareg. Rodd obliged without hesitation. On another occasion he travelled for hundreds of miles with a French Camel Corps patrol across the central Sahara and conducted himself with such uncomplaining good humour that he was created – at a bizarre desert ceremony – an honorary sergeant of a Foreign Legion-type unit of the French colonial army. Rodd recognized in the Tuareg something of his own spirit of adventure and style.

Before he set out in 1922, Rodd had studied the history of the Tuareg's struggles in the nineteenth century to keep the French at bay. He knew of the lost columns of legionnaires. He also knew and admired the story of Charles de Foucauld. This eccentric French officer was a marquis and and a member of one of the smartest and chicest cavalry regiments in the French army; his youth was spent gambling and womanizing in Paris and elsewhere. He made a memorable reconnaissance of Morocco disguised as a Jewish merchant in 1883; and later he joined with fellow officers in leading patrols deep into Tuareg country. In the process, he fell in love with the desert and the Tuareg people and – against every rule of the military and of Parisian society – decided to stay on in the Sahara and become a Trappist monk, devoting his life to contemplation among the rocky peaks of the Hoggar Mountains. Although Father de Foucauld (as he had become) did not attempt to proselytize among the local Tuareg, he certainly used his considerable influence to French advantage, and in 1916 (when France was heavily engaged in the First World War) a band of hostile Arabs and Tuareg from another region – the Fezzan – raided Foucauld's retreat and killed him. When Rodd was there some six years later, these incidents were still fresh in memory and increased his own sense of participating in a dangerous way of life.

Rodd's views about the superiority of the Tuareg were hardly of the 'politically correct' variety. He noted that 'the potency of a noble race among people of inferior class is one of the most interesting phenomena of history'. He admired the way in which the Tuareg 'disdained any weapon except the sword, knife or spear . . . like the knight in medieval Europe, the Tuareg always held that the *armes blanches* were the only weapons of a gentleman'. It was characteristic of them that they respected the lions that still occasionally were found in their regions of the Sahara, but when they had surrounded a lion they would disdain to shoot it but would kill it – at much greater danger to themselves – with sword or spear.

Rodd also noted without any great disapproval that the Tuareg employed Negro slaves to do the sedentary and manual work (in any long-term encampments) which they felt was beneath their own attention as nomadic warriors. The whole process was – Rodd found – fairly relaxed, and in practice the slaves were allowed to possess some property of their own. It was in slave-trading, rather than in slave-owning, that the Tuareg 'sinned against the ethical standards which are usually accepted in Europe'. For the sake of their noble demeanour, one feels that Rodd was prepared to forgive them most things.

He did not even resent the Tuareg's attitude of superiority when it was directed at himself. When approaching a guide he wished to recruit, whose 'birth was noble' but who was extremely poor, Rodd 'was met with a look of disdainful enquiry which said more clearly and forcibly than words could express, "Who the hell are you and what the devil do you want?"' Undeterred, Rodd went on to try to persuade the man to accompany him on a perilous section of his journey, since he had a reputation for knowing every stone and mark on all the alternative tracks over this part of the desert 'as well as one may know the way from Hyde Park Corner to Piccadilly Circus'. The man had already rejected French offers of employment as a desert guide in their Camel Corps, as he felt the French were still his traditional enemies. However, he eventually agreed to accompany Rodd, for as long or as short a time as required, but only with the proviso that he was not paid. He would need a camel provided and of course his food, he explained, because he was poor; an occasional present would not be unacceptable; but he would come only as a friend and not as a servant – and because he himself *wanted* to come. Rodd felt he had met a kindred spirit.

Like anyone who travels for long with the Tuareg, Rodd became obsessed by camels. He spends many pages relating their habits, and he notes with particular attention (perhaps because of his own taste for the substance) that the Tuareg would put snuff into the eyes of their camels to ease congestion of the blood in the head by dispelling the blood pressure. He expatiates at length on the loading of camels, on their brand marks, on their eating and drinking habits, and on everything that affects their usefulness to their nomadic owners. Indeed, he comments that the Tuareg and other nomads of the Sahara are so dependent on their camels that he finds it hard to imagine how they existed without them; and he points out – like the good historian he is – that camels came relatively late to North Africa, in the second century AD. One can look in vain in Herodotus or Pliny the Elder for mention of African camels; they were apparently unknown to Hannibal (who might have preferred them to elephants?), and the Berbers seem to have had no word for a camel that predated the coming of the Arabs with their Arabic names for them.

Rodd finds that the Tuareg 'true nomads' are more dependent for sustenance on their camels than they are on the wells at certain times of year. After the rains, when the pasture is good, they do not trouble to cluster around the wells with their camps but prefer instead to live on the milk of their camels, dispensing with water for weeks on end. The self-sufficiency of the Tuareg is one of their characteristics that appeals particularly to Rodd. Not only do they not rely on the wells for water (at certain times of year at least) but they do not require matches or even flint and steel to kindle a fire: he describes how they rub a small green stick, cut and sharpened like a pencil, on a dry stick; the dust and fibre rubbed off the dry wood collect at one end of the channel that has been rubbed, and when the friction is enough, ignites. No Boy Scout could do it so well.

For one who led an ordered and conventional life, Rodd was remarkably uncritical about the wilder and more antisocial aspects of Tuareg life. He notes that they viewed 'raiding' as an extended field sport, to be indulged in freely once the rains had fallen and (in the case of the more settled among them) once their slaves had brought in the harvest. The most lucrative targets for such raids were of course passing caravans which had their camels 'lifted' by the raiders in regions outside European control. Even when pursued after such raids by the French Camel Corps, the Tuareg usually managed to outride their pursuers, being both better camel men and travelling considerably lighter than the African troops enlisted by the colonial power. When there was a shortage of caravans to raid, the Tuareg raided neighbouring tribes. These would often be far away, and raiding parties thought nothing of covering a hundred miles a day (though a ride of a hundred and sixty miles was recognized as phenomenal even by them). Nor did it unduly disconcert the raiders if they had – for reasons of secrecy – to avoid the wells: Rodd recounts instances of the men going seventy-two hours without water or complaint. Dates – compact and light – were their only provisions. Usually raiding parties would set out in some strength, possibly a hundred strong; but after the raid was accomplished they would split up into smaller parties to confuse their pursuer. The purpose of raids – either on caravans or on settlements – was to acquire camels. Not only were the women and children of target groups left unmolested, but the Tuareg scrupulously avoided killing or wounding the camel owners, unless the latter resisted fiercely. Rodd obviously felt the whole practice was good clean fun and could not bring himself to condemn it.

The Tuareg further consolidated their claim to be considered by Rodd as a gentlemanly people by their affection for dogs. Rodd notes that, unlike in Arabia and the Middle East, there are no pye-dogs among the Tuareg, and their domestic dogs are treated as 'much more companions to man than is usual among Moslems'.

He is convinced that the Tuareg are nomads by choice and not by necessity. They appear to an outsider to want for very little, and certainly they themselves consider they have all they need in life; and Rodd argues that the proof of their happiness is that often, even when they have valuable herds of camels worth many thousands of pounds or dollars, they never think of selling them and changing their way of life, preferring to stay as they are. They are envied by the village dwellers, Rodd says, 'whose sole ambition is to make enough money to buy camels and live in the same way as their wandering kinsmen'.

Subsequent travellers did not always find the Tuareg so contented. But Francis Rodd, soon to become the second Lord Rennell of Rodd, went back to his life in the City of London, to his clubs, his honours and his snuffboxes, feeling that he had encountered in the Sahara a people who were his soul-mates – aristocratic, naturally distinguished, brave and self-reliant.

GEOFFREY MOORHOUSE was already an established writer when he conceived the idea of crossing the Sahara from west to east at its widest point, and writing a book about the trip and the nomads he encountered. He sensibly consulted other authorities on desert travel and nomads before setting out. One such was Wilfred Thesiger, whose comments were realistic and sobering. He persuaded Moorhouse of the impracticality – indeed of the impossibility – of trying to make the trip alone without guides. And he also warned Moorhouse of some of the hazards: his camels would be seen as valuable commodities, and the Tuareg might well 'bump you off without compunction' to secure them.

Moorhouse was not deterred and stuck to his intention of travelling by camel throughout, though he did abandon any idea of going it alone. In Nouakchott, the capital of Mauritania on the Atlantic, he kitted himself out for the adventure, and – despite 'no great taste for fancy dress' – he opted for a variant of Arab costume which included four metres of black cloth to be wound around the head as a protection against the sun. Moorhouse felt not only that local dress was probably the most practical (as Lawrence of Arabia had concluded elsewhere) but that there was no point in advertising the fact that he was a European in a region where Europe was associated with unusual wealth and often with predatory intentions.

Unlike Clapperton and others who had started their journey in the north, Moorhouse was to spend the first weeks and months of his travels not among the Tuareg but with the nomadic Mauritanian Moors. His experience of them did not endear them to him. In particular, he became impatient of their continual demands or requests for gifts - usually tea and sugar in addition to tobacco, cigarettes and medicines of all kinds. One of his guides asked for a gift of a camel, and never let a day go by without hints and reminders of his request. But on many occasions Moorhouse and his guide were taken in and given hospitality in Moorish nomads' tents: frequently the nomads would put up an extra tent for the visitors or let them sleep in the lee of their own tents. On these occasions the call for largesse was not confined to his guides; his hosts, too, would expect tea and sugar with a regularity that meant that the expedition's supplies were seriously reduced by these continual unforeseen demands on them. Moorhouse felt that his guides were ganging up with his hosts to maximize the pressure on him to part with provisions.

Arising out of this, Moorhouse came to deplore the nomadic obsession with food - more particularly with meat - about which they would talk endlessly, often dropping hints about the desirability of buying extra goats from anyone they happened to meet along the route. He put this down not so much to greed as to the fact that for so much of their lives they were living just above the level of famine.

Despite this preoccupation with the basic necessities of life, many of the nomadic families Moorhouse encountered had long strings of valuable camels and, had they sold them, could have afforded to live comfortably in settlements or towns. The fact they did not appeared to be evidence of a preference for this way of life - a preference at least among the Mauritanian men, who treated their women (in most but not all cases) as lackeys to do not only the cooking but most of the heavy work about the camp. It shocked Moorhouse that, if they arrived at a nomad settlement when the men were away hunting or otherwise engaged, his guides would scarcely bother to be civil to the women, while accepting their hospitality as of right.

The Moors were devious in other ways than soliciting food. If they reached a settlement where they had family or friends, instead of asking whether they could stay for a few hours or an extra night, they would prevaricate and delay their loading of the camels so that their stay was extended surreptitiously. These unacceptable traits of the Mauritanian Moors were all the more galling because Moorhouse was so totally dependent on them for his survival; but they provoked him into his own form of revenge. When they criticized or mocked his grasp of their language, he would offer to teach them a few words of English with which they might introduce themselves to future English-speaking potential employers. Mohammed, one of his guides, was coached assiduously to repeat 'I am a cunning little shit'.

But for all their maddening ways, Moorhouse admired the desert-craft of some of the Moors who accompanied him. They often knew when other nomads were nearby long before they came in sight, and claimed that they could smell a camp-fire in the desert from three miles away. On the other hand, he had no great faith in their direction-finding, and attributed any apparent ability they had in that field to their memory for routes they had travelled before. This failing in a sense of direction was compounded by their mistrust of Moorhouse's compass-reading. On the rare occasion he allowed himself and his compass to be set aside in favour of some nomadic hunch about the way ahead, he almost invariably regretted it.

Moorhouse's experience of his nomadic guides changed greatly for the better when he left Mauritania and Mali behind him for (what turned out to be) the final stage of his journey across the frontier into Algeria and on to Tamanrasset. His new guide, who was found for him by the commandant of the garrison at Tessalit (an oasis town on the one road between Oran on the Mediterranean coast and Bamako in Mali), was not a Moor but a Tuareg. Although communication was more difficult with him than with the earlier Moorish guides, because he spoke Tamachek and not French or Arabic, Moorhouse was immediately impressed with his steady gaze and proud bearing. Despite the alarming things he had heard about the Tuareg from Thesiger and others, he felt that this was a man whose support and loyalty he could trust. Ibrahim (for that was the Tuareg guide's name) came armed with a great broadsword, which it appeared was not only carried as a weapon of defence but also as a symbol of manhood. Without it, Ibrahim felt improperly dressed.

Just as the Tuareg men – and even young boys – impressed Moorhouse as more self-reliant and stronger than the Moors, so their camels did the same. They were white (probably indicating that they came from the Hoggar Mountains), woollier, bigger-boned and firmer-humped than the camels he had encountered further west. They tended to be ridden at a 'roistering gallop', partly on account of their own good breeding, and partly because of the spirited nature of their Tuareg riders.

Another feature of the Tuareg, vividly illustrated by Ibrahim, was their good manners. Whereas the Moorish guides had scrabbled greedily with their fingers in the communal eating dish, Ibrahim brought his own spoon and brass dish, using the latter both for his share of the food and as a drinking vessel – instead of swigging at the *guerba* (skin water-bag). Ibrahim had the natural diffidence to roll himself up in his blanket at night at a discrete distance from Moorhouse, rather than lying down in intimate proximity – for mutual warmth – as the other guides had done. Ibrahim did not raid the communal food supplies but waited until offered his share by Moorhouse. And then he even said 'thank you' – an unheard-of phrase among the Moorish nomad guides.

As Moorhouse progressed further eastwards, he was also heading further north, away from the regions he had passed through – in southern Mali in particular – where the Negro population from below the Saraha were penetrating into the fringes of the great desert. This removed one recurring source of friction: the antagonism between the black population of tropical Africa and the paler-hued Arabs, Moors and Tuareg of the desert. The hostility had its roots in history: for centuries the nomadic peoples of the desert had raided the villages of the settled forest and savannah dwellers and carried off black slaves for trading in the markets of Morocco and the Mediterranean seaboard as far east as Cairo. Many of these Africans had ended up in the harems or the galleys of the Ottoman Empire; others had been driven westwards to collection and embarkation stations such as the island of Goree off Senegal, for onward trans-shipment to the New World across the Atlantic. Latterly, since the independence of Mali and other southern-Saharan states, the Negro population had often ended up in the more important and sedentary positions, from which they were able to exert power over the more transient nomadic peoples. Perhaps semi-consciously some element of revenge was being taken; be that as it may, no love was lost on either side. To a traveller such as Moorhouse, with nomadic guides and largely dependent on the goodwill of those among whom he found himself, such divisions were disturbing and likely to lead to unwarranted arrest and detention. Moorhouse went to great pains to avoid encounters with the military, sometimes adding considerably to his mileage by so doing.

Moorhouse endured some fearsome ordeals in the long desert stretches of his journey: it was not for nothing that his book was entitled *The Fearful Void*. More than once he completely ran out of water and came close to dying of thirst and exhaustion, on one of these occasions due primarily to the carelessness of his Moorish guide who had allowed a *guerba* to slip and lose all its precious content of water. By the time he entered Algeria, despite the help of Ibrahim, he was suffering from recurrent dysentery, blistered feet, saddle sores and insect bites, and indeed from general fatigue of a fairly extreme nature. His account of his journey dwells increasingly not on his surroundings but on his own mental state. He understandably and wisely concluded that to continue beyond Tamanrasset was to court disaster. He had already covered nearly two thousand miles, the last four hundred almost entirely on foot to spare the strength of the camels. Honour was satisfied. Having seen the beauty of the Hoggar Mountains – those

Dolomite-like peaks that had for so long sheltered the Tuareg and their aristocratic white camels – he headed for the airport and home. It was to be left to a younger successor to complete the course.

IN the late 1980s, fifteen years after Geoffrey Moorhouse had tried to cross the Sahara from west to east, another Englishman was to make the attempt. Michael Asher was already an experienced resident in the Sudan, where he had lived and travelled with desert nomads. He was familiar with camels and had been invited by the United Nations Children's Fund to advise them on the use of camels in their aid project in the Red Sea hills. The appeal of nomads, familiarity with camels and the challenge of the Sahara were all elements in his decision to try to undertake what no one had managed to achieve before: a lateral crossing of the Sahara at its widest point. Completely by chance he encountered an Italian girl who was to become not only his companion on the trip but (even before he started out) his wife.

Their route took them across five countries: Mauritania, Mali, Niger, Chad and the Sudan. In the course of their journey they encountered numerous different varieties of nomadic tribes, but two tribes or peoples in particular seemed to attract and fascinate Asher – the Moors and the Tuareg. The former dominated the early stages of the journey, the latter the later stages. Both groups wore indigo robes, but Asher confirmed that the Tuareg veiled themselves more effectively from view, winding their indigo headcloths tightly around the lower parts of their faces, exposing only their eyes. This had the effect of concealing their facial expressions and making them appear possibly more threatening than they were. The tents of the two tribes also were different and enabled visitors to distinguish them from afar, the Moors preferring pyramid – or cone-shaped tents, the Tuareg preferring flatter, oval shelters. The Moors hunted, often with Saluki dogs; the Tuareg were more warlike and had a fearsome reputation. The Moors were a more loosely mixed people, partly of Berber descent and partly of Arab blood; while the Tuareg tended to be more purely bred and to have their origins further into the interior of the Sahara, often stemming from the Hoggar Mountains.

Asher was reminded of the ferocious reputation of the Tuareg when he reached Timbuctoo. The story of Alexander Gordon Laing, who had reached the fabled city in 1826 only to be reputedly strangled with a Tuareg headscarf (as related earlier), was not forgotten. The Tuareg may have killed Laing because they thought he was a spy; but this was little comfort to Asher as they often seemed to think the same about him. And Laing's murder was far from the last time that European travellers were to meet this fate at the hands of the Tuareg: only a year before Asher's visit, a couple had been strangled in the same way in another part of Mali.

But the great droughts that hit the region in the twentieth century had driven many of the Tuareg out of the desert and into the settlements, such as Timbuctoo, where their nomadic life had reluctantly been exchanged for a sedentary existence. Where this had happened, Asher and his companion found that they still maintained their faintly menacing manner as they pestered visitors for tea, sugar and tobacco. When away from the oases, Asher had to hobble the camels very close to camp to protect them from marauding Tuareg. The swords and daggers that the Tuareg invariably carried were clearly far from being purely ornamental accessories. One of the aspects of the Tuareg that attracted Asher and his Italian bride was that they were more fastidious than many of the Moorish nomads they had earlier encountered. When they took on a Tuareg guide in Niger, they found (as Moorhouse had done) that he did not snatch at food with his hands and burp and belch like their previous guides.

As Asher made painful progress across his south Saharan route, he encountered nomadic peoples of a wide variety. Many were variants on the Moors or Tuareg but had distinctive characteristics of their own. The Toubou, for instance, were a branch of the black Saharan nomads whose homelands were in the Tibesti Mountains, lying north of Asher's route on the borders of Libya and Chad. The Toubou had always been a divided tribe, which had made them vulnerable to the invasions of the Moors and later of the French; at the time of Asher's trip, they were still divided – some fighting with the Libyans and some with the Chadians. They had been feared far and wide in the Sahara, and still were.

Further east again, Asher ran into the Baggara nomads. This tribe ranged from Lake Chad in the west to the Nile in the east, and they were easily spotted by their woven palm tents. Less fierce than the Toubou, they were also dark-hued and moved silently across the harsh terrain with their cattle.

Unlike Moorhouse, Asher achieved his original objective: he completed the route to the Nile in the Sudan. The obstacles had been formidable indeed: not only the heat, the distances to be covered, the lack of water and nourishment, but also aggressive peoples and predatory animals. The hyenas had been the worst. Always circling their camp just outside the firelight, their yellow eyes easily picked up in the beam of a torch and their eerie cries shattering the peace of the desert night, they menaced and unsettled the camels. And there were just enough stories of their attacking humans to ensure that sleeping in their vicinity without a sentinel was at best unrestful and at worst distinctly rash.

However, the most forbidding hazard of the journey was not any of these things; it was the unpredictable and arbitrary bureaucracy imposed by petty officials at every stage of the route. Often these 'officials' were little more than boys with guns and chips on their shoulders. They relished their unaccustomed power, particularly when confronted with European travellers. Passports were confiscated, visas queried, letters of introduction found unintelligible and rescue flares mistaken for weapons. Europeans travelling on camels were unfamiliar and therefore mistrusted and often suspected of being Libyan spies. Frequently days or even weeks were spent waiting for some distant official to authorize the next leg of their journey; at times it was even necessary to retrace their steps to seek the necessary permits. And all the while money and food were running out. It was a miracle that the trip was completed, and many would have said even more of a miracle that the marriage survived it.

The driving force throughout had been the will to complete the course. But Asher's interest in nomadic tribes had first brought him into the region, and much of his subsequent book about the trip – *Two Against the Sahara* – is devoted to describing their traits. As with so many Englishmen who pursued their interest in nomads to the extent to seeking them out, he ended his trip by feeling more of a nomad himself than many of the peoples whom he encountered:

> The camels shuffled on across the interminable erg . . . it seemed that we had been here for ever . . . I could visualize no end to this journey . . . I could imagine nothing but a life of constant movement, searching for the next grazing, the next water . . . the hundreds of miles I had travelled made me far more like the nomads than I had ever been when I lived with them.

The seeker had become what he sought.

BOTH Moorhouse and Asher had been attracted by the nomads of the Sahara but had been motivated principally by their determination to cross that desert from west to east. Quentin Crewe, who travelled extensively across parts of the Sahara and around its fringes in the early 1980s, was more explicit in defining the purpose of his journey: 'I was setting out to see the last of the nomads, whose way of life I felt sure would have disappeared in another ten years,' he wrote in his book *In Search of the Sahara*.

Crewe was by any standards an unusual adventurer. Having been a man about town, gossip columnist, restaurant critic and writer, he developed a taste for travel in exotic places. The Sahara presents a challenge to anyone, even the fittest and most robust. Crewe was neither. In fact, he was wheelchair-bound with fairly advanced muscular dystrophy.

Having assembled a team of supporters – a mechanic, a photographer, a cook, an 'organizer' and a young man who had just left Eton to push his wheelchair – and acquired two Mercedes Unimog vehicles, Crewe's cavalcade set off from Tunis. They went south into the Sahara, making diversions to Ghardaia, where the Mozabites live in beehive-like desert towns, and headed towards the Hoggar Mountains in southern Algeria. From there they pressed on through Niger and Mali to Timbuctoo, and then across Mauritania to the North Atlantic coast.

It was here – driving over the sand-dunes along the coast – that the party experienced a dramatic disaster that could well have been fatal to the participants themselves as well as to the expedition. Mechanical breakdown, unquenchable thirst, scorching heat, insurmountable sandbanks, scorpion bites . . . all these had been half-expected. What had not been expected was an encounter with a landmine. The leading Unimog driver backed over some sand, to get a better run at a steep slope, and set off the mine in an unmarked minefield near the border between Mauritania and the western Sahara.

Crewe himself was blown out of the vehicle and landed, more or less intact but badly shaken up, some ten feet from the truck. The vehicle was a write-off, and it was probably only because it was the back wheels rather than the front ones that had gone over the mine that none of the passengers had more serious injuries. Crewe got so fed up (he was notoriously short-tempered) with being questioned about how and why they came to be in the minefield that he eventually lost his temper with a Mauritanian *petit fonctionnaire* and called him an idiot and his country 'hopelessly run'. Predictably, he got arrested, but his companions assured the police that he was 'delirious, possibly insane and quite probably on his deathbed'. He was duly unarrested.

The journey was as seriously thrown off course as the vehicle. Crewe and some of his team flew down to Senegal, where he managed to buy two Land Rovers. They had originally decided they would try to return and cross the Sahara from west to east through Libya, Chad and the Sudan. But political problems in Libya and hostilities in Chad made this impossible. So they were obliged to take a more southerly route through Nigeria, Cameroon and the Central African Republic to Sudan. Even this was fraught with difficulties: the consulates that could issue the necessary visas were all in the south of these countries, so their eventual route took them right down to the South Atlantic coast.

Despite all the complications of the revised journey, and despite the hazards – both those expected and the unexpected mine – Crewe maintained his interest in the nomads through whom he was travelling. He quickly discovered (as he would have done in Iran or elsewhere) that 'independent governments disapprove of nomadism': they feel embarrassed by sections of their community that insist on living a lifestyle so far removed from that of the modern states they aspire to become.

Predictably, it was the Tuareg for whom Crewe felt a special fascination. He maintained that one reason why the European travellers, explorers and soldiers who penetrated the Sahara in the nineteenth century were so attracted to the Tuareg was that the Europeans were snobs, and the class hierarchy of the Tuareg appealed to their respect for a stratified society and their wish to recognize aristocratic characteristics in the handsome tribesmen they encountered. The social commentator in Crewe responded to the same sentiments. He describes the Tuareg's different social classes with the minute attention of a gossip columnist and a former assistant editor of *Queen* and author of a book entitled *The Frontiers of Privilege*.

But Crewe, however much he warmed to the superior and warrior features of the Tuareg, was not unaware of their long tradition of violence, cruelty and deceit. Having listed the European travellers who were murdered by them, starting with Major Houghton in 1790 and including a considerable number of other soldiers, explorers, doctors and missionaries, he tells at length the story of the unfortunate Miss Alexandrine Tinne, born in 1839 the daughter of an English merchant. Having been jilted by a young British diplomat, she set off on extensive travels in Africa. She had a highly developed social

216

conscience and was distressed by learning of the flourishing slave trade around Lake Chad, and of the slaving routes that ran north from there to Libya. She decided to try to see what was going on for herself. She set off with an escort of Tuareg (from the Hoggar Mountains) to Ghat, in the south-western corner of Libya, and intended to go on as far as Timbuctoo. Her plans may have been imprecise, but they were certainly brave. One of her problems was that she had a reputation for being inordinately rich (she had cruised the North African coast in her own steam yacht) and it was thought by her escort that her saddlebags contained large quantities of gold sovereigns. Her other problem was that she was travelling through country controlled by a rival band of Tuareg who had no affection for those from the Hoggar. In the end, it was her own Tuareg escort who attacked her while there was some fracas with the camel leaders. Crewe speculates that they did so possibly to stop their rivals getting their hands on her gold. Be that as it may, the attack was particularly treacherous and brutal: when Alexandrine raised her arm (possibly in an imperious gesture of command, or possibly in self-defence) it was severed from her body; the next sabre stroke severed her head. She was only twenty-nine years old, beautiful and defenceless. Whatever the charms of the Tuareg, their gallantry (like Saladin's) was a somewhat unreliable commodity. Perhaps it is because they have over the years had so many murders on their consciences that they are still pathologically afraid of evil spirits: a Tuareg camp must have more than its share of ghosts.

Despite this, Crewe - like Moorhouse before him and Asher after him - found the Tuareg more *simpatico* than the Mauritanian Moorish nomads of the Sahara. He found, like Père de Foucauld, that 'the Tuareg like a lot of laughter'. He found the women (unlike the men – unveiled) attractive and the young girls mildly flirtatious. He sympathized with the Tuareg's plight after the years of drought. But he found them 'pasteurized' - no longer able to support the minimum size of flocks and herds to sustain themselves, and reduced to 'strutting like peacocks . . . in their blue and white robes', often for the benefit of tourists. At the same time, he also noted that some regions were still closed to visitors, at least in part because of the sporadic outbreaks of fighting between the Tuareg themselves. The spark had not been entirely extinguished.

One country where Crewe found that nomads were treated with more respect than elsewhere was Mauritania, largely because of the high proportion of the population (about four-fifths it was reckoned in the early 1980s) who are still themselves nomadic. Indeed, he reported recent efforts by the authorities to encourage those tribes who were purely hunters – like the Nemadi – to take up migratory pasturing of sheep and goats, rather than concentrating on hunting gazelle and other antelope with their spears and the help of their fierce dogs.

Another Moorish tribe of nomads of whom Crewe heard much were the Reguibi, who came from the west of Mauritania and who were among the last to be subjugated by the French in the 1930s. Even that intrepid flyer over the Sahara in the 1920s – Antoine de St-Exupéry – had been terrified of having to make a forced landing among these people. At that period, their reputation for ferocity rivalled that of the Afghans on the North-West Frontier of India.

Crewe found the M'Razig tribe in Tunisia a tame contrast to these wilder and more genuine nomads. He classified them as 'semi-nomadic', and said that although they had previously been wholly nomadic they now subsisted by pasturing their herds in settled parts and by growing dates in the vast oases. Government funding had helped in their settlement – as it was intended to do. Their women tended to spend the cold, hard winters in houses among the palm-fringed oasis at Douz, and only to rejoin their menfolk and the flocks in the desert when the spring warmth returned. However, there was still some movement by the tribe across the frontier into Libya, and some raising of camels: old habits die hard.

Crewe's Saharan adventure had probably turned out both more dangerous and more frustrating than he had initially expected. But he had achieved the object he had set himself at the outset: he had encountered genuine nomads before they had disappeared from the desert. He had also – like so many of his compatriots – succumbed to their appeal, and he had even tried to define what that appeal was. 'Desert exploration offered something more substantial than fame . . . the strange sense of freedom which the nomadic way of life offers . . . Life in the desert is reduced to three essentials – water, the way and, lastly, food . . . It is this paring down that appeals to the British, coupled with the simplicity of friendship . . .' From his wheelchair, Crewe had diagnosed something more profound than many more active travellers.

# Epilogue

THE cavalcade has ended. A cavalcade of bewhiskered Englishmen and eager Americans, of elegant ladies and unabashed adventurers, of eccentric wealthy entrepreneurs and of struggling impoverished scholars – all of them intent on joining the ever-flowing stream of nomadic life.

What, if anything, had they all in common? Perhaps the fact that there was a streak of the nomad in the make-up of all of them. So many were misfits in their own world: social misfits like Hester Stanhope and Jane Digby, intellectual misfits like Doughty and Palgrave, political misfits like Philby and Lattimore, those with physical or psychological problems like Quentin Crewe or T. E. Lawrence, or just inveterate rolling stones like Richard Burton or Bruce Chatwin.

These disparate travellers also had in common a sense of urgency – a sense that the objective of their quest, the quarry of their hunt, was vanishing: vanishing not so much into the sands or into thin air as into a cloud of diesel fumes and an encroaching tide of tourists and tarmac, of concrete and constraints. If the travellers did not get on their Arab stallions or their camels, on their mules, on their steppe ponies or on their Land Rovers, they would be too late – the last nomad would have struck his tent and the last well would have dried up. The obsession with this sense of the hour glass running out was not confined to twentieth-century travellers: Victorian architects of empire felt it almost as keenly as their post-imperial grandchildren.

And what of the nomads themselves? They, too, however far-flung and different their locations and origins, had some things in common. They were all, by definition – having remained as nomads until the twentieth century – survivors. As Bruce Chatwin remarked on one occasion to his friend Michael Ignatieff (as quoted by Nicholas Shakespeare): 'nomad peoples have this amazing capacity to continue under the most adverse circumstances, while the empires come crashing down.'

And another thing they all had in common was that they set a premium on freedom: freedom of movement, freedom from authority, freedom from the habitual anxieties of urban living, freedom from the constraints of organized agriculture, freedom from any convention but their own. With these freedoms tended to be found a taste for adventure ('raids are our agriculture' is a bedouin saying) which appealed to many of the Anglo-American travellers and was forgiven even by those among them (like the missionary ladies and the colonial administrators) who might have been expected to condemn it. It was as if these travellers shared John Donne's relish for 'a wild roguery'.

Islam is the dominant faith among the majority of the remaining nomads of the world. Christianity has been the dominant faith among most of those whose search for them is recounted in this book. But it must surely be left to one who was neither a follower of Mohammed nor of Christ, to the Lord Buddha himself, to encapsulate the relationship between those who tread the trail of nomadism and those who seek to join them: 'you cannot travel on the path until you have become the Path itself.'

# Select Bibliography

—————————

Abbott, Keith E., *Notes taken on a journey eastwards from Shiraz in 1850* (Journal of the Royal Geographical Society Vol. 27), London, 1857

Alder, Garry, *Beyond Bokhara: The Life of William Moorcroft*, London, 1985

Asher, Michael, *Two Against the Sahara: On Camelback from Nouakchott to the Nile*, New York, 1988

————*Thesiger*, London, 1994.

Barth, Fredrik, *Nomads of South Persia*, London, 1964

Bell, Gertrude, *Safar Nameh: Persian Pictures*, London, 1894

Bishop, Mrs I. L. (Isabella Bird), *Journeys in Persia and Kurdistan* (2 Vols), London, 1891

Blanch, Lesley, *The Wilder Shores of Love*, London, 1954

Blunt, Lady Anne, *A Pilgrimage to Nejd*, reprinted London, 1985

————*Bedouin Tribes of the Euphrates*, New York, 1879

Bovill, E. W. (ed.), *Letters of Alexander Gordon Laing 1824–6*, Cambridge, 1964

Brent, Peter, *Far Arabia: Explorers of the Myth*, London, 1977

Briggs, L. C., *Tribes of the Sahara*, Cambridge, Mass., USA, 1960

Brodie, Fawn M., *The Devil Drives: A Life of Sir Richard Burton*, New York, 1967

Bruce-Lockhart, Jamie, and Wright, John (eds.), *Difficult and Dangerous Roads: Hugh Clapperton's Travels in Sahara and Fezzan (1822–5)*, London, 2000

Bulstrode, Beatrix, *A Tour in Mongolia*, London, 1920

Burton, Richard, *Personal Narrative of a Pilgrimage to al-Madinah and Mecca* (2 Vols), London, 1855-6

Byron, Robert, *The Road to Oxiana*, London, 1937

Cable, Mildred and French, Francesca *The Gobi Desert*, London, 1942

Carmichael, Peter, *Nomads*, London, 1991

Chatwin, Bruce *The Songlines*, London, 1997

----*What Am I Doing Here*, London, 1989

Childs, Virginia, *Lady Hester Stanhope*, London, 1990

Cooper, Merian C., *Grass*, New York, 1925

Crewe, Quentin, *In Search of the Sahara*, London, 1984

Cronin, Vincent, *The Last Migration*, London, 1957

Doughty, Charles M., *Travels in Arabia Deserta*, London, 1888

Durand, E. R., *An Autumn Tour in Western Persia*, London, 1902

Gardner, Brian, *The Quest for Timbuctoo*, London, 1968/

Garrod, Oliver, *The Qashqai Tribe of Fars* (Journal of the Central Asian Society, Vol. XXXIII), London, 1946

Gilmour, The Revd. James, *Among the Mongols*, London, 1883

Glubb, J. B., *The Bedouin of Northern Iraq* (Journal of the Royal Central Asian Society), London, 1935

----*The Story of the Arab Legion*, London, 1948

Grousset, R., *Empire of the Steppes*, New Jersey, USA, 1970

Harris, Walter B., *Morocco that Was*, London, 1921

Hopkirk, Peter, *The Great Game*, London, 1990

Hopwood, Derek *Sexual Encounters in the Middle East*, Reading, 1999

Izzard, Molly, *Freya Stark: A Biography*, London, 1993

Kabbani, Rana, *Europe's Myths of Orient*, London, 1986

Keay, John (general editor), *The Royal Geographical Society History of World Exploration*, London, 1991

Keenan, Jeremy, *Sahara Man: Travelling with the Tuareg*, London, 2001

Khazanov, A. M. (translated from the Russian by Julia Crookenden), *Nomads and the Outside World*, Cambridge, 1984

Lattimore, Owen, *Mongol Journeys*, London, 1941

----*Nomads and Commissars*, New York, 1962

Lawrence, T. E., *Seven Pillars of Wisdom*, London, 1935

Layard, Sir Henry, *Early Adventures in Persia, Susiana, and Babylonia* (2 Vols), London, 1887

Levi, Peter, *The Light Garden of the Angel King: Journeys in Afghanistan*, London, 1972

Longford, Elizabeth, *A Pilgrimage of Passion: The Life of Wilfred Scawen Blunt*, London, 1979

Lovell, Mary S., *A Scandalous Life: The Biography of Jane Digby of Mezrab*, London, 1995

Lunt, James, *Glubb Pasha*, London, 1984

Lupton, Kenneth, *Mungo Park, the African Traveller*, Oxford, 1979

Maugham, Robin, *The Slaves of Timbuktu*, London, 1961

Maxwell, Gavin, *Lords of the Atlas*, London, 1966

Moorhouse, Geoffrey, *The Fearful Void*, London, 1974

Newman, Robert P., *Owen Lattimore and the 'Loss' of China*, California, 1992

Opie, James, *Tribal Rugs*, London, 1992

Palgrave, W. G., *Personal Narrative of a Year's Journey through Central and Eastern Arabia* (2 Vols), London, 1865

Philby, H. St John, *The Empty Quarter*, London, 1933
        *Sheba's Daughter*, London, 1939

Powell-Cole, Donald, *Nomads of the World*, Washington, 1971

Raswan, Carl, *The Black Tents of Arabia: My Life among the Bedouin*, London, 1935

Rodd, Francis Rennell, *The People of the Veil*, London, 1926

Russell, Sir John, *The Khan's Road* (Archives of the Royal Geographical Society), London, 1959

Sackville-West, Vita, *Twelve Days: An Account of a Journey across the Bakhtiari Mountains of South-Western Persia*, London, 1928

Severin, Tim, *In Search of Genghis Khan*, London, 1991

Shakespeare, Nicholas, *Bruce Chatwin*, London, 1999

Simmons, James, *Passionate Pilgrims: English Travellers in the World of the Desert Arabs*, New York, 1987

Stark, Freya, *East is West*, London, 1945
----*The Minaret of Djam*, London, 1972

Stewart, Stanley, *In the Empire of Genghis Khan*, London, 2000

Thesiger, Wilfred, *Arabian Sands*, London, 1959
----*Desert, Marsh and Mountain: The World of a Nomad*, London, 1979

Thomas, Bertram, *Arabia Felix*, London, 1932

Tidrick, Kathryn, *Heart-Beguiling Araby*, Cambridge, 1981

Ure, John, *The Trail of Tamerlane*, London, 1980

Wright, Sir Denis, *The English among the Persians*, London, 1985

Witteridge, Gordon, *Charles Masson of Afghanistan*, Warminster, England, 1986

# Index